The Silent Garden

A Journal of Esoteric Fabulism

First Edition

The Silent Garden, Vol. 1 copyright © 2018 by the Silent Garden Collective
Cover artwork copyright © 2018 David Whitlam
Cover design copyright © 2018 Vince Haig
Interior design, typesetting, layout © 2018 Sam Cowan
Proofreader: Carolyn Macdonell-Kelly

"Transcending the Grotesquerie: The Surreal Landscapes of David Whitlam" © 2018 David Whitlam

"Translating The Ritual," by J.T. Glover © 2018 J.T. Glover

"The Raw Food Movement: Comparing Transformative Diets in Han Kang's The Vegetarian (2015) and Julia Ducournau's Raw (2016)," by V.H. Leslie © 2018 V.H. Leslie

"Unstitching the Patriarchy: A review of Camilla Grudova's The Doll's Alphabet," by Rudrapriya Rathore © 2018 Rudrapriya Rathore

"Cinema of the Body: The Politics of Performativity in Lars Von Trier's Dogville and Yorgos Lanthimo's Dogtooth," by Angelos Koutsourakis © 2012 Angelos Koutsourakis

"Lincoln Hill," by Daniel Mills © 2018 Daniel Mills

"Deposition of Darkness," by Mesándel Virtusio Arguelles (Translated by Kristine Ong Muslim) © 2004 Mesándel Virtusio Arguelles. Translation © 2018 Kristine Ong Muslim

"Contortionist," by Mesándel Virtusio Arguelles (Translated by Kristine Ong Muslim) © 2004 Mesándel Virtusio Arguelles. Translation © 2018 Kristine Ong Muslim

"Waystations of the High Night," by Marcel Brion (Translated by Edward Gauvin) © 1942 / 2018 Marcel Brion. Translation © 2018 Edward Gauvin

"Her Blood the Apples, Her Bones the Trees," by Georgina Bruce © 2018 Georgina Bruce

"La Tierra Blanca," by Maurizio Cometto (Translated by Rachel S. Cordasco) © 2017 Acheron Books. Translation © 2018 Rachel S. Cordasco

"Embolus of Cinnabar," by Patricia Cram © 2018 Patricia Cram

"Palisade," by Brian Evenson © 2018 Brian Evenson

"Under the Casket, A Beach!" by Nick Mamatas © 2018 Nick Mamatas

"The Other Tiger," by Helen Marshall © 2018 Helen Marshall

"Coruvorn" by Reggie Oliver © 2018 Reggie Oliver

"Blood and Smoke, Vinegar and Ashes" by D.P. Watt © 2018 D.P. Watt

"The Palace of Force and Fire," by Ron Weighell © 2018 Ron Weighell

"Nox Una," by Marian Womack © 2018 Marian Womack

ISBN: 978-1-988964-05-8

The Silent Garden

A Journal of Esoteric Fabulism

Where Darkness Bends...

"*We went down into the silent garden. Dawn is the time when nothing breathes, the hour of silence. Everything is transfixed, only the light moves.*"
— Leonora Carrington

"*The house was silent, but somewhere in the garden was a swimming pool filled with unsettled water.*"
— J.G. Ballard

CONTENTS

BLOOD AND SMOKE, VINEGAR AND ASHES / D.P. Watt ... 7

PALISADE / Brian Evenson ... 27

LINCOLN HILL / Daniel Mills ... 41

CINEMA OF THE BODY: THE POLITICS OF PERFORMATIVITY IN LARS VON TRIER'S *DOGVILLE* AND YORGOS LANTHIMO'S *DOGTOOTH* / Angelos Koutsourakis ... 43

THE PALACE OF FORCE AND FIRE / Ron Weighell ... 63

UNDER THE CASKET, A BEACH! / Nick Mamatas ... 85

DEPOSITION OF DARKNESS / Mesándel Virtusio Arguelles (Translated by Kristine Ong Muslim) ... 103

THE OTHER TIGER / Helen Marshall ... 105

UNSTITCHING THE PATRIARCHY: A REVIEW OF CAMILLA GRUDOVA'S *THE DOLL'S ALPHABET* / Rudrapriya Rathore ... 119

EMBOLUS OF CINNABAR / Patricia Cram ... 123

TRANSCENDING THE GROTESQUERIE: THE SURREAL LANDSCAPES OF DAVID WHITLAM ... 133

WAYSTATIONS OF THE HIGH NIGHT / Marcel Brion (Translated by Edward Gauvin) ... 159

NOX UNA / Marian Womack ... 177

THE RAW FOOD MOVEMENT: COMPARING TRANSFORMATIVE DIETS IN HAN KANG'S *THE VEGETARIAN* (2015) AND JULIA DUCOURNAU'S *RAW* (2016) / V.H. Leslie ... 189

CORUVORN / Reggie Oliver ... 199

TRANSLATING *THE RITUAL* / J.T. Glover ... 215

LA TIERRA BLANCA / Maurizio Cometto (Translated by Rachel S. Cordasco) ... 223

CONTORTIONIST / Mesándel Virtusio Arguelles (Translated by Kristine Ong Muslim) ... 229

HER BLOOD THE APPLES, HER BONES THE TREES / Georgina Bruce ... 231

ABOUT ... 243

CONTRIBUTORS ... 245

BLOOD AND SMOKE, VINEGAR AND ASHES

D. P. Watt

There are many curious routes to insight; and as many, often more banal, routes to ruin. It was certainly curious to receive a call from Paul ten years after we had divorced. Not that it had been particularly bitter. We just wanted different things. He wanted kids; I did not. We went our separate ways. Such are the everyday manoeuvres of life. He had moved to New York to be with his younger partner, who duly provided him with his required progeny; three of them, all girls. I stayed in Coventry and purchased a flat, from where I managed a little online enterprise making homemade bags and jewellery. And thus a decade passed.

He had called me because his father had just died. There was no one to help. His brother was in New Zealand and was due to go out on a crew ship to Antarctica the following week for three months. His partner was seriously ill and he couldn't leave her, or the kids, with anyone, so that he could make all the necessary arrangements. He was desperate. He needed my help also to deal with the authorities in Poland, where his father had moved to eight years previously. I had studied Slavic languages as my degree, and had begun an MA in Polish Literature, before funds had run out and, on meeting Paul, I'd deferred my place for a year, and then further deferrals until they got fed up with me and terminated my studies. I had only used my Polish a few times in the intervening years, talking with some of the local immigrants and in one of the specialist Polish food shops, but I was still fairly fluent.

I don't really know why I agreed, but then again why wouldn't I? As I said we didn't part on bad terms—I had no grudge against him. He offered to pay me well enough. Perhaps I fancied a change from the routine, and a little glimpse back into the past. I had also liked his father, Dieter—he was a kind, calm and quiet man. I did it as much for him as for either Paul, or myself.

A few days later I found myself stepping off a budget flight onto the frosty tarmac at Krakow airport. Paul had booked me a rental car for as long as I might need it and I slung my bags into the boot and got out the maps I'd printed off for my journey to a little village called Sobolów, some 30 kilometres south-east of Krakow. I'd asked Paul why on earth his father had moved there. He didn't know, he was never one to pry—he was too self-absorbed for that. It seemed peculiarly out of the way; Dieter was hardly a recluse. It was early November and the snows would soon be coming. I needed to get everything arranged for the funeral quickly and then the house up for sale; the rest could be done from a distance.

It was lovely seeing the Polish countryside again. The area around Krakow had always called to me; the great, stunning expanses of land, punctuated here and there by copses of trees that seemed to then huddle together the further you got from the city into long sprawling woodlands and denser decaying forests. It was not simply the natural world that fascinated me about this landscape but its collision with the modern; suddenly train tracks would appear from nowhere and great yards of rusting carriages and engines. Then up would pop, miles from a town or village, an industrial estate, busy with trucks and diggers. And then there were the many isolated little houses—never lit, or with sign of any inhabitation—holiday homes perhaps, the Polish were very fond of their houses in the country. Beyond all of this, or perhaps beneath it, is the ubiquity of the little kapliczki, whether they be elaborate communal things on the outskirts of small villages, or the idiosyncratic wooden constructions that appeared throughout the countryside. Seeing them again reminded me of a road trip I had taken with a friend from university, Daisy Simmons, over twenty years previously. We had travelled Eastern Poland and the Ukraine, taking pictures of all the little shrines we came across. Most do not record the reason for their erection but many that stand by the roadside mark a traffic accident and are memorials for the dead. I remember being particularly affected by a very strange one near some woods a few kilometres from Przemyśl. It had pieces of long coloured twine hanging from it tied to which were numerous small dolls, each in varying states of decay. We stopped and read the dedication; it was a plea to Saint Philomena to watch over the souls of three sisters that had been murdered nearby in 1978. Daisy and I spent an hour sitting there by the roadside, first in tears and then in quiet contemplation. We ended the trip a few days later, that small shrine casting a dark shadow over the holiday.

It was weird to be thinking of Daisy Simmons again as I drove into Sobolów. Her father had been a building developer and he had been one of the first to take advantage of the fall of the iron curtain. He was straight into Poland, employing good tradespeople at good rates, to build countryside bungalows for the growing middle classes. The outskirts of Sobolów looked as though it could have been built by Daisy's father, all orange roof tiles and freshly-painted render. The centre of the village consisted of a great wooden church, a small shop, large restaurant, and a long cemetery that seemed to go on forever up a steep hill leading out of the village—bright with the usual offerings of plastic and real flowers, coloured glass vases with floating candles and numerous pictures of the saints; something about Polish cemeteries seemed so alive, so active, compared to the desolation of the English equivalent; private, isolated affairs, as if to say that none other than oneself might have the privilege of death.

I had got some vague directions to Dieter's house from Paul, over the phone, but these were not to be relied upon; he was never good at explaining things to other people. I thought it best just to ask at the local shop, whilst getting a few groceries to tide me over. The owner was very helpful, a Mrs Szczepanska. She had been a friend of Dieter and was pleased to hear that I had come to arrange the funeral and the estate. If I needed anything I was just to ask, and she would set up an account for me at the shop, even offering to close the shop and go with me to show me the house. I said that wouldn't be necessary; if she could just mark precisely on the map where it was and offer a few pointers to any issues on the way. She duly did and I soon found myself driving down a very steep road, heavily wooded on both sides, which opened out onto a long track through a valley. Given the amount of run-off water already across the road in the wood I guessed that it would be pretty impassable in heavy snow, or icy frost, and resolved again to get my tasks concluded as soon as possible before the real winter came.

Dieter's bungalow was not quite as modest as Paul had described. It had large metal gates that opened onto a curving drive ending with a triple garage; a summerhouse; a large wood store; a shed and the main house itself. There was an ample garden, with many well-tended beds and borders, all carefully prepared for the winter. There was clearly a large allotment area too, that had only recently been dug over, but still with a few winter vegetables now going to seed.

I unlocked the main door with the key that Paul had sent me. The house was very cold and it had that sad stillness about it that accrues after a death—a melancholy compounded by the fact that everything seems to speak of their last moments; as though the objects of the home are somehow questioning where their owner may be. I cried a little. It brought back the sudden death of both of my own parents, five years previously. They had been on their way to Heathrow to catch an early morning flight to Venice as part of a dream cruise they had been planning for years. They ended up in a five car pile-up on the M1. I remembered my first time walking back into the family home after they had died.

I sighed and set to busying myself with practical things. The house was heated by a large stove in the centre of an open plan lounge, dining room and kitchen. This also powered the hot water, Paul had told me. A pile of logs and kindling were stacked neatly beside it. I raked the ashes out from the last fire that Dieter had set, laid a new one, and soon the place was warming up.

I brought my few groceries in from the car, and my bags, and thought it best to get things arranged for sleeping that evening. Two doors led off from the dining room, one into a small bathroom area with a lovely walk-in shower. The other opened into Dieter's bedroom. Again, it looked sad; the bed still dishevelled from the last night he had slept there, a half-drunk glass of water on the bedside table, and a green hardback book open next to it. I closed it and read the spine, *Of Herbs and Spices* by Colin Clair. *A little odd*, I thought; *Dieter had never been one for cookery*. I opened it again and the title page fell open. There was a simple, coloured print of a foxglove in green and pink, striking and attractive. I flicked through. There were many coloured plates of plants and even more in black and white. The whole thing was filled with Dieter's annotations, in pencil, blue and black pen, and even in places in a thick felt tip. I put the book down again and thought I'd look over his marginalia later. For now I needed to get the bedding changed and think about some supper.

There was plenty of clean bed linen and once I'd hung a few of my own clothes up on the rail it was starting to look a bit more like my room. I went through to the kitchen and put a can of soup on to simmer and cut some thick pieces of bread to go with it. There was a small utility area off to the side and I dropped the dirty bedding in there, to put on to wash later. Just beside the washing machine a small door opened into a large pantry cupboard, big enough to walk into, cooled by unplastered outer walls. As I opened the door a pungent waft of herby air rushed out. I saw above me an old clothes drying rack, tied up to the ceiling on a pulley. Hanging from it were bunches of dried herbs of every kind imaginable. It had clearly been well used, the sagging wooden shelves had a good number of tins and cans—beans, fish, sauces and soups—neatly arranged in rows. There were also packs and packs of salt and many jars with spices and further dried herbs, all neatly labelled up by Dieter. Beside the salt there was bottle after bottle of every type of vinegar one could think of. More practically there were some cartons of UHT milk and various powdered products; bottles of juices and water and a few wines and bottles of beer. I spotted a row of at least six green bottles with a very distinctive shape—Becherovka! God, I hadn't had any of that in years. It was a wonderful, herbal Czech spirit that again brought back memories of Daisy Simmons. We had spent an outrageous New Year in Prague in 1998 and had got so drunk on it in a touristy restaurant, endlessly supplied with shots of the stuff by roving waiters that seemed to deposit the glasses like water at our table.

With everything that was stored in the pantry one could have easily lived for a few months without venturing from the house. At the back there was a tall metal rack on which many kilner jars were stacked, each crammed with various pickled vegetables and fruits. The whole rack had a strange air about it; as though I had walked back into another century. As my eyes scanned the jars I had an awful sense of eeriness; pickled eggs bulged against their glass prisons like dead cows' eyes; pickled cucumbers floated in brine like the fingers of drowned men, gnawed by long fronds of dill; sliced beetroot was stacked like shavings of rotting flesh submerged in blood; brown chutneys were pocked like piles of dark manure—all of it a desperate attempt to halt the inevitability of rot and the relentlessness of decay. I shivered.

In the furthest corner, beside the metal rack of preserves, there was a small wooden cabinet—more like a bedside table—with a cupboard below and a drawer above. I tried the cupboard. It was locked. The drawer opened easily enough and inside I found a green account ledger with well-thumbed pages. A darkened sticker on the front read, in Dieter's familiar script, 'Dieter Helm ~ Other Preserves ~ January 2005-May 2017.' I flicked through; neatly copied out recipes, scraps of notepaper with little recollections of old memories, a few newspaper clippings about gardening, mushrooms, foraging, and further recipes ripped from magazines and other odd bits a bobs. It looked rather intriguing so I decided to take it back through to the main house and look at it in more detail later that evening, along with the annotated book on herbs and spices.

My soup had caught in the pan but enough was salvageable to keep hunger at bay. I opened a bottle of red wine from the pantry, which was quite decent. As the silence of the dark evening wrapped about the house I realised there was one further room to check. It was on the other side of the building, beyond the lounge. It was supposed to be a second bedroom, and had a small ensuite, but Dieter had used it as a study and it was crammed with his books on Marxism and Socialism and his stacks of paperwork and notes. He had been an historian and I had always found his books—he wrote only a few—to be meticulously researched and written with a passion and energy that was absolutely infectious. I looked across the shelves at all the editions of Marx and Engels; *Kapital* in German, Polish and English translation, and so many different editions of *The Communist Manifesto*. Other book spines revealed the names of the great and the good, and indeed the downright bad and wicked, of the Revolutionary Ideal; Trotsky, Lenin, Lafargue, Kautsky, Pashukanis and the wider, associated thinkers, writers and theorists; Gorky, Benjamin, Habermas, and Marcuse. I noticed a whole shelf of books by Ted Grant. I knew they had been great friends until Grant's death a few years before Dieter moved to Poland. I took out a well-worn copy of *The Unbroken Thread* and opened it up. It was inscribed, 'To my good friend Dieter, A little token of my vanity! With all best wishes, Your comrade, Ted.' The book was very dusty, as indeed were all of the books on these shelves.

The other side of the room seemed more used. On the few, low bookcases there I found many books on cookery, gardening, herbs and spices, folklore and myth. It seemed that these latter books were all fairly recently read and clearly marked something of a new departure for Dieter in his interests, and chimed with the book I had found on his bedside table. Perhaps he had given up on the project of a socialist utopia; finally realising it was impossible in a world obsessed with itself. Or maybe he had merely become absorbed in a new project for a while, before intending to return to his politics and history. I would never know now. I smiled to see a half-full bottle of Becherovka on the desk and next to it a sticky shot glass. I plucked up the bottle and took it through to the lounge to toast the memory of Dieter. I closed the door on the study; it would take a lot of sorting out.

I sat down with Dieter's book of 'Other Preserves' and looked at the first entry. It was in a green ink and was dated December 2004:

1. Herb and Spice Blend – For Other Preserves

Ingredients:

A whole Nutmeg, grated
One Cardamom, ground
Three inches of Cassia bark, ground
A good head of dried Yarrow flowers

Ten leaves of fresh Rosemary
Fresh Mallow root
1tsp dried Lavender
One stem of Lovage
A spike of Plantain seeds
A drop of Oil of Sage

[Caveat: the provenance of the ingredients is of little importance, as long as they are of good quality, apart from the Oil of Sage, Mallow, Rosemary and Yarrow, which should always be picked by the one producing the blend; the latter should be dried for a minimum of thirty days, in total darkness, before use. The Oil of Sage should be made in the month of May and matured for at least six months.]

The entirety should be ground inside a mortar crafted of the rough-scraped skull of a red stag; the pestle of the base of a thick young Ash tree, taken no more than one inch from the root in one fell of an iron axe, and then, crudely, and swiftly, wrought, so that its sap may contribute to the making of the blend. For the duration of the grinding, which should take no less than one hour, but not more than two, the names of the maker's nearest deceased kin should be intoned, in a ceaseless mantra. Use only the given names, and never the family names (the latter can attract unwelcome, violent spirits!). The nature of the ancestral link is of vital import! Of most powerful application to the blend is the naming of the maker's parents, should they be departed. Beyond that proximity through the matrilineal is to be favoured. Never, under any circumstance, reverse the lineage… do not—DO NOT—invoke the names of departed siblings, or offspring! I cannot emphasise this last point enough!

The whole powder should be mixed to a paste with Fennel water using the same pestle and mortar and then dried again on a thin metal tray over a very smoky fire using thin sticks of well dried cedar; when the fire begins to light too much dowse with a little of the fennel water to create as much smoke as possible. Once dried, and before fully cooled, return the blend to the mortar and grind again to a fine powder in small batches. The entire blend should then be mixed together for an hour with a bone spoon (fashioned from the tibia of the same beast used for the mortar) and stored in a solid silver casket used solely for the purpose.

(Note: use precisely as directed in the recipes. If the described effects of each are not achieved it will be a result of a failure in the blend. The defective blend must be discarded, along with the silver casket,

which will be forever tainted by it. A new blend must be produced in precise adherence with the above instructions.)

I put the book down, a little unnerved. It was so clearly Dieter's writing, but the subject was so strange, so oddly pagan and irrational that I could only think it was part of some fiction he was writing. He had always been an atheist, and certainly had no interest—when I knew him anyway—in anything to do with magic or mysticism. But this seemed to be like a kind of, well, *witchcraft*—I could not think of any other word for it. I flicked through the annotations in the bedside book on herbs and found little notes, again in Dieter's hand, about the efficacy of herbs in given months, for certain ailments, but I also found odd little diagrams and insignia; the kind of thing I had seen only in those tacky 1970s books on the occult—popular pulp on the supernatural. I sat, staring into the fire, topping my glass up regularly, listening to the wind howl about the house.

The following morning, nursing a rather sore head, I put all thoughts of strange preserving methods and silly superstitions from my mind. I concentrated on getting arrangements made for the funeral. It would be a simple affair, I told myself—probably just me and the priest at the graveside, a few short poems and prayers and then on to sorting out the will and the house. I gathered many of the necessary documents from Dieter's study through the morning and thought it a good idea to have a decent warm meal in the village. The restaurant was owned by a Czech man, Marek, and his Polish wife, Teresa. They welcomed me and said how much they had loved Dieter, who often dined there. A plate of steaming pierogi appeared for me, with a vast bowl of barszcz czerwony, without me even placing an order. They talked and talked as I tentatively ate, enjoying the intense evocation of memory that the food gave me. Mrs Szczepanska made an appearance as I was trying to force down the last of my pierogi. She was with another of Dieter's friends, a younger woman called Marta, probably in her mid-thirties, who had helped Dieter with his garden and vegetable patches. Once they all knew I was arranging the funeral they all began planning the wake, which they insisted take place there in the restaurant, and entirely at their expense. They started listing names of Dieter's friends, both locally, and in towns and cities further away, all of whom must, *they insisted*, be invited. As I began to protest Mrs Szczepanska held up a hand, as though to silence a moody child, and asserted that she would deal with it all and provide me a list of the guests the following day. All I needed to do was make the arrangements with the authorities and everything else would be dealt with. I was then presented with a large slice of excellent cheesecake, peppered with fat raisins soaked in brandy—the deal was done, apparently.

BLOOD AND SMOKE, VINEGAR AND ASHES / D. P. Watt

An Alchemist, (1661) by Adriaen van Ostrade

And so it proved to be. I had a couple of difficult days in Krakow, trying to deal with overzealous bureaucrats, entailing two return journeys to Dieter's house to find documents that then were deemed to be unnecessary. But finally all was in place for the funeral the following Friday. As I had no mobile reception at Dieter's house, and there was no internet connection either (Dieter and computers just never seemed to click) I spent a lot of time in the main village, making plans with Marek, or Teresa, as they offered their thoughts and opinions. I kept Paul informed as I went along. He was happy with whatever I suggested. I had chosen everything to be as basic as possible, as he had instructed—simple coffin, no flowers, and so on; just frugal and functional. The turnout though was quite overwhelming, at least fifty people, all of whom seemed to want to introduce themselves to me and just assumed that I was still married to Paul. The wake was far from austere. I think Marek and Teresa had planned to feed at least a hundred, and provided wine and vodka for nearly two hundred. It became a superb celebration of Dieter's rich life; he was clearly well respected and loved by these people. I understood now why he had moved here. If I could ever find such care and friendship I would do the same.

I left the wake while it was still in full swing, tired from all the planning, and just relieved to have seen it all go off ok. I slipped away from the crowd, a little tipsy, and drove back to Dieter's just as it was getting dark; a gentle snow was beginning to fall.

Back at the house things seemed even quieter than they had before. I had left the fire blazing well, but it was now reduced to a few embers. I stoked it up again and realised that in all the preparations for the funeral I had neglected to get any more food in for myself. I would have to fall back on Dieter's pantry. I rummaged around to find something appetising. A can of vegetable broth would do. I also found a few hard cheeses wrapped in cloth and grabbed a pack of crackers. A jar of Dieter's homemade piccalilli would go well with them. I hadn't had piccalilli in years; it always reminded me of Christmas at my parents' house. The preserves were on the higher shelves and as I took the jar down a small key slid off the shelf and jingled on the tiled floor. I found it soon enough and realised that it should fit the cupboard door of the little cabinet unit.

As I opened it a waft of musty air escaped; vinegar and mould, damp leather and the mushroomy scent of soil. Inside there were two shelves, on the lower one very small jars were stacked, higgledy-piggledy, on top of each other. Beside them were a number of brownish muslin cloth packages, loosely bound with green twine. On the shelf above there were some very odd things indeed; a small twig all splayed and crushed at one end, where it was also blackened, as though from a fire; a thin knife—I guessed it was silver—very crudely wrought, and clearly much used as its blade was exceedingly worn. There was a hand axe, again well-used, its cracked handle held together with black electrical tape. There was also a small silver box. I recalled the ludicrous recipe I had read the night I arrived. *No, surely*, I thought, *you can't be serious, Dieter. You didn't believe this drivel, did you? You didn't actually try to make that stuff.* I opened the box. Sure enough, there was a fine brown powder within. I scoffed in disbelief. I started looking at the little jars. They were each labelled with numbers, mostly number five, and a few sevens, many had the initials D. H. on them, and two had P. H.; each was dated. One, half consumed, read '5. Marta, 15/05/15, A delight!' I didn't know what to think. I wondered what could be in the muslin packages. My hand was shaking a little as I reached for them, but I pulled myself together. *It's just a load of hocus-pocus*, I assured myself. I undid a couple and the stale smell became stronger. In one there were long, thin strips of meat with white, mouldy rinds, tied into bundles; small labels were tied to each strip, again numbered, initialled and dated, all with the number three and the initials D. H.; the dates were all within the last six months. My hands shook again as I unwrapped another package. Meats again, but knotted into roundish, dry sausages, almost black, but with a yellowish mould. The labels on these were stained with grease and were harder to make out. They all seemed to have the number twelve, and again the initials D. H., but with dates from 2014 to within the last three months. I looked at the contents of the cupboard, now spread before me on the pantry floor. Suddenly I had an overpowering sense of dread and scrambled to my feet and ran through to the kitchen where I poured a large glass of red wine and, in an attempt to get my composure back, busied myself getting some cheese and crackers together to eat. *It really is all just some silly nonsense to do with something Dieter was writing about*, I kept thinking. *He was such a stickler for research; he must have got rather consumed by it all and started experimenting so that he could get the details right.*

I sat down with my supper—*get a bloody grip*! I thought. The snow was really coming down now and the wind was getting up again. Against my better judgement I reached for the ridiculous book I had taken from the pantry cupboard and flicked further on.

12. To Relive a Memory from Youth – A Blood Pudding.

Ingredients:

A pint of one's own blood (or that of another requesting the sausage and who is trustworthy with the knowledge of such things.)

4oz of hard back fat, finely diced
4oz shallots, finely diced
1tbsp fine oatmeal, soaked in caraway water and goat's milk overnight
1tsp herb and spice blend (of the kind previously described)
1tsp salt
1tsp white pepper
1 head of coriander flowers, finely chopped
Natural casings
I buttercup, I daisy, 1 dandelion (dried together in five days of midday sun and then ground into a powder in a pestle and mortar)

Method:

Rub the required length of casings in the powder of buttercup, daisy and dandelion and set aside.
Sweat the fat, with the shallots, until they are tender, remove from the heat and spit upon it (or add the fresh spit of the one requesting it). Stir in the drained oatmeal, herb and spice blend, salt, pepper and coriander flowers.
Sieve the blood to remove clots and stir into the cooled mixture.

Fill the casings using a funnel and wooden spoon, as they are easily broken. Do not overfill as you will need to separate into smaller sausages tied with homespun twine. Leave room for the mixture to expand upon cooking, which should be for merely ten minutes in boiling water freshly taken from a free running spring. This quantity will make twenty small sausages. Under no circumstances must they be reheated, or chilled. They should be stored in a cool, dry place. They will be preserved from undue decay for up to three years by the blend, but will taste of rot when eaten. This is normal.

(Note: Should a specific memory be desired then care must be taken to recall this [as best one can] during the consumption of the sausage. A light reverie will ensue, during which one will feel as though one were present at the memory, sometimes this may involve a dislocation from it, especially if many years have passed, and one may feel as though one witnesses the event, rather than it being one's own experience.)

'Oh, you are fucking joking with me, Dieter, "*A pint of one's own blood*",' I laughed, glancing up at the heavens. 'You silly old man! You don't think I am taking this crap seriously do you?' I urgently looked further back in the book.

5. <u>To Dwell in Another's Dreams</u>

Ingredients:

1lb Apples (any variety)
2-3 ripe plums
1 large onion finely chopped
1lb demerara sugar
½ pint white wine vinegar
A pint of spring water
A whole garlic bulb, roughly chopped (including skin)
A large stem of ginger, roughly chopped (including skin)
1tsp herb and spice blend (as previously described)
A single strand of hair from the chosen dreamer (this may be procured from a hairbrush or anywhere really. The length of hair is immaterial.)
One long dark root of Wormwood
A larva (any species will do, but beware, maggots will invariably result in the production of a nightmare—if this is what is required then a blow fly maggot will be sure to deliver! I have found mosquito larvae particularly useful for this purpose and merely leaving a bucket of water outside within a week or two there will be ample larvae to select from.)
A handful of ashes from a Laurel Fire

Method: Rough cut the apples into 1 inch chunks. Halve the plums, retaining the stones. Taking a large pan place all the ingredients in (save for the hair, wormwood root, larva and ashes) and bring to the boil, stirring continuously, then simmer for at least two hours, stirring occasionally until the surface of the mixture retains a furrow when a wooden spoon is dragged across it. Allow to cool for half an hour before adding the live larva, hair and wormwood root. Allow to cool fully before adding the ashes and then mix thoroughly before bottling into small jars.

(Note: The finished preserve will last up to five years but must be labelled with the name of the person and the date of bottling. Do not consume beyond the point of five years as it will induce frightful hallucinations. Only a little need be consumed—say, a teaspoon—before sleep, to enable the dreams to be reproduced. These will be in full and may come from any age of the person selected. It may take some time to become fully acquainted with these dream patterns, but once one has done so it is frequently possible to guide the dreams to a particular period in their life. Remember that childhood dreams frequently move back and forth into more nightmarish territory and care is advised in seeking out these dreams.)

'Right, then,' I said, angrily. 'Let's put you to the test, Dieter.'

I threw the book down on the sofa and stormed through to the pantry. I rifled through the little jars and found the one labelled 'Marta'.

I took it through to the kitchen and got out a small spoon. I unscrewed the sticky cap and sniffed at the gloopy brown mess inside. It had a sweet aroma to it, but the abiding smell was fungal. I scooped up a loaded spoonful and swallowed it. It was smooth, and quite sweet, but the aftertaste was woody, like damp bark.

I swigged some wine straight from the bottle to wash it down. It did not take the taste away.

'There you go, Dieter,' I shouted. 'Let's see what dreams may come, eh?'

Despite my bravado I had a sudden feeling of regret, followed by an irrational fear. What if it were poisonous? Surely it wouldn't actually work and induce dreams, but maybe the mix itself would do me some harm. The nearest other bungalow to Dieter's was nearly half a kilometre away and with the snow coming down like it was at the moment it would be unlikely that anyone would find me for days if I did get sick.

I panicked and wandered the house, desperately trying to find a place with a signal so that I could at least send a text to Paul to make him aware that I may be in danger. There was no signal anywhere. I stared at the darkness outside, watching the great flurries of snowflakes being plastered across the whitening countryside. I was alone. I would have to deal with it.

It took me many hours to get to sleep, mainly because my mind was racing with all of the connections I was making between the things I had read in Dieter's recipe book and what I had found in the small cupboard. It just couldn't be possible that this little spoon of homemade chutney would induce another's dream. It just wasn't possible.

I awoke at nearly midday, feeling better than I had in years. I did dream; the clearest, most lucid dream I could ever recall; and I recalled it in great detail. There were a group of us, children, playing in an alpine landscape. We were holding hands with badgers and bears, owls and otters, all of them the same size as us, chanting nursery rhymes and singing nonsense songs. We were dancing around a single giant daisy that grew from a mound of purple soil, ringed with white rocks, almost glowing with their brightness. The sky kept changing colour, as though going through phases of sunset; dark oranges, bright reds and then an ominous mauve that darkened everything about us. We children then also became animals and we all then dispersed into a wood to hunt. I seemed to be some kind of bird and flitted through the dark trees in search of insects, which appeared to my birdish sight as little glowing specks of red in the gloom. When I had had my fill I burst into a shower of glittering embers that cascaded to the woodland floor, from each erupted a huge block of grey concrete that shattered the trees around it. As my dream sight floated up into the sky, below me the whole earth was splintering into a dull block of greyness. Then all was darkness.

 I shuffled through to the kitchen in my nightdress to make a coffee. The house was illuminated with the brightness of the snow outside. I looked out. It must be at least three feet deep. The sky looked dark though, heavy with another impeding bout of it. I was here to stay for the next few days, at least. But I had survived the night, and chided myself for my foolish fit of terror, and impetuous risk in consuming the damned thing in the first place.

 I wandered about in a daze. Had the dream been mine, or Marta's; how could I possibly know? It was certainly unlike any dream I had had before, and the sense of it too was somewhat alien, as though I did not belong there. I sat down with a pot of coffee and re-read the two recipes from the previous evening. Again I sank back with incredulity. Did this really indicate that sitting through in the pantry, in an old bedside table, there were little pots of people's dreams—that the strings of nasty looking sausages were dried up chunks of childhood memory; *preposterous*, I affirmed, but the doubt was already within me, quite literally.

 By mid-afternoon the snow was back again. I had spent the previous couple of hours trying to occupy myself with anything to avoid thinking of the book and the things in that cupboard. I couldn't wait a moment longer though and suddenly rushed through and grabbed the package of small sausages. I searched for the most recent label I could find, '12. D.H., 20/03/17.' I cut it into small slices and crammed one in my mouth, chewing rapidly. As it described in the recipe there was a rotten taste, indeed that was the only taste; similar to the chutney, but much more intense, and without any relieving sweetness, or fruity flavour. I stood there at the kitchen sink, wondering whether I should just stick my fingers down my throat to bring the awful thing back up again. Then I began to feel very light-headed. I stumbled through to the bed to lie down, again admonishing myself for such rash behaviour.

What happened in the following hour was simply magical. I seemed to drift beside a large ship moving steadily through light, dark waves. I kept swooping in towards the deck, as though I were a gull. I was circling around a man and a small child. The man looked so much like Dieter, I was amazed. But Dieter was tall and thin and this man was short and quite heavily built. He also had a thick, brown moustache. Dieter had always been clean-shaven. On the horizon land appeared, and a city came into view, just as evening began to descend. As the ship drew closer, my sweeping, free-roaming perspective got closer and closer to the little boy, until it seemed that I was looking through his eyes. On the skyline the glimmering lights of the city came into view, and I was filled with a sense of awe and trepidation, of excitement and joy. Then there was a striking image—the Statue of Liberty. We were approaching America.

I had not been asleep during this; merely in some kind of stupor. It was as though it happened inside my mind, the way I would recall my own memories. But this, this I knew belonged to Dieter. He had talked of it at great length on any occasion we had seen him. He had travelled to America with his father, from England, in the late 1940s. His mother had died shortly after he was born and his father, a dedicated socialist, was in danger in the Germany of the late thirties. He had fled to England in 1939, with Dieter still a baby, and had stayed somewhere in Kent, with a distant relative. Despite his clear opposition to Hitler he was interred in a holding camp for much of the war and never really forgave the British for what he saw as an unnecessary cruelty. Dieter, in those early years, had been raised by this relative but on his release Dieter's father had planned the move to America, which promised a new life for them both. This image came straight from the description Dieter had always given. Or, was it possible that I had merely projected this, given the intensity of my current emotions?

I then remembered the thin strips of meat, labelled number three. What were they intended for? I felt as though I were drunk, tottering through to the lounge to find the entry for them in Dieter's book.

3. To Recapture a Recent Moment

Ingredients:

Either 1lb Venison Loin or fillet of Beef (venison will recall more cerebral or emotional experiences, beef the more corporeal)
30% brine solution

3tsps herb and spice blend (as described for these purposes)
2tsps Salt
2tsps Pepper (coarsely ground)
The sweat of your body
Required for air drying to further preserve (see below):

3tsps ground coriander seed
A pint of cider vinegar
Enough salt (mixed with one tbsp saltpetre) to roll the joint in and entirely cover

Method:
Soak the meat for one day and night in the brine. Remove and pat dry. Rub the meat all over your body gathering as much sweat as possible. Rub together the blend, salt and pepper and rub over the meat. Cover and allow to stand in a cool place for a further day and night.

To smoke the meat one must use a crude smoker. This can be fashioned from any wooden crate, the principal being that there must be much aeration. Choose a windy day to do this. Light a fire of alder wood and allow to smoke. Suspend the meat on hooks from the top of the crate, ensuring that there is at least a foot above the smoking wood. Leave for four hours. The meat is ready to use as soon as it is cool. See below though for notes on its consumption at this stage.

To further dry to the consistency of biltong (which is recommended) then soak the cooled meat in the cider vinegar for one day and night. Then pat dry and roll in the salt and saltpetre mixture. Leave for one hour. Rub in the ground coriander seed and then leave for a further hour.

Finely slice the entire meat joint and thread onto wooden skewers, leaving a half-inch gap between each. For the drying box one can use the same crate as for the smoking. Simply suspend the skewers from the top of the crate and leave in a cool, airy space to dry. This is best assisted by the use of a cable lamp, if the latter is used drying should take 2-3 days, if not then it will be 6-8 days.

Note: This will recapture experiences within the previous 6-12 months of the life of the producer. It is best to keep some of the first smoked cure to access those more distant memories (of 8-12 months) and the drier meat for the more recent. The former will last 2-3 weeks in a sealed container, the latter up to a year. As only one sliver need be consumed at a time this should produce enough to recall many moments. The first cure will also produce an intensity of experience that is shorter in duration—normally a few minutes. The tougher, dried meat will produce a longer recollection—even up to an hour—but one that is rather clouded, as though viewed through a slightly distorted window.

If a specific memory is required then care should be taken to begin to recall it immediately upon eating, otherwise the meat will randomly activate memories dependent upon one's mood.

I rushed through and grabbed the bundle. I took them into the kitchen and shaved slivers off of a few of them with a potato peeler. I put them on a plate and sat on the sofa, pausing a brief moment before I took the first one. It was quite chewy, and didn't have that rotten taste the other two had. A few seconds later I was experiencing a sensation of intense lust and then my eyes fogged a little before closing. I seemed transported to Dieter's bedroom. What I saw there revealed a rather deeper relationship with Marta than I had initially thought. A few minutes later I was back to myself again. It felt strange to be a voyeur into recent moments in Dieter's life, but the urge to do so was compelling. I took another sliver of meat and was walking through the woods, looking for herbs and mushrooms. I looked down to see Dieter's boots striding through emerging bluebells, and then glanced up into the trees at shards of bright sunlight. On and on I ate, binging on moments of another's existence, from the most ordinary to the most private and intimate. It appeared that Dieter had been quite the man about town; numerous recollections involved some of the women I had seen at the funeral, but there seems to have been a genuine passion for Marta.

After a few hours I stopped. The fire had burnt out entirely and a blizzard was raging outside. *What am I doing*, I thought. *What kind of madness is this*? I must stop.

I tried everything to occupy myself. Nothing worked though. All I could think about were those shards of meat and the fantastical visions they promised me; ways of knowing another person that one could never achieve otherwise.

The storm howled on, and inside its icy inferno I fell into an addict's wonderland. No drug, no drink, no physical pleasure had ever given me anything as intoxicating as this. I binged on spoonfuls of fantasy; loitered through other lives and minds in a crazy kaleidoscope of images, memories and moods. Days passed as I dozed on the bed, sipping Becherovka and nibbling shavings of the past or inducing hours of dreams, or nightmare.

I was awoken, quite when it was I cannot say, by a loud hammering at the door. I pulled on a thin dressing gown and answered the urgent knocking.

It was Mrs Szczepanska, looking distraught. She warbled on about how they had been so worried about me, with it being almost three weeks since the snows had arrived and nobody had been able to make it down to this part of the village. She hoped I had survived on the well-stocked larder that she had helped Dieter to assemble. On and on she rattled, her words jumbling together into a bizarre, hallucinatory incantation. The real world was crumbling around me, in favour of another realm.

When she had finished I stirred from my reverie.

'What do you want,' I said, curtly. 'I've got to sort through Dieter's affairs, I'm very busy.' It was true, in so many ways. All his affairs were magically arrayed before me to indulge my prurience; yet also, I was meant to be dealing with his estate. The latter could wait.

She was visibly shocked, probably as much by my appearance as by my attitude. I did not care. She left in a huff of bewilderment.

After I had seen her off I returned to those other's realities. Perhaps it was a few days later, in a rare moment of lucidity, that I recalled the other recipes in the book. Why were there only jars of a certain recipe, and the, rapidly dwindling, stocks of the two types of meat? There were other pages to explore; perhaps further stashes of even more revelatory things might be discovered.

The other numbered recipes were disappointing, and seemed to be of relatively mild effect, compared to these astounding concoctions. There were love potions, and cures for various ailments—number thirteen was for a potent poison made from simple soil. The last entry, number fifteen, tempted with something else entirely though:

15. To See Beyond the Threshold

1lb of flesh of the departed
1lb Saltpetre
3tsps of herb and spice blend
Enough grave clothes, or the shroud of the same departed, to wrap the flesh to cure

Method:

The departed must have been known to the one making the cured flesh. The stronger the bond the deeper the knowledge revealed will be. The deceased must be no more than six months gone and the flesh retrieved on the first night of a waning moon. The cut of meat is of no matter, but it must be whole, rather than comprised of smaller pieces. Often a lower limb is the most convenient for this purpose.

Wash the flesh in a stream for an hour at dusk, then rub with the soil from the roots of an oak tree. Immediately rub the blend into the flesh and then rub again with more soil. Pack the saltpetre around the flesh and wrap tightly in the grave clothing, or shroud, and then bind with ivy at intervals of one inch.

The wrapped flesh must be hung in a cool, dry place to cure. The cure will take only five days.
(Note: Once the curing is complete then one must observe the following strictly! The meat must only be consumed on the first night after the cure is complete. A day beyond and nothing will happen, a day before and you will sicken and die within three days. On that very particular night a single thin strip of the meat should be sliced, using a bone knife fashioned for the very purpose. The meat should then be left to infuse for one hour in red wine of any kind alongside root of valerian and the whole plant and flowers of Euphrasy. Upon the completion of that hour the whole strip of flesh must be consumed at once, without the aid of any liquid to assist. It will taste foul but must not be spat out, or regurgitated, or a terrible sickness will afflict you. Go to sleep immediately and the reality of the life beyond will be revealed to you. Immediately upon awakening you must take the remaining flesh and bury it beneath the root of an elder tree. The root must be as thick as the meat itself. If this final task is not done you will be forever plagued by nightmares so foul that your waking hours will be entirely lived in terror of them. Your mind will wither until your existence cannot be tolerated a moment longer and you will, if you are lucky, be able to take your own life, before being taken to the madhouse. The production, and consumption of this meat is only to be undertaken by those knowing in the craft, in the full awareness of what it is they do, and the ultimate nature of the truths that will be revealed to them – you have been warned!).

And so I sit here, Eve with the apple; what am I to do? Given the promise of such knowledge how could anyone resist? I must see! Tonight the moon begins to wane. I have a spade and shall shortly make another visit to Dieter to see what final teachings he has for me. Soon I shall know the truth of paradise or abide forever in hell.

PALISADE
Brian Evenson

I.

At first it struck Basz as the same as any of the other islets, barring the peculiarity of the house erected in the center of it—a house, according to his uncle, long unoccupied.

"How long?" Basz wanted to know.

"Don't know," said his uncle. Seated behind him in the canoe, Basz could not see his uncle's face. Even had he been able, the man's face rarely gave much away.

It wasn't the only islet on the lake with a dwelling on it. Indeed, there were, rightly speaking, perhaps a half dozen such islets. Most were little more than forty of fifty yards across, cresting just slightly above the water, heavily wooded except for a patch cleared at the highest point. At that spot, a modest cabin might be built. But those cabins were all occupied this time of year, smoke curling up from the chimneys. And this wasn't a cabin: it was a solid, albeit deserted, house.

The islet was on the large side, about double the size of the others they'd seen, and it rose much higher from the water. Unlike the cabins, the house wasn't made of logs: it had stone walls and a slate roof, green with damp and moss. The trees surrounding it had been hastily cut down, the stumps left standing to rot, the logs having been used to erect a stockade just beyond the house. Assuming it was a stockade. A palisade, anyway.

"What's that about?" Basz asked, pointing at it. "Was that there when you lived up here?"

His uncle shrugged, his shoulder blades momentarily jutting out of his back.

"What do you suppose they kept penned in there?" Basz persisted.

"How the hell should I know?" his uncle said.

No point having livestock out here—not enough land for them to graze. Perhaps a garden, Basz thought. But why would you wall a garden in? Surely there were no animals on the islet that they needed to protect the plants from, and tall walls would diminish the sunlight.

His uncle dipped his paddle back in and, grunting, dragged it through the water. Basz took his own paddle up from where it rested athwart the gunnels and began pulling it through the water on the boat's other side.

The closer they came, the bigger the house seemed.

"Why would they abandon it?" Basz asked. "It's the only decent house out here."

His uncle didn't bother answering.

"Is this a good idea?" asked Basz a little later, when they were nearing the shore.

His uncle shrugged again. "Beggars can't be choosers, Basz," he said. "Keep paddling."

The way Basz saw it, as they pulled the boat onto the dark squelchy mud of the islet's shore, as they unloaded the boxes of food, was that he wasn't the beggar: his uncle was. Basz was, basically, just along for the ride. He was not the one who needed to hide. He was not the one who had gotten himself into, in his uncle's words, "a minor bit of bother," and then made it much worse by knifing the man who came to try to talk some sense into him. All that had been his uncle, not him.

True, Basz had been present, but he hadn't been involved. At first, he'd just watched from the sofa as the two men argued at the door. But once his uncle flicked out his knife and pushed it deep into the man's side, he had leaped up quickly enough to grab his uncle's wrist and keep him from stabbing the fellow a second time.

Basz settled the stabbed man carefully onto the floor, then found a towel that the man could hold tightly against his wound.

"We should just kill the fucker," said his uncle. "Easier all around."

But Basz talked his uncle out of it. That was usually his role with his uncle, talking him down. The wound was bad but not too bad, Basz argued. Barring sepsis, the man would recover. Perhaps in time, he told his uncle, the incident would be forgotten, or at least minimized.

"So here's what you do," said Basz. "You call 911. Tell them there's been an accident and to send an ambulance. Then hightail it out of here, find a place to hide until you know if he lives or dies."

His uncle stared at him a long time. For a moment Basz imagined he'd just push him aside and slit the fellow's throat—easier all around—but finally his uncle nodded and put his flick-knife away.

"Where we going to hole up?" his uncle asked.

"We?" said Basz. "No, just you."

His uncle shook his head. "I don't want you giving people the wrong idea about these events when I'm not around. I'm keeping my eye on you. You're coming."

"But I—"

"You're coming," said his uncle.

From the floor, the stabbed man regarded him weakly. The towel, Basz saw, was already sodden with blood. Almost certainly the man would die.

"So, where?" asked his uncle.

"Don't know," said Basz. "Got any ideas?"

His uncle thought a long moment. "One," he finally said.

The man was still alive when they left, though no longer conscious. It had been a long drive, six hours, maybe seven. At first Basz was worried about pursuit, but he'd been vague enough in the 911 call that it no doubt took some time for the police to figure out what had happened and who had been responsible.

On the drive, Basz got a little information out of his uncle, but the man, laconic as usual, didn't give up much. It was like bleeding a stone.

There was a lake up there, his uncle said.

A lake?

He had lived near there one summer, years ago, in the town next to it.

The whole family had? Basz's mom and grandparents too?

His uncle shook his head. Just him.

But why just him?

His uncle shrugged. "Long story," he said.

"We got time," said Basz.

But his uncle didn't take the bait. Instead he just let the road markers flick by. How long was it before he spoke again? A dozen minutes, maybe two dozen.

"It's sparse up there," his uncle said. "People mind their own business. But there's a safe place to stay."

"Who we staying with?" asked Basz.

"Nobody," said his uncle. "It's not that kind of place."

"What do you mean, it's not that kind of place?"

"Nobody's living in it."

"Why not?"

"There's stories," said his uncle.

"What kind of stories?"

"The usual shit," said his uncle. "It don't mean anything. Don't worry about it." And a few minutes later: "The stories are good for us. They'll keep people away."

It was early morning by the time they drove through what passed for a town, little more than a single street three or four blocks long. They had barely entered it before they were out again. His uncle slowed to a snail's pace, peering into the bushes and ferns lining the road. At a certain point, he stopped, reversed a little, then drove the car off the road and onto a little path until it was completely hidden.

They got out and walked back into town. His uncle jimmied the back door of a Mom and Pop grocery. In the back, he found two crates, began to fill them with supplies.

"Should you really break in and steal shit near where we'll be hiding out?" asked Basz.

"Don't be a smartass," said his uncle. But when they were leaving, his uncle was careful to clean up, to make it less immediately obvious there had been a break-in.

They each carried a crate. They walked out of town and down the road past the hidden car and to the shore of the lake. There, they stole a canoe.

Breakwater in Jersey (circa 1850–1855) by Victor Hugo

II.

His uncle wasn't following him. He turned to see him still standing on the muddy shore of the islet. He had put his crate down in the mud and was just pushing the canoe out into the lake.

Basz walked back to him. His uncle was watching the canoe float away, bobbing gently.

"What the hell?" Basz asked.

His uncle turned. "Anybody sees a boat on the shore it'll just let them know we're here. Now we're safe."

"We could have just hid the boat in the bushes," said Basz.

There was an instant where it was clear from the sheer astonishment on his uncle's face that he hadn't even considered this, but almost immediately the expression was gone. That was his uncle's problem, thought Basz—he didn't think. That was why his life was such a mess.

But what's my excuse? Basz asked himself. *Why am I here?*

"How are we going to get off?" asked Basz.

"We'll cross that bridge when we come to it," said his uncle. *But there is no bridge,* thought Basz. *That's why we had the canoe.* His uncle bent down and in a swift fluid motion hoisted the crate to his shoulder. "Come on," he said. "Let's get a look at the house."

The front door was padlocked shut. They used the solitary window to get in, his uncle plucking a rock off the ground and breaking a pane, then reaching through, unlatching it, lifting the sash.

"In you go," he said, and so Basz clambered in, cutting himself in the process, though not too badly. It was nothing to worry about, he told himself, as he tried to staunch the bleeding.

The house was stagnant inside, a layer of grime thick on every surface. It stank of mildew. The rooms were bare: no furniture, nothing but the stone walls, a fireplace, a packed dirt floor. No beds in the two small side rooms. No shelves, no cabinets, nothing to cook with or in— which made half of the foodstuffs they had stolen useless. In the center of the main room's dirt floor, someone had gouged what looked like a crude drawing of a face. The face looked somehow familiar. Basz stared at it until his uncle called his name, then went over and took the two crates that he passed through the window.

"See if there's a key in there for the padlock," his uncle said.

"Why would they keep the padlock key inside the locked house?" asked Basz, but he looked anyway.

There was no key. He examined the door, looked to see if it might be easy to remove the hinges, but they were tight. Without a hammer and chisel he doubted he could get the pins loose from the knuckles.

He returned to the window.

"Well?" said his uncle.

"It's empty in here, totally barren," he said.

His uncle shrugged. "No key?"

He shook his head.

"What about the back door?" his uncle asked.

Back door? Yes, there it was, the wood so blackened and grimy that in the dim light from the single window he had thought it a discolored portion of the stone wall. It was held shut by a single hook and eye. He slid the hook out then turned the handle and pushed it ajar.

"I'll come around," said his uncle, and disappeared from the window.

But the door, as it turned out, didn't open onto the outside.

There was a short passage, roofless, walls made of vertical palings, logs perhaps eight feet tall, tapered at the tips. Or probably a great deal more than eight feet tall, considering the part of them that must be buried in the ground. Basz went down the passage, looking for a door in the side of it, but there was no door, only an opening at the very end, leading into the palisade.

He entered. It was hard to say what it had been: a courtyard of sorts, perhaps, or a garden. Whatever it had been, it was now overgrown, thick with plants that seemed like ferns but were squatter, more fibrous. They twisted and curved in a way different from any ferns he had known. They looked tortured. They grew to the height of a man and were so thoroughly and angrily interlaced that it was hard to see through them. He could see the top of the palisade and could see that the logs had been set vertically here as well and were sharpened at the tips. He could just see, in the far wall, over the torrent of green, the upper edge of a crude doorframe. At least that's what it seemed to be from here.

The ferns, if they were ferns, were wet. His feet sank into the ground as he stepped forward and into them. A half-dozen steps and he could no longer see where he had come from. He took a few more steps and tried to orientate himself by the walls of the palisade, but the floor must have been curved like a bowl, sloping down as you moved toward its center. The farther he got from where he had begun, the more the ferns seemed to thicken not only before him but over him as well. Soon, he could see nothing, neither before nor behind. All he could see was the ghost of the sunlight through the fronds themselves, dimmer all the time.

And then a cloud must have passed across the sun: suddenly, it was hard to see anything at all. He stepped forward and found a trunk in his path, thick and broad. He tried to sidle around it but there it was again, much wider than he'd thought—doubled, perhaps, two trunks that both were and weren't the same plant. Or perhaps the second belonged to another plant entirely and he'd somehow missed the gap between.

He took another step and this time passed around it. It seemed even darker on the other side. His face and jacket were soaked through now. A frond brushed by his face and left it tingling and going slowly numb. Was it just the cold and the damp making it so?

Surely he must be near the wall now. But no, here was another trunk, and another, and another, tightly together, but not arranged regularly enough to be a wall. Somehow he had managed to step into what seemed a closed circle of trunks. But it couldn't be truly closed—if it was, how could he have gotten inside? All he had to do, he told himself, was feel his way around them, slowly, carefully, until he found how he had first gotten in.

The light brightened momentarily, whatever cloud had been between the sun and the ferns now gone. The trunk directly across from him had a strange protrusion on it, just level with his eyes. It looked almost like a face. Almost, funnily enough, like his own face. How strange, he thought, staring. And then the light shifted again, which made it seem like the eyes of the face were opening.

He felt sleepy. That was understandable, they had travelled all night and the last twenty-four hours had been a nightmare. When was the last time he had truly slept? He would push his way to the far wall, open the door for his uncle, but after that he'd go back inside and rest.

Where was the wall? Or was this, what he was thinking of as trunks, the wall after all? Maybe he was already there.

He reached out, feeling for a latch, but there was nothing, only what felt like the curve of a shoulder but strangely damp, strangely cold. Was this his uncle, already in? Was it is his own arm he was feeling? He reached up and touched what felt like a beard, a nose, the contours of a face. It felt like his own face. But if it was his own face, what was it doing in front of him?

He could hear the sound of his uncle calling out, shouting his name. His face was pushed against something and he was lying down. He had fallen somehow. His arm was tingling, his face too. He tried to answer his uncle but his tongue was no longer his own. After a while, the cries faded, coming from a greater and greater distance.

He managed somehow to get to his feet. Where was he exactly? Was the man still bleeding somewhere on the floor? Had his uncle, frustrated by Basz's attempts to hold him back, stabbed him as well?

What's wrong with me? he wondered.

It was too dark to make much out. He felt around and found he was not inside after all but in a tight grove of trees. The bark of each was strange, warm, gnarled with protuberances in one spot alone, at head height, in a way that reminded him of a face. What face? Even by touch it was somehow familiar.

He tried to push his hands into his pockets, but his fingers were numb and he couldn't get them to go in right. Or, rather, he couldn't feel them enough to be sure if they were in or not. There was a lighter in there, in one of the pockets, if he could just get it out.

He shook his hands, felt his fingers tingle, could discern their limits just long enough to close them around the lighter. They dragged it out. He thumbed the spark wheel, threw a few sparks. He tried again, then a third time, focusing now on the plastic lever behind the wheel, and suddenly there was a flame, his knuckle close enough to it that he could smell the hair burn off it. He lifted the lighter up and saw that yes, it looked like a face. Not only a face, but his own face, ashen and dumb, on the trunk of the tree. And there, again, on the tree beside it, and again on the tree beside that. He lifted the lighter higher to get a closer look and the eyes clicked open, like a doll's. Not just in the face in front of him but in all the faces surrounding him. And then his thumb slipped, and the flame was snuffed out.

III.

It just took him a single goddam minute to make it around from the window to the door at the back of the house, but by the time he got there, the door was closed again. Where was Basz? What was the bastard up to? He tried the door, hammered on it, but there was no answer.

He went back and looked through the window, but Basz wasn't in there. Maybe in one of the two side rooms? But the door to each was open and from the window he could see most of each room—if Basz was in one of them, he was pressed against the wall, hiding out of sight. Why in the hell would his nephew do that?

He walked a little way down the slope, scanned the lake. Maybe Basz had decided to cut out and had swam for it. He hadn't wanted to come in the first place—if he had had his way, he would have stayed behind and betrayed them—and so, maybe he had left to do just that.

But he couldn't see anything or anyone in the water, just a few loons and the gently lapping waves.

Why, he idly wondered, *did I let the canoe go?* It had seemed to make sense at the time, but it was almost like someone else was doing it, not him. Why had he ever thought it was a good idea?

He went to the back door. Maybe Basz had gone into that structure, the stockade or pen or whatever. There was a gap of about fifteen feet between the stone house and the palisade, and from what he could tell from the two half-filled parallel trenches running from one building to another, there had once been a walled passage of some sort running between the two. Now, the logs that must have formed the walls of that passage had been piled in front of the entrance of the palisade, blocking the way in.

"Basz?" he called out. "Basz?"

He walked around the structure. There was no other entrance. What was it they had said about the house, years back when he had spent that summer at the lake? *Nobody goes there,* was all the old bastard he worked for had said at first, and then, when pressed, *it's not the house but the island, what lives on it.* Which was why, he gathered, they had chopped all the trees down. But since, as the old man said, it wasn't the house that was the problem and the trees were already chopped down, he figured the house should be all right to stay in, even if the stories were true, which they weren't. Beggars couldn't be choosers.

The logs were too heavy to roll. There were spikes too, he now saw, driven into a few of them, holding them in place. Because of the way the logs had been piled against the door, he could clamber up them. A little tricky—slippery in his boots, and a couple times he almost fell. But in the end he climbed high enough that he could just peer over the wall and down into the palisade.

It was empty inside, muddy, nothing but mud, certainly no Basz. What had the structure been for? What had been kept inside? And why had they felt the need to barricade the entrance?

He climbed back down, walked back to the front of the house. Still no sign of Basz. He lifted the sash and, grunting, started to work his way through the window, then thought, *Why bother?* Instead, he kicked the front door with his boot heel until the hasp holding the padlock tore loose.

"Basz?" he called.

But the house seemed empty. It smelled faintly of mildew and something else. Sap maybe. The two side rooms—bedrooms probably, though there were no beds in them—were empty. Nothing in them. Nothing in the main room either, as if nobody had ever lived here.

Maybe nobody ever had. Maybe he would be the first.

He would lie low for a while, not even leave the islet until he ran out of food. How long would that be? Two weeks maybe if Basz showed back up again, probably a month if he was on his own. Then he would figure out some way of discovering if that fucker he'd stabbed was still alive and how much trouble he was in. Sure, he knew he owed money, that was fair, but there was a right way and a wrong way to ask for money and that man had asked in a very wrong way.

What about Basz? he thought later. Was he gone or would he be back? What had happened to him? He didn't know, but one thing he did know was if Basz went shooting his mouth off, well, then, he'd sure as hell do something about it, nephew or no. He wouldn't let Basz be the death of him.

He pushed the crates up against the front door, to keep it closed now that the latch was broken. He unlatched the hook holding the back door shut, checked to make sure the knob would hold it. He'd come and go through that door. That'd make him less visible from the water.

The wind rattled the doors in their frames. It got on his nerves. He stood, started to pace.

There was, he suddenly realized, a design of some sort scratched into the dirt floor of the main room. At first it was just lines. It took walking around it, staring at it, to make sense of what it was. But then, suddenly, the lines all came together for him: a face.

Why would somebody do that, scratch a face in the floor?

A man's face, certainly. Vaguely familiar. He shook his head, turned away. All faces looked more or less the same, didn't they?

He propped himself in a corner of the main room to sleep, near the front door. Could he risk lighting a fire? Probably not. There was no bedding, nothing to wrap up in but his jacket. Probably he should have thought of that. Basz was always telling him that he needed to think things through, but he'd just been eager to get the hell out before the police arrived. And Basz to be fair hadn't thought of it either. Besides, if Basz had let him do what he wanted, he could have just finished the bastard and dumped the body and then they both could have stayed put. He wouldn't have had to hide out at all.

He settled deeper into the corner and tried to sleep. After a while, despite the damp, despite the cold, he did.

It was dark when something woke him, a creaking sound. At first, he didn't know where he was or what the sound could be, but then all at once he remembered he was on the islet, in the stone house. The sound, he realized, must be the back door opening.

"Basz," he called. "Is that you?"

He heard a grunt that he took for a yes—after all, who else could it be? He heard a shuffling and saw the hints of a dim shape as Basz crossed the floor and settled into the darkness to one side of him, in the other corner or somewhere close to it.

"Where the hell you been?" he asked.

But Basz didn't say anything.

He waited a long time for an answer but for once Basz outwaited him.

"We'll talk in the morning," the uncle finally said. He was too tired tonight to care.

There was a grunt of assent from the corner, or at least the uncle thought so. And yet, at the same time, there was the same creaking sound from across the room, as if the door was opening again. *Am I dreaming?* he wondered. The same shuffling, going this time to another corner of the room. So, maybe this was Basz, and he had imagined or dreamt what he had first heard. Or maybe Basz was restless and hadn't settled in the corner as he had originally thought.

"Hello?" he said, his voice tight.

The door squeaked again, if it was the door. Something squeaked anyway. The same shuffling or a similar sound, as if Basz kept going in and out through the back door. And yet he was hearing movement from different parts of the room, too. Was he really hearing it?

The smell of sap was stronger now. Perhaps the back door had been left ajar.

He scooted over until he touched the crates, felt around in them until he came up with a box of matches.

"Basz?" he said again. "Close the door, Basz."

No answer. He fished a match from the box and dragged it along the box's side.

But even with all the warning he'd had that something was wrong, he wasn't prepared for what he saw: his nephew but not his nephew, right face but wrong body, no body exactly to speak of, not a human one, wandering aimlessly through the room. And not just one of him, but many.

As soon as he lit the match all the faces turned toward him. Panicked, he blew it out. Almost immediately, he realized the mistake he had made. But by the time he managed to get another match lit it was already too late.

LINCOLN HILL
Daniel Mills

1.
In April, he came down the track
out of the fog on Lincoln Hill.

He passed beyond the lumber mill,
a woman on his broken back —
with child, yes, but thin with lack,
where he was seventy and ill,
but still he carried her until
they vanished in the tamaracks.

The snow looked ashen in that light,
then crimson in the place they lay,
with dawn above them, hard and bright,
when came a wailing from the white,
like that of birds at breaking day
or of a babe born in the night.

2.
Blue irises and lilies grew
up in that bloodied clearing where
we buried them with muttered prayers.
There my Elise and Anna flew
to pull the bramble and the blooms
they wore like gemstones in their hair.

Elise, eighteen, stripped herself bare
to meet a man nobody knew
while Anna listened, terrified,
until at dusk she ran for home
and begged for me to come outside.

Elise made no attempt to hide
but waited, waking, in the grove —
and with such dreams behind her eyes.

3.
A windstorm shook the naked trees
the night he knocked upon our door
and shouted to the upper floor
that he had come back for Elise.

He brought with him the winter's freeze:
we huddled in our cloaks and furs
and cried to hear those holy words
she whispered underneath the wheeze
of chimney-wind and dying flames.

"I do," she said. A hush like death
receded to a hissing rain,

and fire flared to show the stains
of loving on the wedding dress
her mother wore and wept for pain.

4.
Then sickness took him and the glow
went out from him, a dying coal,
and winter stripped away the soul
to leave the hair and teeth, the bones.

Such hell for her to watch him go
to pieces as the year turned cold:
the roof-beams creaked and could not hold
the weight of years, the drag of snow.

The gusts were blowing high and shrill
through empty rooms, a lonesome sound,
and Anna, dreaming, watched until
her sister danced him past the mill

and whirled the old man from the ground
to join the wind on Lincoln Hill.

CINEMA OF THE BODY:
THE POLITICS OF PERFORMATIVITY IN LARS VON TRIER'S *DOGVILLE* AND YORGOS LANTHIMO'S *DOGTOOTH*

Angelos Koutsourakis

Both in Hollywood and European cinema there has been a growing tendency to simplify narrative and characters in favour of a more visual dramaturgy, rather than a text-bound one which focuses on a cause and effect narrative structure. In Hollywood this practice is evidenced in high concept, e.g., *Top Gun* (1986) and blockbuster films, e.g., *Avatar* (2009), and serves strictly commercial purposes.

Narrative simplification aims at prioritising style over story, creating moments of visual excess which can be appropriated for marketing and advertising reasons. According to Justin Wyatt high concept films are the product of the synergy of the industry, resulting in objects which appropriate televisual aesthetics, as well as music video tropes. The narrative is superficial and gives way to flashy images which can be reproduced in high tech trailers, TV commercials, music videos and publicity posters.[1] By contrast, the minimisation of text-bound dramaturgy in contemporary European Cinema proposes a more austere type of filmmaking.

Certain contemporary European filmmakers, such as Lars von Trier, Béla Tarr, Yorgos

Lanthimos and many others show preference for a fragmented narrative structure which reduces the narrative to the bodies of the actors. This aesthetic places emphasis on the performance of the actors as a formal and thematic element, demonstrating a preference for a paratactic style, which does not aim at unifying all the episodes, but opens the narrative to moments that go beyond dramaturgical consistency.

The differences with the Hollywood paradigm mentioned earlier are more than obvious, since Hollywood high concept films aim at minimising ambiguity; conversely the reduction of the narrative to moments of performative excess, which permeates the works of contemporary European filmmakers, aims at maximising ambiguity and assigning a more productive participation to the audience, a gesture which I understand to be political. I shall return to this argument later in my detailed discussion of *Dogville* (1998) and *Dogtooth* (Kynodontas, 2009). Before turning my attention to the specific films, it is important to provide a theoretical framework which can elucidate this performative turn.

Normally, the term performance and performativity describes the passage from text-bound theatre to performance art. However, performativity is a term which has been acknowledged and discussed by film scholars too. In particular, Gilles Deleuze's distinction between "the cinema of action" and "the cinema of the body" has been quite influential in contemporary discussions of film performance. Deleuze discusses the "cinema of the body" as a type of cinema which privileges gestures, postures and attitudes over concrete character and plot development. Deleuze's key contention is that "the cinema of the body" is performative, that is, it cannot be simply understood as the reproduction of a script. Performativity replaces narrative causality.[2]

Within this framework offered by Deleuze, one can define performativity in the cinema as the camera's interaction with the actors' performances in ways that the communication of content is not prioritised. The camera interacts with the performing body in space for reasons that exceed narrative coherence. In many respects, performativity refers to a process in which the act of showing an action is privileged over the action itself, and it is not accidental that Deleuze's definition of the "cinema of the body" centres on Bertolt Brecht's concept of gestus and the film practice of John Cassavetes. Brecht's concept of *gestus* refers to a physical acting style which opposes the clichéd dramatic one according to which the actor "becomes" the character he/she embodies. For Brecht, a gestic acting minimises psychological traits and offers a simplification of character through an exposition of attitudes and postures which allow the audience to place emphasis on the social characteristics of the individual instead of the psychological ones. According to Brecht, a gestic acting aims at showing an action, that is quoting it instead of imitating it, with the view to exposing characters as the products of forces and laws that cannot be understood in the phenomenology of human relations.[3] Cassavetes, on the other hand, approaches the filmmaking process not as the narration of a story which strictly adheres to a pre-existing script, but as the exploration of questions, tensions and ideas that emerge throughout the filmmaking process.[4]

Deleuze refers to Brecht and Cassavetes so as to clarify the ways that 'the cinema of the body' describes a filmmaking process according to which the mimetic mirroring of identity is replaced by performative moments that fragment the body and destabilise the narrative. It is worthwhile quoting a passage from Deleuze's argument:

It is Brecht who created the notion of gest, making it the essence of theatre, irreducible to the plot or the 'subject': for him, the gest should be social, although he recognizes that there are other kinds of gest. What we call gest in general is the link or knot of attitudes between themselves, their co-ordination with each other, in so far as they do not depend on a previous story, a pre-existing plot or an action-image. On the contrary, the gest is the development of attitudes themselves, and, as such, carries out a direct theatricalization of bodies, often very discreet, because it takes place independently of any role. The greatness of Cassavetes' work is to have undone the story, plot, or action, but also space, in order to get to attitudes as to categories which put time into the body, as well as thought into life. When Cassavetes says that characters must not come from a story or plot, but that the story should be secreted by the characters, he sums up the requirement of the cinema of bodies: the character is reduced to his own bodily attitudes, and what ought to result is the gest, that is, a 'spectacle,' a theatricalization or dramatization which is valid for all plots. *Faces* is constructed on the attitudes of the bodies presented as faces going as far as the grimace, expressing waiting, fatigue, vertigo and depression.[5]

Deleuze's definition of "the cinema of the body" synopsises an interest in a film language which is not concerned with the mere duplication of a story. It is rather a film practice which is keen on registering performances, unforeseen elements and materials not firmly controlled by the narrative and the director. The effect is that the entire process generates variations from the script that transcend distinctions between filmic and meta-filmic reality, staged and real events. In this context, "the cinema of the body" refers to a self-reflexive filmmaking process which valorizes the process over the finished product. Jonathan Rosenbaum describes it as a "cinema of doubt,"[6] which is more interested in posing questions rather than offering answers. The filmmaker and the performers discover and explore new paths throughout the filmmaking process, while the audience is given time to think and reflect on the portrayed actions instead of passively following the storyline.

DOGVILLE:
THE POLITICS OF PERFORMATIVITY

A glaring example of a film which firmly belongs to the category of the "cinema of the body" is Lars von Trier's *Dogville*. The film's austere form and its ascetic aesthetics, as well as the references to the theatre practice of Bertolt Brecht give rise to a film style which does away with the tropes of narrative cinema, such as detailed plot, narrative causality and psychological character portrayal. *Dogville* employs a minimalist aesthetic with respect to the set and was shot in a hangar in Trollhättan, a Swedish town. The hangar is used so as to resemble a theatre space where chalk marks are used to define scenography, while the actors act realistically in a set which is far from being realistic.

What needs to be pointed out is that this austere setting combined with the film's extensive use of voice-over narration, which replaces plot, have their effect on the representation of the individual. Characters are reported by the voice-over making them look like textual constructs. Von Trier does away with psychological portrayal, an effect that is strengthened by the set, whose minimalist scenery gives the spectator the chance to detect the interactions between individuals. Equally important is to emphasise that this is also reinforced by von Trier's shooting style which allows the actors to work in a more physical way rather than in a dramatic realist one. A cautious analysis of his camera-work since *Breaking the Waves* (1996) can illustrate this point more clearly. The release of that film coincides with von Trier's preference for a less polished filmmaking style and a less stylised acting which incorporates filmic and extra-filmic responses. The actors were not aware whether they were on frame or not (as Dziga Vertov would say they were shot "unawares"[7]) and this gave them freedom since they did not have to follow a specific plan. This shooting style reassesses the role of the script. The script is the starting point for the exploration of gestures, attitudes and materials not necessarily scripted.

As such, the camera is not solely busy capturing material, but is also concerned with provoking reactions and gestures, which blur the boundaries between the diegetic and the extra-diegetic identity of the actors. This acting style produces an effect of interruption

Scene from *Dogville* (2003) / Trust Film Sales ApS

and not a seamless reproduction of unified characterization.

Von Trier offers the actors the possibility to produce more than what lies in the script, something which is very much related to a whole shift from acting to performance. In an interview he gave me, I asked von Trier whether this *modus operandi* is deliberately interested in making the actors act out of character. Von Trier responded:

I am very interested in this. I am interested in capturing the actors when they are in and out of character. The borderline between the private individual and the character is very intriguing. Especially, when it overlaps and you cannot tell whether a reaction can be attributed to the actor or the character. That is where I try to go very often.[8]

The camera becomes performative and adds a sense of mobility that is not concerned solely with the simulation of actions; it is rather interested in provoking responses, attitudes and gestures that function as a meta-critique of the portrayed actions. This is a practice that can be identified in the films of Cassavetes—Deleuze's major example of a director whose films belong to the category of "the cinema of the body."[9]

The aforementioned comments on a film practice which aims at provoking reactions rather than simply capturing narrative material are crucial to our understanding of von Trier's use of the camera as a performative tool that foregrounds the performance of the actors and highlights the process of creating a character by provoking uncomforting feelings to the actor while she/he is in the process of impersonating a character. This clarification provides the impetus to reveal Dogville's politics of performativity and comprehend the film's focus on gestural and performative contradictions. I do not want to get bogged down into issues of content, but let me briefly summarise the film's story. *Dogville* tells the story of Grace (Nicole Kidman) a young fugitive who finds refuge in a small town in the Rocky Mountains. When Tom (Paul Bettany), a young self-appointed intellectual, meets Grace chased by a bunch of gangsters, he protects her and decides to accommodate her in Dogville. To do so, however, he has to gain permission from the people. Grace will be their chance to prove that they are committed to community values. The people accommodate her and Grace for her part, and at Tom's suggestion, volunteers to help the citizens of Dogville with any errands that need to be done. Initially, nobody accepts her services, but eventually people consent to let her do things "that they do not really need," but can make their lives better.

The people decide that Grace is entitled to stay, but when they realise that there is a large amount of money offered to anyone knowing of her whereabouts, they start abusing her in various ways. Grace is coerced to work longer hours, to accept a pay cut and she eventually becomes the victim of sexual assault on the part of the male population. In the last chapter, the citizens of Dogville decide to deliver her back to the gangsters. The "big man" (James Caan) turns out to be her father and after a brief conversation between them, we learn that the two of them had disagreed about his brutal methods. The reason that Grace left him was because of her willingness to prove that human beings are essentially 'good'. Now that her experiment has failed her father offers her the possibility of sharing his power with her. Initially, Grace hesitates but eventually she accepts his offer and orders the gangsters to burn the town and execute its citizens.

The film has provoked various critical readings, but there have not been any discussions concerning the ways that the minimalist setting and von Trier's shooting style thematise the very theme of performativity, making the audience rethink any essentialist preconceptions of identity. I have chosen to discuss two scenes from the film which may clarify this. In the first one, which takes place in chapter eight, Grace publicly discloses the abuses she has suffered from the citizens of Dogville.

Humiliated by her speech, Dogville's residents ask Tom to side either with them or with Grace. Frustrated by their response, Tom returns to Grace's house. Initially, we get to see both characters lying in bed assuming that they share an affectionate moment. When Tom explains to Grace that he has been asked to choose between her and Dogville, the camera alternates between the left and the right angle of the frame. This alternation is followed by Tom's radical change of *Haltung* (the German word for attitude and posture that Brecht employs repeatedly to show how the body's postures respond to social stimuli). Tom's soothed *Haltung* is replaced by a posture of aggression and he starts making sexual advances towards Grace. He imposes himself aggressively on top of Grace and the camera zooms out to capture the material via a high-angle shot. The camera shows the characters from a great distance and eventually zooms in bit by bit. This antithesis between distance and proximity highlights Tom's exaggerated *Haltung* and divides the character with the purpose of externalising his actions and revealing their social significance.

Tom's change of *Haltung* cannot be understood in terms of psychology. The scene produces a corporeal energy that can be observed in the character's postural behaviour and in the sudden camera movement that decreases the magnification of the image and then zooms in so as to adopt an analytical stance towards the material. Here, von Trier's representation of the body follows the Brechtian practice, according to which the body's *Haltung* and *gestus* can reveal a set of "interpersonal" and social relations that help the audience identify the social laws motivating an individual's actions. The social law that regulates Tom's relation to Grace's body is the law of exchange-value. Tom implies that by rejecting everyone else, he acquires the right to enjoy her body. He is siding with Grace hence his attempted rape becomes a reward for his loyalty to her. However, at the level of actions, he is siding with the community by oppressing Grace, and his attempt to force himself on her ratifies this. The contrast between image and communicated speech puts this forward very strongly. Tom defends his lust for Grace, arguing that it is the ideals they share that made him choose her, whereas he is portrayed as unable to suppress his carnal passion.

In effect, a natural instinct, namely sexual desire is estranged, and calls attention to the connection between sexuality and power. Von Trier does not treat sexuality as natural, but as part of a relationship founded upon exchange value, which is heightened by Tom's use of language that alludes to an economic terminology.[10] It is this performative contradiction that is stressed by the camera, which shows an action and simultaneously analyses it so as to question it. This particular scene showcases how the camera's interaction with the body of the actor de-individuates an action and embeds it in a social context. At this point, the performative contradiction, or the false relationship between the character's pronouncements and his social practice is rendered visible by von Trier. Tom, the embodiment of a liberal attitude of 'openness and acceptance' adheres to Dogville's mental outlook and proceeds to impose his sexual desires on Grace following the capitalist law of making profit through exchangeability that he introduced to the town. When Grace refutes his sexual advances, Tom aligns himself plainly with Dogville and decides to deliver her to the gangsters so as to benefit from the financial reward. This performative change offers an implacable autopsy of the "financialization of social relationships." Of particular note is that this point is communicated mainly by means of a physical acting which highlights the contradictions between the character's somatic attitudes and his pronouncements. The camera makes conspicuous the character's body so as to "disembody" him and to prevent a direct equation between an action and the individual. It is rather the social gesture that is emphasised with the intention of revealing the link between the individual and the social laws that generate certain responses and actions.

Throughout the film the social law that reveals the individual as alterable is the establishment of a capitalist ethic of making profit through exchangeability, which is introduced to the town by the time Grace and Dogville enter into a "reciprocal exchange." In stressing the fact that the characters become more violent after being conditioned to the capitalist ethic of exchange value, von Trier shows the individual as the product of conflicting social forces and not as self-determined.

The view of the individual as performative is also evidenced by Grace's portrayal and her shift from a person acting 'good-heartedly' to a mass-murderer. Grace as a character stresses the tension that arises when one is dedicated to enforcing values upon people not prepared to accept them. Apparently, the film's critical reception has not really identified this idea, something that led von Trier to elaborate on it with more clarity in *Manderlay*,[11] which is the second part of a (still incomplete) trilogy titled "USA: Land of Opportunities" and shares thematic and formal similarities with *Dogville*. Taking up the story of Grace and her father after the end of *Dogville*, *Manderlay* is set in the early 1930s in a plantation in Alabama, within which slavery has not been abolished. Grace is shocked to hear this and insists on staying in the estate to ensure the slaves' transition to freedom. She naively believes that the empowerment of the former slaves will end their oppression, whereas the members of the community use their democratic rights to their own advantage and eventually lead it to self-destruction. Commenting on Grace's behaviour in *Manderlay,* von Trier stated something that applies to her attitude in *Dogville* too. As he says: "The idea of spreading your values to other places is that's what in the past used to be called a mission and is problematic."[12]

This standpoint is clearly articulated by *Dogville*'s ending in which Grace decides that the "world would be a better place without Dogville." In the midst of a lengthy camera movement, the lighting changes and we get to see a high-angle shot of Dogville. The camera slowly zooms in and in a choreographic movement pans from right to left to capture the people of Dogville in a state of bewilderment. This movement intensifies the antithesis between the camera's mobility and the static position of the actors. The following frame shows Grace, who performs a circular movement that heightens stylisation. The tableau here focuses on the characters' change of *Haltungen*, and the uninterrupted camera movement generates contradictory processes that question any essentialist notions of identity and the moralist viewpoints advocated by the main character. When Grace comes to her final conclusion, she walks backwards in a steady and stylised movement which becomes rhetorical and prognosticates the forthcoming catastrophe. Grace's stylised movement towards her father's car becomes a gestural exposition of an attitude and a rhetorical statement that uncovers the thin boundaries between moralist reformism and violence. This rhetorical statement is intensified by the ironic voice-over which asserts that it was one's duty to reinstate order "for the sake of humanity and for the sake of other towns." What confounds matters more is that Grace legitimises violence using her standardised moralist rhetoric. The sound and image counterpoint de-individuates Grace and places emphasis on the performative contradiction of effacing a whole town "for the sake of humanity."

Action, images and the recited text are in conflict and the effect is that Grace's identity is deprived of any notion of interiority or psychological motivation. Her identity is performative and here my understanding of the term is informed by Judith Butler's discussion of a performative act as an act that is simultaneously "dramatic" and "non-referential."[13] A performative act is "non-referential" because it does not describe an act deriving from an inner essence or a fixed identity. By contrast, identity emerges out of the performing of specific acts and thus it is performative, that is, subject to transformation. Butler appeals to the concept of performativity to discuss gender construction as a process that reproduces cultural stereotypes regarding gender identity. From this perspective, Butler concludes that gender identity is performative and as she says, "it is real only to the extent that it is performed."[14] For Butler, the revelation of the process of performativity is of political importance, because it may give one access to the very falsity of "identity normalization" and uncover processes of social construction that are not visible.

Butler's view of identity as performative exposes the connection between identity and society, because a performative action follows certain social rules which negate the bourgeois understanding of the individual as static and self-determined.

Butler's analysis sets up the terms that help us understand the ways that von Trier's camera interacts with the restricted space and the actors' bodies so as to uncover them as performative constructions. The film's deconstruction of the characters' identities by means of performativity shows individuals as the outcome of conflicting forces and interests. *Dogville*'s experimental form, which reduces the narrative to the bodies of the actors and does away with settings, aspires to debunk the capitalist understanding of the individual as self-determined, and to unveil the characters' dependence on broader social structures. Consequently, their changeability cannot be reduced to a change in moral attitudes. Concomitantly, von Trier's analytical observation of the characters' *Haltungen* concentrates on the primacy of social and political relationships motivating their actions and questions their moralist rhetoric implying that the moralist amelioration of the system is a simulacrum given that ethics cannot be separated from politics.

DOGTOOTH: PERFORMATIVITY AS EXPERIMENTATION

In the previous section, I discussed the ways von Trier's reduction of the narrative to the bodies of the actors brings to the fore contradictions which defy the view of the individual as unified. In Yorgos Lanthimos' film *Dogtooth*, the director follows a similar practice and shifts the interest from dramatic action to performative happenings. The actors' bodies are not simply the carriers of dramatic agon, but the medium through which the filmmaker captivates the most ordinary aspects of human behaviour, so as to dissect them and analyse them.

Dogtooth tells the story of a family living in the outskirts of an unspecified town somewhere in Greece. All the characters in the story are nameless and the family consists of the father (Christos Stergioglou), the mother (Michele Valley), the older daughter (Aggeliki Papoulia), the younger daughter (Mary Tsoni,) and a son (Christos Passalis). The kids have not been outside the house's tall fence since they were born and their education is the outcome of a "home-schooling," without any influence from the world outside the house. The father keeps on warning them of the dangerous world beyond the limits of their villa and has taught them that they can only leave their house securely once their dogtooth falls. The situation is perplexed by the fact that the language system that the kids have inherited from their parents is illogical and has no representational attributes. It is a rather invented vocabulary which attributes different meanings to common everyday words. For instance, the youngsters are told that zombies are "yellow flowers," "the sea is a sofa" and keyboard is the definition for female genitalia. Christina (Anna Chalaintzidou), a security guard working in the father's factory, is the only person from the outside world who enters the house, in order to fulfill the son's sexual desires. Her presence in the house will eventually provoke a series of events that will challenge the family's serenity.

Tired of offering her sexual services without having an orgasm, Christina offers the older daughter a headband, asking for oral sex in return. The latter's eventual discovery of sexual pleasure provokes curiosity for the world outside her house.

Initially, she practices the same "game" with her sister and offers her a headband in exchange for oral sex. However, the lexical and hermeneutic boundaries offered by her family cannot satisfy her anymore and she decides to break her right dogtooth so as to explore the world outside her familiar environment.

The film's critical reception so far has focused on issues of content rather than form. Many critics have referenced the Fritzl child imprisonment case in Austria, which was

Scene from *Dogtooth* (2009) / Boo Productions

discovered in 2008.[15] Despite the fact that the content has captured the public's and the critics' attention, I suggest that it is through a study in form that we can comprehend its political complexity.

Lanthimos' work is heavily influenced by von Trier's post-Dogme 95 cinematic practice, which I described earlier, and in particular by his preference for a minimalist aesthetic, which manipulates the actors' performances, with the view to exploring things instead of communicating unambiguous dramaturgical assertions. When viewing *Dogtooth*, one is faced with a series of problems that derive from the fact that the film does not create a coherent fictive cosmos produced by means of mimetic reproduction of a script. Without being an anti-representational avant-garde film, *Dogtooth* has a very loose and open-ended dramaturgy. The film starts showing us two sisters listening to a tape recorder and learning some new words by rote. Among the paradoxes of the language system that they inherit from their parents is the explanation that motorway stands for a strong wind and that road trip is a highly durable material used for the manufacturing of floors. The initial audience response is that of bewilderment and even laughter given that the language spoken by the characters is not necessarily representational.

The film's blockage of linguistic communication affects its narrative to the extent that the final cut looks like a collection of happenings, which relinquish the idea of a discernible beginning, middle and end. Furthermore, there are times that the camera treats the characters as props for the mise-en-scene. A prominent example of this is the first sexual encounter between the son and Christina. Initially, the camera focuses on the lower parts of the characters' bodies without showing their faces. The characters start undressing in an emotionless way as if performing a task. The camera remains immobile and the sole movement in the frame derives from the actors' gestures in the diegetic space. When both characters lie in bed, Christina starts exciting the son's genitals in a mechanical way. Both characters' gestures are stylised and do not intend to reflect clear-cut feelings and attitudes. As such, the gestures are not mimetic and strip performances from emotional and rhetorical unity. From this perspective, the characters' postures and their bodily attitudes are not reproductive but explorative. Representational stability is downplayed in favour of a process that experiments with the characters' gestures and postural attitudes, so as to produce shock and disorientation in the viewer.

In the first section of this article, I discussed Brecht's concept of gestus and the way Deleuze analysed it so as to propose a cinema of 'attitudes and postures'. For Brecht, gestus was an efficient way of presenting the body, not as the reflection of a predetermined content, but as the locus of dialectical explication. Meg Mumford defines gestus as "socially encoded expression"[16] which indicates that the body is in a constant dialogue with the social environment. Thus, a character is not an individual with fixed and unchanged characteristics, but is always defined by the social context in which he/she is embedded. This short return to Brecht's theory and practice can help the reader perceive the ways Lanthimos builds upon Brecht's predilection for a physical acting, without sharing the former's social certainties. Here it is crucial to note that Brecht's aspiration to make the familiar strange strived to help the audience achieve *Aufhebung* (dialectical enlightenment). The term *Aufhebung* refers to Brecht's willingness to distance the audience so as to unveil cognitive revelation, and truth which are predicated upon the Orthodox Marxist interpretative system. Brecht's denaturalisation of the material by means of gestus aimed at challenging the audience's understanding of reality so as to reveal, as David Barnett explains, that social reality is not static, but is shaped by the laws of historical materialism.[17] On the other hand, Barnett explains that post-Brechtian performance practice retains Brecht's emphasis on a denaturalised performing style, but does not share his epistemological certainties, and thus the body is not simply reduced to a producer of concrete social gestures as it is the case in orthodox Brechtian practice.[18] Instead, the body becomes a provocateur of gestures that connect it with the social reality, but the reference points to decode the material on stage are no longer given.

Lanthimos, a film director with a performance art background treats the body as a potentiality in a way that the very act of performing is thematised. In a master- class he gave in Sweden Lanthimos explained that he started his career by filming theatre and dance performances. As he says:

I guess that helped me understanding (sic) the physicality of things much more. It is something I like very much. That's why I mostly work that way with the actors—more physically instead of intellectually or theoretically [...] We just do things physically. I challenge them to go to rehearsals and try this or that without explaining why.[19]

This physical way of working has its effect on *Dogtooth* which is like an assemblage of various happenings loosely connected with each other, in which the isolated teenagers perform various tasks, quote words that have no meaning per se, only to end up learning that the boundaries between performing an identity and being somebody are quite hazy. The film's locus dramaticus becomes a meta-performative space, in which the actors do not dramatise situations, but perform activities, which undermine identity and reveal it as a mere act. The kids are shown performing various exercises, and games that are part of their home schooling, but it is by means of these games and their quotability that they get acquainted with their sexual and violent side, which has been suppressed by their family.

A closer look at another scene may clarify things further. During a conversation between the two sisters one of them complains that she feels unwell. The younger one volunteers to examine her and while offering her medical advice (that she has obviously quoted from an unidentified source), the camera focuses on the lower part of the characters' bodies. The camera's disinterest in the characters' conversation is made conspicuous by the fact that once again we are denied access to their faces. Accordingly, the separation between voice and body is heightened and the produced frame fluctuates between being part of a narrative structure and part of a performative instance that disorganises the narrative.

The latter function of the scene draws attention to the body as an ontogenetic force and not as a vehicle that solely serves narrative requirements. The result is a physical rather than a text-based dramaturgy, which focuses on the possibilities stemming from the actors' unaffectionate performances. To paraphrase Kristin Thompson, the film generates a performative excess which aims at questioning the dominant frame of representation. Thompson employs the term narrative excess to point to the use of dramaturgical tropes which are not necessarily used to communicate story-telling material. As she explains, identifying moments of excess in a film can open up the audience's attention to the politics of form, and the ways a film negates the dominant frame of representation. As she says:

An awareness of excess may help change the status of narrative in general for the viewer. One of the great limitations for the viewer in our culture has been the attitude that film equals narrative, and that entertainment consists wholly of an 'escapism' inherent in the plot. Such a belief limits the spectator's participation to understanding only the chain of cause and effect. The fact that we call this understanding the ability to follow the narrative is not accidental.

The viewer goes along a preordained path, trying to come to the 'correct' conclusions; skilful viewing may consist of being able to anticipate plot events before they occur (as with detective story, which becomes a game in guessing the identity of the criminal before the final revelation). This total absorption in narrative has some unpleasant consequences for the act of viewing.[20]

For Thompson, moments of excess in a film aim at disorganising the cause and effect narrative and introducing gaps in the story-telling process. These gaps reject traditional plot, character and setting; they refuse to reduce the film narrative to interpersonal interaction in dialogue and to a causal articulation of the chain of events. Whereas Thompson's understanding of excess refers mainly to a visual excess, which has been co-opted even by the Hollywood industry, Lanthimos' film engages in a dialogue with performance art so as to communicate a performative excess. The actors' performances combined with the structuring of the story as a connection of happenings loosely connected with each other simplify the fabula and place attention on the very performative process. Lanthimos' employment of performativity instead of concrete dramatic tropes aspires to reveal the tension between language, the body and the speaking subject, so as to render the act of interpretation problematic.

Scholarship has acknowledged the ways that performative excess can disturb narrative coherency by joining together 'real' and representational images. The view of performance as "negativity,"[21] that is, as a means of resisting the dominant strategies of visual representation has been proposed by performance and film commentators. Among them Peggy Phelan and Elena del Rio suggest that performance art strategies become the means of resisting the reproduction of ideological certainties. They achieve this by placing emphasis on the very performativity of the communicated material and on moments of non-performing and acting.[22] In other words, performance and performativity are, as Britta Timm Knudsen says, bound up with a 'constructivist/productive world view' and not a reproductive one.[23] Then again, while the aforementioned theorists mention performance in relation to acting, it is noteworthy that performative excess can also derive from the performative use of the camera, as I mentioned earlier in my discussion of Dogville; this practice is something that we can identify in Dogtooth too.

My description of the aforementioned scenes clarifies that Lanthimos' camera is not concerned with presenting the body as a neutral reproducer of dialogue and actions. The body is seen as a potentiality, something which is directly related to a preference for thematising the very act of performing. Lanthimos employs these series of performative tricks, and his characters are continuously in search of a script in the diegetic and in the meta-level too. In his previous film, *Kinetta* (2005), he followed the same *modus operandi* and presented an austere story, in which a policeman in a Greek resort town enlists a cameraman and a hotel maid to help him resolve some crimes by means of performative re-enactments. The film's employment of long-take cinematography and slow camera movements fits exceptionally well with the actors' slow-motion re-enactment of the crimes. In the end, the director deprives the audience of a narrative resolution of the crimes; through these performative re-enactments, the audience becomes aware of the micropolitics of everyday life in this rural part of Greece. On this basis, performance operates as a means of social discovery and Lanthimos puts forward the conjecture that an isolated incident that involves "victims and perpetrators" cannot be perceived outside a broader social context.

Similarly in *Dogtooth*, Lanthimos' emphasis on the body—reinforced by the blockage of linguistic communication—draws the audience's attention to the fact that what passes as "real" cannot be understood outside socially constructed representational systems. Like Brecht, the director suggests that individuals are not one-dimensional/unchanged and different social circumstances and representational systems can produce different social beings. Lanthimos' minimisation of dramaturgy is still committed to the Brechtian employment of performance as a means of exploration rather than reproduction, but his *modus operandi* avoids the simplification of the Orthodox Brechtian practice.

CONCLUSION:
THE POLITICS OF PERFORMATIVITY

The examples of the films I discussed indicate that both Trier and Lanthimos engage with modernist experiments of the past, as well as with a realist film style, which builds upon the long-take documentation of the actors' performances, inviting the actors to develop themes during the filmmaking process. Here realism does not refer to dramatic realism, that is, the causal linkage of a sequence of events, which consist of a series of coherent psychological motivations. By contrast, Trier's and Lanthimos' realism is more in line with a filmmaking practice which clings into indexicality in order to incorporate the performative contingent. The films' penchant for austerity and their focus on performativity aims at destabilising the narrative, so as to refuse to offer the audience material for consumption. Evidently, both filmmakers reference modernist experiments of the past (Trier includes obvious references to Brecht's epic theatre, while Lanthimos' intentional abuse of the language system and his employment of the performers' body as a means of discovering social gestures has evident references to Brecht, as well as to 1960s Happenings).

Both filmmakers combine references to modernism with a realist use of the camera—in the Bazinian sense which refers to an aesthetics of reality that undermines the role of the script in favour of the presentation of fragments which have a material connection with their referent.[24] Despite the fact that Bazin's writings on realism were considered reactionary by the 1970s film theory, it is important to understand that contemporary geopolitical changes, neo-liberalism's apotheosis of mobility and the predominance of the media have changed the dominant understanding of realism. It is not accidental that present-day film students find more "realistic" narratives that might have nothing to do with the everyday material reality (such as blockbusters), rather than films which manipulate realistic conventions (e.g., long-takes and continuity editing). In this context, von Trier's and Lanthimos' performative realism can be seen as a gesture of negativity; they intend to minimise dramaturgy so as to discover—to paraphrase Giorgio Agamben—the social gestures[25] and the micropolitics of everyday life that have been smoothed by contemporary cinema's employment of technology as a reproductive tool. Consequently, the idea of the filmability of the performative contingent goes against structure, meaning and rationalisation—the stock in trade of capitalist mass culture. To understand this performative realism as a gesture of negativity, we need to turn our attention to the Hollywood paradigm.

There has been an ongoing discussion among film studies scholars which centres on the ways Hollywood has de-radicalised certain formal experiments initially introduced by filmmakers who worked on the margins of the industry. Thus, in recent years we witness the fact that Hollywood has reappropriated radical formal experiments, not to open up human perception and thought to new roads of discovery, but to reproduce a set of relationships as natural, as well as to celebrate the expansion of the industry. Thomas Elsaesser's discussion of *Avatar* is very much a good starting point to see how Hollywood engages with modernist experiments such as self-reflexivity, not to liberate the audience from the confines of conservatism, but to reproduce the very ideas of consumerism and to promote marketability. As he says:

As far as Hollywood is concerned, it wants audiences to interact with images, while Hollywood itself acts with the images. Which is to say, for the industry that makes them, images are instructions for actions—they trigger further moves, purchases and events—rather than pictures to contemplate or immerse yourself in, however much 'immersion' might be the stated objective. In this respect, Avatar the film functions itself as an 'avatar' in the larger system, of which it is the most successful representative. Hence my argument that when Hollywood films allegorize their own conditions of possibility, which are by necessity contradictory, they perform cognitive switches or enact a reversibility of roles: a master–slave relationship that never stabilizes itself.[26]

Elsaesser's comments provide the methodological framework to understand something that has been also pointed out by scholars in American cinema, that is, Hollywood's absorption of modernist and art cinema experiments aims exactly at a new way of commodification, which strives to serve the needs of diverse audiences.[27] Geoff King, for instance, mentions how Hollywood blockbusters have manipulated Sergei Eisenstein's concept of dialectical montage, not to make the audience conscious of the contradictions of capitalism, but to increase the pleasures of narrative consumption. Hollywood valorises spectacle and special effects instead of narrative, so as to minimise the complexity of the stories it tells. Moments of incoherence, as King rightly observes, are not signs of complexity but they have to be seen as "a symptom of offering something to everyone."[28]

Minor European cinemas can resist Hollywood's ability to assimilate even the most radical experimental forms, by focusing on the roots of European art cinema and its preference for a filmmaking style which holds onto indexicality as a means of registering contingency and the plurality of the real. My understanding of the term Minor cinema derives from Deleuze's discussion of minor literature, as a form of literature which intends to subvert a dominant culture from within.[29] As the examples of contemporary filmmakers, like Lars von Trier, Béla Tarr, Yorgos Lanthimos, Nuri Bilge Ceylan, Costas Zapas and Benedek Fliegauf, indicate, Minor cinemas benefit from returning to a performative cinematic austerity, which manipulates film performance as a means of resisting ideological and market-driven narrative certainties and clichés. Apart from the two objects I have used as case studies, contemporary films like *The Turin Horse* (*A torinói ló,* 2011), *Dealer* (2004) and *Minor Freedoms* (*Mikres eleftheries,* 2008) employ a performative corporeal realism that focuses on the productive aspects of representation, rather than the reproductive ones, so as to show the real as contingent and changeable. This type of performative realism references the modernist experiments of the past to construct an anti-commodity aesthetic, which resists reproduction and asks the audience to rethink the staginess and the in-authenticity of everyday forms of human interaction. I suspect that there is some very interesting research that needs to be done on the interrelationship between the current economic crisis and the emergence of films, which belong to the category of "the cinema of the body," in countries like Greece, Hungary and Romania.

NOTES

1. See Justin Wyatt, *High Concept: Movies and Marketing in Hollywood* (Austin: University of Texas Press, 2003), 18.
2. See Gilles Deleuze, *Cinema 2: The Time Image*, trans. Hugh Tomlison and Robert Galeta (Minneapolis: University of Minnesota Press, 1989), 191-92.
3. See Bertolt Brecht, *Brecht on Theatre: the Development of an Aesthetic*, ed. and trans. John Willett (New York and London: Methuen, 1964), 57.
4. See George Kouvaros, *Where Does It Happen?: John Cassavetes and Cinema at the Breaking Point* (Minneapolis: University of Minnesota Press, 2004).
5. Deleuze, *Cinema 2*, 191-92.
6. Jonathan Rosenbaum, *Movies as Politics* (Berkeley and Los Angeles: University of California Press, 1997), 53.
7. Dziga Vertov, *Kino-Eye: The Writings of Dziga Vertov*, ed. Annette Michelson, trans. Kevin O'Brien (Berkeley and Los Angeles: University of California Press: 1984), 71.
8. Interview with Lars von Trier, personal communication, 12 Nov. 2010.
9. See also Kouvaros, *Where Does It Happen?*, 134.
10. Robert Sinnerbrink also discusses the idea of exchange in the film, but while I see the act of exchange as a social law that motivates the characters' physical actions, Sinnerbrink discusses it in different terms, that is, as the 'libidinal economy of desire' that infiltrates the system. See Sinnerbrink, "Grace and Violence: Questioning Politics and Desire in Lars von Trier's *Dogville*," in *SCAN/Journal of Media Arts Culture* 4:2 (2007), http://www.scan.net.au/scan/journal/display.php?journal_id=94.
11. See Katja Nicodemus, "I am an American Woman," in *Signandsight.com*, http://www.signandsight.com/features/465.html.
12. Von Trier qtd. in Carsten Bramsen, *The Road to Manderlay* (2005), in *Manderlay* DVD extras.
13. Judith Butler, "Performative Acts and Gender Construction: An Essay in Phenomenology and Feminist Theory," in *Performance: Critical Concepts in Literary and Cultural Studies*, ed. Philip Auslander (London: Routledge, 2003), 106.
14. Ibid.
15. See Peter Bradshaw, "Dogtooth," *Guardian*, 22 Apr. 2010, http://www.guardian.co.uk/film/2010/apr/22/dogtooth-review. See also Philip French, "Dogtooth," *Observer*, 25 Apr. 2010, http://www.guardian.co.uk/film/2010/apr/25/dogtooth-film-review.
16. Meg Mumford, *Bertolt Brecht* (Abingdon: Routledge, 2009), 53.

17. See David Barnett, "Toward a Definition of Post-Brechtian Performance: The Example of *In the Jungle of the Cities* at the Berliner Ensemble 1971," in *Modern Drama* 54:3 (2011): 340.
18. Ibid., 337.
19. Yorgos Lanthimos, GIFF master class, http://www.youtube.com/watch?feature=player_embedded&v=_tLCgibK8jI.
20. Kristin Thompson, "The Concept of Cinematic Excess," in *Narrative, Apparatus, Ideology: A Film Theory Reader*, ed. Philip Rosen (New York: Columbia University Press, 1986), 140.
21. Peggy Phelan, *Unmarked: The Politics of Performance* (London: Routledge, 1993), 165.
22. See ibid., 165. See also Elena Del Rio, *Deleuze and the Cinemas of Performance: Powers of Affection* (Edinburgh: Edinburgh University Press, 2008), 17.
23. Brita Trimm Knudsen, "It's Live: Performativity and Role Playing," in *Performative Realism*, ed. Rune Gade and Anne Jerslev (Copenhagen: Museum Tusculanum Press, 2005), 270.
24. See André Bazin, "An Aesthetic of Reality: Neorealism," in *What is Cinema?*, vol. II, ed. and trans. Hugh Gray (Berkeley and Los Angeles: University of California Press, 1971), 21.
25. I am paraphrasing Giorgio Agamben's argument that "[i]n the cinema, a society that has lost its gestures seeks to reappropriate what it has lost while simultaneously recording that loss." Giorgio Agamben, "Notes on Gesture," in *Infancy and History: The Destruction of Experience*, trans. Liz Heron (London: Verso, 1978), 137.
26. Thomas Elsaesser, "James Cameron's *Avatar:* Access for All," *New Review of Film and Television Studies* 9:3 (2011): 261.
27. Warren Buckland and Thomas Elsaesser, *Studying Contemporary American Film: A Guide to Movie Analysis*, (New York: Oxford University Press, 2002), 78.
28. Geoff King, S*pectacular Narratives: Hollywood in the Age of the Blockbuster* (New York: I.B. Tauris, 2000), 105.
29. See Deleuze and Félix Guattari, *Kafka: Toward a Minor Literature*, trans. Dana Polan, (Minneapolis: University of Minnesota Press, 1986), 19.

This essay was originally published in
Cinema: Journal of Philosophy and the Moving Image

THE PALACE OF FORCE AND FIRE

Ron Weighell

It was almost midday, and the Tour Guide was busy not having a drink.

His group had left for Piazza Amerina just before eight, which meant that he had been not having a drink for four hours. If he kept the promise he had made to himself that morning, he would continue to not have a drink for at least five hours more.

It was proving to be a mistake.

The Sicilian sun was already beating down as they toured the spectacular mosaics of the Roman Villa Imperiale, and by the time they reached the Valley of the Temples at Agrigento, the heat was scorching. There was, of course, all the chilled mineral water you could drink, if that happened to be all you needed. A break was customary, too, between the Roman Villa and Agrigento, but that would have entailed watching his charges sinking beers and wine, an experience he chose to avoid until he could join in. Besides, his thirst was legendary in every Trattoria on the itinerary, so any request for a non-alcoholic drink would have produced either hilarity or catatonic shock.

He had gambled on the fact that the Roman Villa was not too badly haunted, and that the tour of the so-called Valley—it was in fact a ridge exposed to the sun and wind—always started at the end furthest away from the stone-rimmed pit that was for him the epicentre of the darkest magic. But the afternoon developed into an endurance test in more ways than one.

The local expert booked to talk them through the Temples was, of course, native Sicilian, so he arrived zipped into an anorak with a woolly hat pulled over his ears against what he clearly felt to be an inclement wind, and delivered his initial talk beside the temple of Concordia in the full glare of the sun, while the Tour Group wilted visibly.

"The Vaddi di li Tempri is the most outstanding example of Greek architecture. A national monument of Italy, and a UNESCO world heritage site, it is the largest archaeological site on Earth, and this Temple, dedicated to Concordia, the most complete and beautiful …"

Knowing the talk by heart, the Tour Manager found a spot in the shade that was comfortably out of earshot, and prepared himself for what was to come. The magnificent structure under which he sheltered was, comparatively speaking, devoid of horrors, though Concordia's role as patron of marriages didn't exactly endear her to him. But the walk through the ruins that snaked along the ridge would, as he well knew, be a progressive escalation of darkness and fear culminating at the Sanctuary of the Chthonic Deities: a game of snakes and ladders with all the ladders removed.

He felt obliged to climb with them to the supposed Temple of Hera Lacinia, but he was already struggling inwardly. Just ten steps up and nothing to be worried about, he told himself, but it felt more like descending into a pit. He adapted the counting system that helped him keep his drinking under control, reciting the Sephiroth backwards to create the illusion of ascent; and, as a bonus, prove that, for all the warnings of doomsayers concerning alcoholic consumption, that his memory was unimpaired.

"Malkuth—Yesod—Hod—Netzach—Tiphareth—Geburah—Hesed—Binah—Chokmah—Kether."

But it couldn't convince him that in mounting these steps he was ascending into glory. All the ladders had been removed. Despite its name, no one really knew which deity the Temple of Hera had been dedicated to, and close by was an altar on which countless oxen, pigs, goats and dogs had been sacrificed. And other victims never recorded. It was like walking into a gigantic, horribly haunted abattoir.

The Sicilian, quite oblivious to all this, led them on inexorably towards the complex of temples dedicated to Hercules, Zeus, Castor and Pollux and Hephaestus that clustered like dead satellites about the black Sun that was the Sanctuary of the Chthonic Deities. The Sanctuary had a square altar long used for blood sacrifice, and a massive round altar with a well in the middle that he had learned to avoid looking into. His innocent charges experienced it all as a mere walk through sun-bleached Classical ruins. They were quite impervious to the atmosphere of darkness and dread that haunted the stones, the foetid memory of Holocausts of pigs—and much worse—butchered and flayed, and to the impending presences they were designed to propitiate.

"I give not that thou shouldst give, I give that thou shouldst depart."

As they stood by the Temple of Castor and Pollux, the inevitable memories arose. Castor and Pollux had been the name that either Yvonne or Kenneth or Prok had given to the obnoxious twins whose facial similarity had been such a source of amusement because one was a rabid Communist and the other a grasping Capitalist. What had Kenneth called them? Two sides of a very greasy coin. They could bury their differences when it suited them, though. How they had bled Kenneth for every last penny in return for access to the Villa Santa Barbara, with its potent chamber of nightmares!

He diverted these inconvenient thoughts to the more acceptable consideration of the general idiocy of his Group. That people still clung to the pathetic chestnut about travel automatically broadening the mind amazed him. For all its lingering terrors, this was a place of architectural wonder, and as often as not members of the Group would shuffle around nattering about their gardens back home; what was the best treatment for greenfly, and how to get a better yield of tomatoes. They also exhibited an instinctive urge to defend their country against the pretensions of foreigners, talking up the architectural wonders of their local shopping centre, and the subtly elegant *contrapposto* of its sub-Giacometti municipal sculpture.

Faced with a magnificent temple that had withstood earthquakes, natural and social, for two thousand five hundred years, one Little Englander had turned to another and asked, "Have you seen the Bristol Suspension Bridge?" He had then wondered aloud why the "bits on the ground" had not been "stuck back on?"

Such inanities had once enraged him. Now they were a welcome distraction, a respite from what was already menacing the edges of his vision. In any case, he now saw that the wiseacre in question had an unseen passenger on his neck, suggesting he would soon be needing all the sympathy he could get.

But then there was Dollarton. The portly American was an enigma. He made a play of being the brash Yank, responding to a reference to the horns on a statue of Pan by shouting, 'I've been known to get a little horny myself'. It would have been easy to write him off as a cliché, but on a couple of exchanges he had shown real knowledge and insight. And he seemed to keep himself to himself. He was the only one, apart from the Tour Guide, who had sought shade, and was standing alone.

That self-imposed abstinence was almost the undoing of him. Things that he would have preferred not to have experienced were besieging his senses by the time they left the 'valley' for the last lap to their hotel.

In fact the whole day's coach journey across the parched heart of the Island had been barely endurable. An all too familiar landscape had opened up before his eyes, bleak and unforgiving as the smouldering plains of Hell. Endless fields of stubble burned brown, and loud with cicadas. Here and there a derelict mansion that had crumbled into ruin, abandoned by its rich owners for fear of kidnap and ransom demands, while ramshackle hovels of corrugated iron and clinker blocks, populated, it seemed, only by pariah dogs, spread relentlessly like a cancer. There were sudden, inexplicable weed-grown stretches of motorway that went nowhere; concrete flyovers that terminated in mid-air like Piranesi nightmares, aborted because the money and the concrete had been put to darker uses.

Wheels within wheels, rolling towards the Abyss.

And all around, an ignored and insulted Nature of breath taking beauty, above Human right and wrong. Nature that endured, and had learned not to care. Impossibly, the pariah dog packs had seemed to be gaining on the flying coach. In desperation he had reached for the microphone.

"Did you hear the one about the travelling salesman…?"

He was surely justified in seeing a drink as medicinal after all that. Quite understandable, then, that he should obey his favourite piece of medical advice, once given to Inigo Jones by his Doctor, to "drinke clarratt wine exterourdinary much at dinner."

And "exterourdinary much" he did, not Claret but Typhoeus, the potent Sicilian red grown in volcanic ash on the slopes of Aetna. More than a bottle, naturally, but surely not as many as three, because, after all, there were so many bottles scattered about the group table, and who could prove conclusively how many of the 'dead men' piled up at the end of the evening were due solely to him?

Enough, probably, to bring on what that good Doctor had called 'the vomiting melancholy' tomorrow morning.

The Typhoeus label, black and pyramidal, featured an old engraving of a monster with serpentine legs, a grotesque bearded face and a squat body plumed with many snaky protrusions terminating in the heads of wolf, boar, leopard, bear and lion. He knew it well, a depiction, fittingly, of Typhon, father of all monsters, favoured as an image of the Universal Spirit of Mercury in several volumes of alchemy that had once made up part of his long lost library, where The Primal Power in Man, or the Kundalini Shakti rubbed shoulders with volumes of Agrippa,

Blake and Sir Thomas Browne, and the Egyptian and Tibetan 'Books of the Dead' stood cheek by jowl with The Sacred Magic of Abramelin, the Amphitheatre of Dead Sciences and the Natural and Unnatural Magic of Faust.

For the moment he was liberated from the visceral horrors that haunted him, and all was well; all was exceeding well. The jokes and anecdotes poured off the production line of his lubricated mind even as the glass in his hand rose and fell with the smooth regularity of the practiced 'lifter'. It would not be long before he reached that rapturous moment when we quit ourselves entirely.

And who could tell? Tomorrow he might choose not to drink at all.

The man who had ended up a Tour Guide for a British travel company had once seemed destined for Academe; a man, as was once said of Sir Kenholm Digby, 'skill'd in six languages, and learn'd in all the arts'. He had been well educated in the Classics, but had chosen to pursue post-graduate research in the area of Renaissance studies then pioneered by Dame Frances Yates and D P Walker. His days had been spent immersed in the Hermetic and Neoplatonic magic of John Dee, Marsilio Ficino and Giordano Bruno. Who could possibly have guessed where that would lead?

In his case it had led, eventually, to that Villa owned by Castor and Pollux, and to the chamber of Typhon. It had been, in a way, a beginning as much as an end. In fact it was because of actions undertaken in that painted chamber of nightmares that he now found himself a haunted man, with the inertia of the Universe firmly set against him.

The itinerary had started manageably enough at Syracuse, birthplace of Archimedes, and home of the alchemist and Hermetic astrologer Abulafiah whose works had once held a worthy place in that lost library. The amphitheatre there had been the scene of glorious dramas. When Syracuse had fallen to the Normans, they had soon been seduced by the lifestyle of their predecessors, and adopted lifestyles of oriental luxury and intoxication, with Harems and fabulous gardens. As usual the air was thick with the Will o' the wisps that were the unmistakable signs that much blood had been spilt in the past, but the memories that haunted Syracuse were in the main very much to his liking.

After the delights of that coach journey across the interior and of Agrigento, their next stop was Segesta, where he had a couple of particularly bad moments. There had been many guesses why the Greek temple there had been left unfinished, but none that even hinted at the real cause, which he had glimpsed, coiling and flapping blindly among the columns. And the Theatre there had once been the scene of a particularly bloody rite that was either brilliantly staged, or horribly real.

At the Mountain village of Erice there was free time to wander around. The Tour Guide, whose delicate condition meant that he usually progressed slowly, with a somewhat precarious ice-walking gate, denied himself the questionable pleasures of a stroll, choosing instead to find a Trattoria and allow himself just one chilled Birra Baretti, very cunningly chosen because it was not really alcohol at all in the true sense. More of a soft drink with an edge, even if it did help to lay the ghosts. Cunning indeed. In the days of the Grand Tour a Guide with his education would have been called a Fox Leader.

He liked Signor Baretti's beer. The man himself was on the label, wearing a green velvet coat and a matching Tyrolean hat with a feather. He had become an old friend. The waiter proved to be something of a fox himself, because in no time there were six jolly fellows in green Tyrolean hats smiling at him. The sneaky devil seemed to have somehow smuggled an extra five empty bottles onto his table, and would no doubt expect him to pay for them.

Well, it might be a little difficult to prove he hadn't drunk all of them. He himself was not entirely certain.

"Let me buy you a drink, pal."

Somehow the American, Dollarton, was sitting beside him.

It would have been unforgivably impolite to refuse, and only a fool would choose beer when he could choose wine, or expect his generous benefactor to buy it by the glass rather than the more economical bottle. And by a singular stroke of luck they had Typhoeus.

Dollarton raised his glass.

"So it's Palermo tomorrow. Anywhere you particularly recommend?"

Dollarton was the only one among his party that seemed to be doing more than ticking Sicily off an anonymous list of necessary places to say that you had seen. So it was with more than a sense of obligation that he offered his deep knowledge of the city's history.

There was undeniably much about Palermo to recommend. In Norman times it had been a centre of Christian, Muslim and Judaic learning, producing Latin versions of ancient texts that enlightened the world. Later the Holy Roman Emperor Friedrich had studied Hermetic magic there, and couched his 'Sicilian Questions' concerning the Eternity of the World, the limits of Theology and the immortality of the Soul. A rich mingling of Cultures was just as evident in the very architecture.

Yes, there was much that was admirable in the history of Palermo, but even as he recounted the City's wonders, another list was forming in his mind, the unspoken list of places that had proved better for him to avoid, because they remained indelibly tainted by the terrible events of the past, and the creatures that still invisibly fed there. It would have been difficult to specify the exact moment, but it had surely been in Palermo that he had first realised that the worst of the horrors that plagued him were not the DT's, but invaders through an invisible gate that he had opened years before by certain acts undertaken in that chamber of Typhon.

Might it have been in the suburb of Bagheria, at the Villa Palagonia, that the realisation had come? The grotesque sculpture that covered its façade—dubbed Palagonic by Goethe -was generally interpreted as a quaint example of Mannerist morbidity, but he had immediately known better. The Prince of Palagonia, who must have been cursed with the same vision as himself, had witnessed the monsters that crawled over the building and, like Duke Orsino, creator of the statuary in the garden haunted by Etruscan horrors at Bomarzo, had simply known enough Hermetic magic to placate them by providing forms of stone in which to live.

Not that this realisation, that he was all too sane, and the horrors he saw quite real, had ever been much comfort. Sometimes he reflected on how much simpler life would have been had he joined that lucky group of drinkers delivered, by galloping cockroaches and imaginary scorpions, into the tender arms of St Dymphna.

It was then that he had begun to perfect the fine act of balance, a narrow funambulatory way, by which he could abstain enough to maintain a semblance of physical health, but drink enough to shut off the visions.

For their first day in Palermo, he decided he would learn from his foolish abstention at Agrigento and drink just enough to keep the horrors at bay. To this end he enjoyed a liquid breakfast, and began the tour with a place in the City that he did not fear to visit. Piazza Pretorio, with its spectacular Fountain of Shame. Even the most Philistine tourist was always knocked on his heels by the sheer mass of water- soaked statuary—deities, monsters and nymphs—which had been moved from a private garden near Florence in the 16th century. Its provocative name came from the outrage of Church congregations, and a nearby convent of nuns who complained of being forced to look out at the nude bodies all day.

He chuckled drily at the thought of so many holy prudes complaining about the nude figures, but making no attempt to stop looking. Bricking up their windows would have solved the problem, but then they couldn't have peeped, and their main source of lascivious pleasure would have been denied.

For all their aquatic appendages and elaborate gestures, the oceanic fauna in the fountain did not move once. The tremors in his hands were gone, too, and his step was as steady as could be reasonably expected. There was no denying it. Drinking in the day agreed with him. The rest of the walk passed without unpleasant incident.

Unfortunately the Tour Brochure promised an experience of Palermo by night. Even at 1 am the tables outside the bars and restaurants were full, and the atmosphere vibrant, but he walked with a sinking heart. Despite the fact that he could boast a deep knowledge of the history of every building around them, his Group had insisted, as so often on this particular excursion, that priority must be given to the famous 'walking tree'. He struggled to see the attraction of a parasitic growth that strangled a host tree and left its rotting corpse clutched to its heart in a crushing cage, but he complied. Near Piazza Marina was a massive Banyan that had been putting down subsidiary 'legs' in a stealthy progress of centuries. The thing was generating out of itself a forest of trunks that by some nightmare logic were joined to the parent body not by the roots up but from the branches down.

He must have left it just too long since his last drink. Solid as the bark of this monstrosity might be to the others, he could only see a stalking horror that crept on distended, serpentine legs, draped and festooned in swags and dewlaps and goitres of wrinkled flesh like some epiphytic Elephant Man. The Group posed for pictures in the very maw of this gigantic octopoid monstrosity, this mother of monsters, oblivious to the menace of the sagging tentacles, to the fat roots that slithered with sinister intent about their feet.

After the freedom of the next day "at leisure", which he spent in a trattoria located where his Group were least likely to venture, dinner was an unavoidable communal affair in the hotel. He decided to make the best of it, and was soon, as an acquaintance from the Antipodes had once put it, 'drinking with both hands'. Well into 'the care forgetting vintage', just lubricated enough to be coherently eloquent, he found himself recounting the anecdote of his Wedding Day long ago in France. He had gone to exceptional lengths with his appearance, dressed in an immaculate white suit that had made him look, in his own young opinion, 'aces'.

Naturally he had been nervous before the Ceremony, and had steadied himself with a few fortifying libations. Inevitably he had then required urgent use of the facilities, which were, as was often the case in France, a hole in the floor with 'footholds' on either side. The aim of previous patrons had not always been careful, and he walked on tiptoe in his cream suede brogues towards the hole. But Fate had chosen that of all moments to reveal that his balance had become less than perfect. He had found himself on the floor, the white fabric of his suit soaking up yellow liquid.

In the telling, he gave the episode the air of a silent comedy routine, but his bride, Yvonne, had somehow failed to see any humour in the situation. The atmosphere at the Ceremony had been foul in more ways than one, and their married life had begun under what could only be seen in retrospect as a star of ill omen. How could either of them have understood then the full nature and significance of the uncontrollable mystery that had been acted out on that sodden lavatory floor?

Sometimes he allowed himself to consider what might have been if he had done things differently. A distinguished academic in crumpled linen, his erudite library intact, admired for his scholarship and envied for his publications and even, perhaps, television appearances: not least for his beautiful wife. But the beautiful wife was long gone, and that imagined academic status in the world of Classical scholarship would surely have been precarious at best. He had always been too attracted to the path less trodden: always too much at home with the divine madness of The Dionysiaca and the darker demi-gods: too obsessed with the little Olympus within the greater. And, of course, with the libations of Bacchus.

Using the usual method by which he suppressed such thoughts, he subjected his Group to cynical scrutiny. What would they have made of the library he had collected from his youth? The Museum Hermeticum and the Religio Medici; works by Eleazer of Worms and Isaac Luria; a treasured Jacob Boehme, left, he now remembered, somewhere in Paris; copies of Sandivogius, Thomas Vaughan and Michael Maier: and, of course, the subscriber's edition of Magick in Theory and Practice.

That naturally turned his thoughts back to the Villa Santa Barbara—he never referred to it, even to himself, as The Abbey—and he wondered what had possessed him so long ago. The irony of the word 'possessed' raised a smile, but not of pleasure. Was it not rather the opening of the interior eye that had left his vision, unless under liberal sedation, populated with so many new and startling inhabitants? The author of the Demonialitate had been right. Indeed there were in existence on earth rational creatures besides humans. In fact Sinistrari had not come near to guessing the half of it.

There were the spirits of those who had lived, of course, innumerable, some of them vaguely resembling conventional ghosts, each with a lambent flame burning within. Often they were victims of violent death, displaying eternally their wounds. Then there were the things that had always inhabited the ancient places, Genius Loci; and worst of all, creatures drawn from the unthinkable Elsewhere, nourished by passion, spilled blood or bodily excretions.

"These are they that can dwell in any part of the Earth, and are called Pilosi."

When the interior eye was left unfettered, the world swarmed with monstrosities like the slick Mantis-like horrors that scuttled erect among the unknowing crowd. Creatures that approached with boneless undulations the couches of the sleeping and the dead. Things that stalked backwards, with idiotically-rocking heads on many jointed limbs, at one's shoulder; or crouched rottenly over unknowing diners, dripping unseen liquid decay on their food. He had grown to dread more than any of them certain aerial reptilian Harpies whose shrieks could not be heard, impinging on his senses as horripilation and the taste of excrement.

Would that not be enough to shatter anyone's equanimity? The knowledge that at any moment such forms might appear? It tended to breed nightmares, and the one he had that night was particularly memorable.

He was leaning against a tree, and Yvonne, looking as she had when he had first known her, was singing to him. It was the same lovely voice he remembered, but the sounds she made were visible, and they gradually formed a richly coloured web in the air between them. It grew to envelope him and the tree, conjuring horrible change. Grey, gnarled stems, like the trunks of ancient elephants, descended, rooting in the ground and swelling to form a constricting cage around him.

It was the Banyan, of course, and she soon had him trapped in its rotting heart. Rats, serpents and spiders of alarming size skittered and slewed about the narrow space. The rotten core of the tree began generating many blazing images: jagged mountains; bejewelled forests; corpse women and satyrs: the ugly heads of vividly-haloed saints or gods. The colours became unbearably intense, concentrating themselves at last into one volcanic blast of heat and crimson light.

He turned on the lamp and reached for the medicinal hip flask.

It couldn't be denied that the Tour had been put together with a certain expertise. Just when the walking and the heat were getting too much for the older members of the Group, Culture gave way to natural beauty with a leisurely afternoon visit to a deep cloven valley where an icy river meandered swiftly through forests shady, cool and ancient as the hills: the beautiful Gorge of Orphne.

The sides of the Gorge were far too steep for descent on foot. He counted them into the Lifts, descending with the final group.

Families were wandering through the trees that crowded in over the rushing waters. There were pebble banks where it was possible to take off your shoes and wade in the cold shallows, but he had warned the Group not to venture too far along the valley, where a deeper torrent raced, and only more experienced hikers went.

A savage place, holy and enchanted, if ever there was one.

His charges safely dispersed, he himself wandered in the direction of the deeper waters. The rippling surface and refracted light were pleasantly soporific. A group of young girls with long hair and flowing hippy-like dresses overtook him. They were capering and dancing around an older, staid looking man in dark clothing gathered up above his knees. They were pulling and pushing him through the shallows, deeper into the Gorge. Students, perhaps, the worse—or was it not the better—for drink, teasing a lecturer on a day's outing from College. Their flowing garments looked anachronistic, but wasn't hippy stuff coming back in?

The man was only grudgingly allowing himself to be dragged deeper and deeper, where the chill waters ran wild, building towards a roar that suggested rapids somewhere. Why should the fool struggle? Could it be, he thought, that the young women had in mind something that required privacy?

But this was surely an old lecher's fancy. As likely as not they were his daughters, trying to stir the man from the safe stupor of middle age and into holiday adventure.

When they disappeared from sight, he sat down with his feet soaking in the soothing water. Something was needed to make the moment perfect. A bottle or two of Typhoeus.

"The honey trickling river turned to wine?"

He had to satisfy himself with an occasional swig of ardent spirit from his hipflask.

Later he watched the girls trail back, flushed but calm, one of them swinging a branch of some ruddy blossom-heavy foliage. As they passed, she raised it over her head with an oddly graceful crook of her elbow. Several of them, he now saw, were crowned with plaited strands of the same flowers. Their garments were wet to the waist. But where was the man? Was he left behind because he was older and slower? Close up, their hands were stained, perhaps with crushed blossoms.

He thought of spilled Typhoeus.

Something shifted in the trees on the farther bank, low and running hard. The Tour Guide felt a qualm, and some words arose into consciousness.

"I have fulfilled his red and bleeding feasts."

He could not help himself. Rising, he made his way unsteadily back where the girl's had just come, to where the waters grew deeper, the gorge walls steeper and closer: into chilling gloom.

Of course, he was worrying unnecessarily. Nothing untoward had happened. He would find the man sitting on the bank where the water began to boil, or even poised brooding, like the Romantic figure above the maelstrom in Caspar David Friedrich's famous painting.

He imagined a river falling down caverns measureless to man.

But there was no sign of him. Only, on a promontory of damp earth, the prints of bare feet, and next to a pyramid of gathered pebbles the remains of a small fire and what might have been a hoof print. Something sweet had been burned there. Then he saw what had been placed carefully at the apex of the pebble pyramid. A small terra cotta head of Silenus. Such things were sold in their thousands in gift shops, faces of gods and demi gods reproducing ancient votive offerings, but this looked old, and finely detailed.

Surely a case of finders-keepers?

He did not pick it up, though. The cold and the roar of the waters was becoming oppressive, so he turned and made his way back.

He had not gone far before he saw Dollarton wading towards him through the shallows, trousers rolled, tasselled loafers in hand, for all the world like a fat man at the seaside. The American glanced back in the direction the girls had taken, waved his walking stick and smiled at him.

"Behold the snake his mystic rod entwine."

He was too stunned to reply. Dollarton's habit of chiming in with his own thoughts could be unnerving. He made straight for the Lifts. The Group were not due to leave for some while, but, the heat notwithstanding, he felt a desperate need to get out of the Gorge.

Up in the blazing heat of day, as he finished the hip flask, he found himself pondering the serpentine nature of Time.

Evening in Cefalu found him guiding his charges into a hall where an ornate miniature theatre had been set up for a puppet show.

In his childhood he had loved Punch and Judy, but he could not see one now without thinking uneasily about his marriage. Not that he could remember giving in to such wild excesses of anger or violence, but his memory was not altogether infallible, and he couldn't entirely avoid the suspicion that if he looked into Judy's face he would recognise the look in her eyes.

If his Tour Group were expecting Punch and Judy, however, they were in for a shock. The traditional performance they were about to see had its roots in Ariosto and Tasso, and would feature Charlemagne—Carolus Magnus—his Queen, and his Paladins fighting the Turks in a formulaic battle between Cristiani and Pagani.

The curtains opened to reveal a backdrop of crimson mountains, brilliantly coloured forests and a volcano belching smoke. He felt an immediate qualm. The scene was not traditional, yet disturbingly familiar.

The magnificently detailed puppets were soon about their business, a welter of confrontation, braggadocio and dismemberment. He had been thinking how much more pleasant the experience would be if he had taken the opportunity to have a bracing bottle or so before leaving the hotel. It had looked like being a long evening. But he was soon riveted by the spectacle that presented itself. The puppeteers seemed to have deviated drastically from traditional form. Charlemagne and his Queen were clad in Sorcerer's robes, and appeared to be conducting some sort of rite. The dragon, when it appeared, or was summoned, was a grotesque creature with many heads and serpent legs, a fiendish challenge for any puppeteer. An angel somehow became involved, and the dragon creature seemed to be controlling events. There were subsidiary figures, one holding a lance, enacting such a revelation of the secrets of Carolus Magnus as might once have invoked the wrath of the Holy Vehm.

Then things began to happen that he found increasingly familiar; things that must surely shock the audience: yet no one reacted. The realisation grew in him that they could not possibly be witnessing the same scene. There was another thing; Sicilian pronunciation could be near impenetrable, even for other Italians, but was the central character now being referred to as Carolus Magnus, or Caroli Magus? He locked his hands together to keep them from shaking.

The memories flooded back unbidden. He saw himself with the burden of drunken years fallen from his shoulders and his mind not besieged. Instead of that careful, high-stepping ice-walk, a firm, untroubled step. His grey hair black; his cheeks unmapped with veins and benefitting daily from a hand that could wield a steady razor. He was with his fiancée, Evienne.

God, what was wrong with him? It was Yvonne that he had been with; not Evienne, Yvonne. They were very young, though already serious students of the Path, and he an addicted collector of magical texts. Had it been chance or fate that brought them into the orbit of Kenneth and Prok? Kenneth had been acting as Prok's guide through Rome, Palermo and Sicily when they met.

In any case it had been Kenneth who led them through the ancient wonders of Cefalu; the fragments of Greek temples, Roman walls, remains of Saracen and Norman buildings. Westward lay Palermo, and to the east the sea. To the north loomed the bulk of Cephalodium. They had come at last to that legendary place below the temple of Diana, more derelict from without than he had expected, truth to tell disappointingly ordinary, but my god there were wonders within.

In the central chamber the dark red circle with the blue pentagram at its centre was still visible on the floor. Kenneth had spent many days cleaning the whitewash off the walls and doors, revealing a stunning tableaux of Heaven and Hell. Jagged mountains, bejewelled forests, monstrous puppet heads leering demonically. Corpse women and satyrs. Eruptions of colour like earthly orgasms engendering demons. Our lord the Devil. The head of the Scarlet Woman under the hoof of the Goat. And the Four Degenerates at Prayer.

Under Kenneth's aegis the four of them had performed many rituals in that chamber of nightmares, the first time such a thing had happened in thirty years. Most ambitiously there had been the full Mass with Kenneth as Deacon, he and Yvonne as Priest and Priestess and Prok fulfilling as best he could the functions of the Acolytes. A sacred marriage enacted with full commitment; an act, ironically, that should have represented a great uniting, or coming together. Hriliu indeed! It had been the beginning of the process that had driven them apart.

Was that really the start, though? There had been many other rites, including a solitary ritual of congress with the demon. Might that not have been the act from whence all his troubles had come? The slumbering serpent, at best only weakly active, had duly risen, but through unpropitious channels, awakening, in its erratic passage, untoward, barely controllable appetites.

There was really no one to blame but himself. He had been less than completely honest with Kenneth about the degree of his previous attainment. His application to the grind of mastering Asana and Pranayama had not been all that it should have been. Every ritual had the nature of a pact, and he had subsequently sworn, hand on a carefully chosen selection of treasures from his library, even as the Monotheist might swear on his holy book, to devote himself exclusively to the Great Work, and to treat every event in his life as a particular dealing of God with his Soul.

THE PALACE OF FORCE AND FIRE / Ron Weighell

Fallen Angels in Hell, (1841) by John Martin

He had committed himself to the service of ancient powers as surely as if he had signed a document in blood, but even the most generous examination of his life could hardly conclude that he had kept that pact in any meaningful sense. Unless of course one thought in terms of ritual libation, the wine of rapture and the loss of self that makes one glorious, like the Orphic Dionysus? Might it not be said that even now he was reborn every day from the blood of Mithras?

Such cynical thoughts had become habitual, but deep down they disturbed him. Those who broke their Oath and left the Path were considered Black Brothers, and henceforth the Inertia of the Universe would be against them. Had that not been his exact fate?

"Indeed, indeed, Repentance oft before I swore, but was I sober when I swore?"

His doubts about Yvonne's faithfulness had started then. Of course, she had been safe with Kenneth, whose interests were actively pursued elsewhere. It was surely Prok, so avid to locate the Mage's sex diaries, claiming the only sexual perversion was not doing it at all, who must have been the seducer. Had he turned her into another statistic?

The head of the Scarlet Woman under the hoof of the Goat?

He knew very well what Kenneth would have told him.

'Persecution and humiliation are the chosen lot of the dedicated Cabbalist.'

Beautiful Taormina, teeming with happy souls taking their ease where Odysseus's men had slaughtered the cattle of the Sun. Sitting at a bar, almost nearly sober, the Tour Guide decided that he would show his self-control by counting twenty, and let the next living thing to come round the corner in that time decide what, and how much, he would drink next. In the event it turned out to be a big black pariah dog skulking along the gutter. He decided that was an acceptable herald of Typhoeus, and ordered a bottle.

For a while all was well. Soon he ordered a second bottle, and as he drank, his thoughts turned to D H Lawrence, who had lived in the town, working, no doubt, on his Apocalypse, with its approving references to The Orphic mysteries and the invocation of Dionysian ecstasy. And of methods of getting out of the body to experience the beyond.

Could it be that Lawrence had himself experienced some spontaneous initiation, or had he just discovered the blessings of Typhoeus? He had understood enough to opine that the Orphic initiates had attained the same state of consciousness as Einstein many centuries before him, and that every such initiate must die his own death, to be reborn through Hades. Perhaps that was why he had seen that snake in his garden as a missed opportunity?

"In Sicily, black snakes are innocent, only the gold are venomous."

Dollarton could have given Jeeves lessons in shimmying up silently. Here he was again, already settled beside him, refilling his glass and gesturing to the waiter for another bottle. And, in paraphrasing Lawrence's poem, apparently reading his mind.

"Lawrence thought that when he shunned that snake he missed his chance with one of the Lords of Life. But even if he had been more receptive, I wonder what message it would have brought? How would it have been communicated?"

At last, the danger of an interesting conversation! He drank the glass back and went in at the deep end.

"Well, Sir Thomas Browne wrote about how surprised Eve must have been to hear a serpent speak, and even speculated on how the voice came out of it. He concluded that it would be no challenge to a Being that had spoken from the belly of the Pythonissa, or the oak at Dodona."

Again Dollarton managed to surprise him.

"Ah, good old Sir Thomas! 'Hell is where I am, Lucifer and all his legions are in me.' But I was thinking of an even older wisdom. Rabbi Eleazer of Worms and his Ashkenazi brethren spent a long time pondering the nature of Eve's tempter. If a body shares the eternal stability of the unchanging soul, how can it be fluid enough to change its form? Yet Satan was supposedly changed from a two legged to a crawling, legless thing for tempting Eve. They wondered how that was possible. Do you know their answer? As long as the eyes remained the same, everything else could change. They even pondered Werewolves, and came to the same conclusion. If everything changed but the eyes, something of the integrity of its form remained. Incidentally, the wolf form emerged, they said, from between the man's shoulder blades!"

He refilled the glasses.

"Who was it that said the very act that condemns a man's soul to Purgatory brings the Yogi salvation? I suppose we're talking about the power of the Beast here, aren't we; a different path to wisdom? Mephistopheles in bestial form? I was told that the power of the Beast was particularly strong in some temple or other that used to be around here. I don't know who told me that. Some old Crow."

The American was playing with him again, and he was growing sick of it.

"Just what *is* your game, Dollarton?"

"Oh, I've played many games, my friend. And I'm not talking Las Vegas. Siang K'i, Fanorana,

Tablut, Saturankam, Nine Men's Morris, Ashtapada. I'm considered a master at Brandubh, and Throwboard, Fidchell, Oente Grammai and Enochian Chess; even Pachis with living pieces. I learned Dog and Duck from the master. I've even diced with the author of the Book on Games of Chance, and played the Game of Globes with its inventor, though that was a long, long time ago. If games are what you want, I'm definitely your man."

He saw with some confusion that Dollarton had somehow palmed a well-worn pack of cards, which he was shuffling expertly. Dealing them out into groups of three, he began to move his hand around the table, tapping their vividly painted images as he went.

"Let's see now. The Fool, flanked by The Empress and the Two of Cups. What could have been a happy, loving relationship with a wonderful woman: with the woman. Ah, but then there is Lust. Not entirely what some might think; spiritual intoxication; the invocation of Divine Ecstasy.

"All still going well, but oho, here comes the Three of Swords! Sadness. And could it be that the cause of it is a three-sided relationship? The old Eternal Triangle?"

His hand traced the coils of a widdershins serpent over the cards, tapping each in turn. He did not seem to be looking at them.

"Five of Wands. Strife, bitterness. Ten of Swords, oh, a broken heart! Anger and pessimism; even fears of insanity. Seven of Cups. You keep trying to block out the past with excessive indulgence, but with no success. Nine of Swords; guilt and self- recrimination. Five of Cups. What a surprise! Unfulfilled aims and the loss of equilibrium, in every sense of the word."

The hand went on, relentlessly circling.

"Never fear! Hope dawns! The Hanged Man; the end of old ways. Art; the alchemy of transformation. The Tower; destruction of established patterns. But how? Ah! The Knight of Wands; fieriest of all fire cards. Change must surely come. And not just change; at the end there must be Judgement."

He could feel the anger rising in him. Up to then Dollarton had been a mildly interesting irritant, but this little performance, so tauntingly delivered, was at the least an unforgivable invasion of his privacy. It was high time the man learned a few home truths in return. But the table was bare, and the chair opposite was unoccupied; somehow Dollarton had managed to make himself scarce.

There followed a night spent drinking and brooding on the American's callously frank reading. Next day was the last of the holiday, and he had decided at some point during the night that he would not accompany the group to Mount Aetna. It was a dereliction of his duty, of course, and would probably get him sacked if he let them go unsupervised, but he no longer cared. He would, in any case, never be able to return to Sicily.

The decision seemed to calm him. He was actually able to shave next morning, and looked younger without the wispy grey beard that he had allowed to grow. It confirmed what he had always believed. That the dangers of drinking were ridiculously exaggerated. His condition was stable.

No harm, then, in a few celebratory glasses in the bar to start the day. As he waited to be served, he decided he would count to twenty. If the first person to pass him in that time was a woman, he would drink only Birra Baretti. If it was a man, it would be a bottle or two of Typhoeus.

The first person to pass him was a man, but he was running, and wearing an odd kind of garment soaked in red. Peering round the bar in the direction from which the figure had come, he saw a body lying in a widening stain of dark blood. The fact that guests were walking calmly through the glistening ruby pool, even walking right through the corpse, told him that neither existed in their World.

Something came undulating smoothly across the floor to the fallen body. It was huge, glistening and somewhat slug shaped, and it began to feed on the fuming blood. As he turned away, he saw that slaughter was going on all around, attracting a growing horde of horrific parasites.

This degree of incursion into normality so early in the day was alarming. He staggered outside, expecting blazing sunlight, but a black veil had been drawn over a sky from which blazing meteors were raining. The shades of armed invaders were pouring in through the long-demolished Cuseni Gate. Somewhere, he realised, Bishop Procopio was being hunted, and when he was captured, Ibrahim would tear out his heart and eat it.

Tauromenium was falling, and with it the last vestige of the Byzantine Empire.

There was only one fragment of the present left in his field of vision. Before he knew what he was doing, he had pulled himself up into the waiting coach. The ironic cheers of the Group told him it was too late to turn back. The door closed behind him and the coach was pulling away. He forced himself to go through the customary headcount, followed by his usual sardonic, "So many, I had not thought that Dreamtours Holiday Company had undone so many."

They were all seated in pairs but for Dollarton, who was at the back of the coach, as usual sitting alone. But no extra, unwanted passengers. A few more jokes and resultant groans, and he was calm, and more or less back in his stride. He might have been forced to go with them this last time after all, but he no longer had to spoon- feed them pap. He reached for the microphone.

"Since I have a captive audience, let's have a few facts about today's visit. You may know that we are about to see what is currently the World's most active volcano. What you might not know is that the lava that flows down its sides is Gorgon's blood, for Aetna is the mother who nurtures Typhon, from whose union with Echidna all monsters come …"

Up from the wine dark sea they climbed towards the smoke that sullied the crystal air. As they ascended, the arid vastness of the uplands was increasingly penetrated by tentacles of black lava: dread flows that creeping monsters send aloft.

A new stop had been added to the journey, a dwelling that had, miraculously, been spared in the last eruption. They had already passed several structures engulfed in solidified debris, but here a wall of solid blackness six feet high marked where the molten lava had stopped within arm's reach of the house. A sign, surely, of a benevolent God. The locals had already raised a shrine to the Virgin there, and the flowers were plentiful and fresh.

The Tour Guide wondered at their inner certainty. No one seemed to have noticed the odd piece of graffito on the wall that faced the lava flow. A crudely painted monster, livid mustard yellow against a blood red background, surely made to placate the god of the volcano. Reassuringly, it seemed to have worked. But when he looked at that threatening mass of darkness all but engulfing the frail structure, he saw another message more personal, and much less comforting.

Climbing on, the coach entered a region of unrelenting blackness broken only by the occasional stubborn plant forcing its way back to the sun. Their destination was a smouldering side crater of the volcano, looming over a cafeteria with stalls selling unspeakably tasteless novelties carved from black lava; souvenirs of some dead planet from which all colour and good taste alike had been banished. There, on the side of a great black pyramid with a mantle of fumes and fire belching from the very forge of Hephaestus, the gaggle of humanity poured as one into the gift shop and began to buy.

He turned and climbed away from them, up into silence and absolute stillness. Legs that were still capable of a stately progress on flat ground were soon struggling. He paused breathless on the rubble strewn acclivity, alone in a world entranced under some ancient obsidian spell.

Something began fluttering for escape from his chest, then clenched agonisingly. The world spun away and he was face down against rough pungent blackness.

It seemed the story of his life; falling into the mire.

"Do you remember me? Abe, your old friend Abe."

It was Dollarton, drawing him up.

"Not far now. We can go the last part together."

He resisted the American's help. Clearly the man had not noticed the other poor soul who was sprawled on the slope close by.

"Shouldn't we help him?"

"We are, pal."

Despite all that had passed between them, he heard himself saying.

"I'm scared, Abe."

"Remember what Meister Eckhart said. If you fear, you will see devils. If you have made your peace they come as angels."

It seemed to be a day of pratfalls. No sooner had Dollarton spoken these dignified words than the noble effect was destroyed, for it was the American's turn to stumble, collapsing forward onto all fours in the black dust. The Tour Guide, whose condition seemed to have undergone a sudden improvement, reached to help him up, and saw that something was emerging from between the crouching man's shoulder blades.

'He's been such an arsehole.' thought the Tour Guide. 'Don't let them be wings.'

But it was a pair of paws, black and cruelly clawed. A dark lupine head and a broad, shaggy back followed. The beast rose up on its hind legs, and looked at him with Dollarton's eyes.

The chambers deep beneath them boiled and roared; Ignis Gehenna belched from a dozen fumaroles.

The dark beast with Dollarton's eyes set off through the swirling vapours, striding firmly on what now seemed to be crudely-shod human feet. He found to his surprise that he could keep up easily, for all his self-inflicted infirmities had apparently fallen away.

The big black form led the way into the crater. For a second it turned to make sure he was following, and all that could be seen was the noble outline of the great snout and pointed ears before it vanished from sight.

Gaining the rim the Tour Guide paused, and looked deep into a black, smouldering crucible. The fumes that rose into his face stank of sulphur, but he breathed them deep, and his whole being was purged of the poison in which it had soaked for so long. For the first time in many years he felt no need for a drink.

Stepping over the edge, he began the long descent.

UNDER THE CASKET, A BEACH!

Nick Mamatas

The beach was so close. Alexandra had been every day so far, but this morning her cousins Kimon and Kalliope were virtually kidnapping her for some ridiculous reason—her terrible Greek and the cousins' mediocre English could usually meet in the middle for most vacation-themed planning, but not now. Something about money and their dead grandfather. Alexandra was in the back of Kimon's tiny pickup truck with a pair of shovels and a literal bucket of sticky-sweet wine, but the beach was tempting her, just past the winding dirt road and down the cliff. She was tempted to throw her long legs over the side of the cargo bed and roll for it.

Kalliope stuck her head out the passenger side window. Her hair swirled madly in black tangles around her face, her long nose. "Hey! How you doing, z'alright?" Alexandra had gotten a little carsick on her first day on the island, but that was after a ten-hour flight and a twelve-hour ferry ride.

Alexandra said "*Kala!*" *Good*, in Greek. Kalliope was good about keeping things simple. Her brother Kimon would just chatter away at Alexandra like a machine-gun, and end every utterance with "eh? Eh? EH?" as if it were a helpful prod toward understanding.

"Don't drink too much *krasi*, we need it for pappous!"

Were they going to pour wine on the grave, or serve it to other relatives and friends for some gravesite memorial ceremony? Then Alexandra realized the purpose of the shovels clattering next to her on the floor of the pickup's cargo bed.

"We go to beach after and swim off the sweat," Kimon said. Kimon was a little guy; all Alexandra's relatives in Greece were short. He looked like a dwarf from *Lord of the Rings* digging away at pappous's grave. Neither Kalliope nor Alexandra betrayed much interest in the shovel that Kimon had dropped at their feet.

"*Para poli orea*," said Kalliope, which Alexandra couldn't help but mentally translate as "Very a lot nice."

"Or maybe by the time we're done the sea will dry up," Kimon said, looking pointedly at both women.

"Why are we doing this now?" Kalliope demanded. "It's too hot for this work."

"We have to do it now. You know, you know…" Kimon said through gritted teeth. *Kseries, keseries!* Kalliope glared like a statue, but Alexandra pursed her lips and decided to help. She wasn't very good at shoveling, but the grave wasn't very deep either, and it took only thirty minutes. It was hot now, and Alexandra could practically feel the marrow boiling in her bones. Kimon told Kalliope to get the wine. Amazingly, she had somehow produced a pack of cigarettes and was smoking one, though she wore only a tank top and a pair of cut-off jeans. Alexandra wanted one, but didn't have the breath to ask. Kimon barked at her to move her ass, and Kalliope cursed and brought over the bucket.

"What are we even doing?" Alexandra finally asked. Whatever it was, there was clearly no need to be devout about it.

"Washing pappous's bones in the wine," said Kalliope.

"And then taking them home for a while," said Kimon, then Kalliope immediately started screaming at him. The Greek flew by too fast and too idiomatically for Alexandra to know what they were talking about, but she did know that in rural Greece—and the island was rural enough that she hadn't even seen a single Tweet since arriving two days prior—exhuming bones, washing them, and then sealing them in a small ossuary was not uncommon. On an island like this one, which is mostly impassable mountain ringed by a handful of small villages along the shoreline, land was at an even higher premium.

Then Alexandra heard her name, and money, and her name again, and money again, and then both her cousins, red in the face and sweating heavy tears, looked to her.

"He's not…ready yet," Kalliope said. "You understand?"

"Pappous is dead for four years," Kimon said. "He is not only bones yet…We bought more time for him, made the rent longer…"

"Extended the lease," Kalliope, who loved American television, clarified.

"But now we need more money. We're selling it."

Kalliope snorted at that, but her contempt wasn't for Kimon. "You're an *engoni* too, Alexandra," she said, the x in the name a hard click on her tongue. "We only need a thousand dollars."

"Kalliope thinks all Americans are rich, cousin," Kimon said.

"A thousand isn't rich. How much it costs to come here?" Kalliope said.

"About a thousand bucks, but I saved for months to do it, and I took all my vacation time too, and I have a roommate and student loans and…" Alexandra trailed off. She did not have a thousand dollars. She did not save anything for months; Greece was credit card territory and depended on a strategy of staying with her mother's family in Athens on either end of the trip, and in between living out of a dufflebag while bopping from cousin to cousin. When Kimon and Kalliope got tired of her, which seemed to be happening before her eyes, she'd spend interminable hours waiting for the water taxi to take her around the bend, to the other side of the island, to the next relative.

"He's your pappous," Kalliope said, gesturing toward the grave. The cousins had cared for him in his final days, and still lived in the old man's house. Kalliope had lost her job thanks to austerity, and the elders who paid Kimon to do work with their gardens and goats had suffered from pension cuts and so hired him much less often. A thousand dollars…

"I mean euros," Kalliope said, catching herself.

"I'm sorry, I don't have it."

"*Theos*…" Kimon ventued.

Now Alexandra snorted. It was a family trait, she realized. "My dad *definitely* doesn't have it!" The cousins looked suspicious, bemused. "Gambling," she said, and then the cousins understood. Pappous had been a *pallikari*, a real man, who as teen during the occupation had crawled on his belly down the side of the mountain with a knife in each hand to slice Nazi throats, who fished daily to feed his family and who punched tax collectors during the junta, and who lived till the age of 101. His son though was nothing but a big fat American disappointment who worked in an auto parts store and donated fifty percent of his income to Atlantic City.

"We have to get him home before it gets too hot," Kimon said. "We all lift."

Kalliope groaned.

"The…" Kimon struggled for the word. "Meat. The meat will get hot and smell."

"What about the wine?" Alexandra asked.

"We'll do it at home."

Alexandra had to sit in the cargo bed of the pickup with the plain box holding the remains of her grandfather all the way back. Her shovel had left a couple scars on the lid. The beach still looked great, but she couldn't smell it anymore; nothing but the sickly-sweet burning dust of the long dead filled her nostrils. The cousins had told her that they'd figured she had money in her fannypack—they'd guessed that was why she always wore it—and that she would pay off the deposit for the lease extension on the spot. Alexandra had only met her pappous twice, and both times as a child. When she was four years old, he pinched her cheeks and forearms way too hard, and sounded like Dracula when he spoke. When she was twelve all he could remember of her was that she had once liked picking up long twigs and pretending to be a witch with a magic wand-slash-flying broomstick. A teenaged American who could barely carry on a conversation just bewildered him, and for her part Alexandra didn't like jokes about how he was going to build a box for her *prika* when she came over to Greece to meet the husband he'd picked for her.

She felt bad for the old man, and for herself. "*Lypámai*," she told the casket. She decided, as the truck pulled up to her grandfather's little white house, that she would help Kalliope and Kimon wash the bones, and that she wouldn't freak out. She promised herself, she promised the spirit of pappous that she would do it like a good Greek girl might, and not like an obnoxious American who didn't even have the wherewithal to be rich.

She did not realize that a skull could still have hair on it.

There was a shoe too, and a pair of socks, that had managed to resist rot in the dry climate. Alexandra blanched quickly, and was offered a towel by Kimon. Confused, she made to heave into it. "Don't *sernó* there," Kalliope said, her hands pantomiming a spray of vomit. "Wave the insects away with it."

"What about pappous's…"

"Yes," Kimon said, in English. He left the small concrete patio overlooking the hilly vegetable garden and came back with the block of knives from the kitchen counter.

"But why," Alexandra said. "Why why…" *Giatí giatí*.

"He has to go in the…bone, ehm, guard," said Kalliope. She held her hands in a way to suggest a box. The ossuary, she meant. "But with skin and flesh they won't take him. We can't afford the grave lease anymore. That's it. No other way."

"Cremation?"

"No place in Greece for that," Kimon said. "The church says ashes won't be resurrected on the last day. Everyone believes it."

"Plus expensive to ship to Bulgaria, and then get him back. Five thousand euros," said Kalliope.

"What do people do?"

"Most *pay*!" said Kimon, angry now. "Or have American relatives pay."

Alexandra forgot the Greek word for "whatever" and wasn't sure it would work idiomatically anyway. She flapped the towel as hard as she could. Kimon's work took a long while, and he often made mistakes and growled curses about fucking the Mother of God. Twice, he resorted to the cleaver, and hacking. By the time the cousins needed the wine for the clean bones, night had fallen, and half the bucket had been drunk.

What to do with the flesh was a problem, but Alexandra decided that it wasn't hers to deal with. Kimon was convinced that burying it in the garden would somehow negatively influence the growth of the vegetables that the cousins have become increasingly dependent on since austerity and depression hit, but Kalliope thought that was ridiculous. She wanted to take the remains to the beach and throw them in the sea.

"For the birds to eat?" Kimon shouted.

"Yes! Who else? The tourists, or the refugees?"

Alexandra left them to their argument and headed down to the beach herself, picking over the rocky incline in the blue dark. There was never a cloud in the sky during a Greek summer, and the moon was large, so Alexandra was able to step carefully and find her way. It was quiet, except for the waves. This night, for a few minutes at least, the beach was empty, and the sea untraveled upon. That's what she really craved—to be the only person in the entire world, or at least the momentary illusion of the same. The only thing that would have made the experience better would have been a hot day of topless sunbathing, long swims, comical German tourists, and Balkan disco music pouring forth tinnily from cheap smartphones and cheaper radios. For the contrast.

When Alexandra closed her eyes, she thought, *Is this what the grave is like?* It wouldn't be so bad, really. Cool and dark and contemplative. No chance of being interrupted. Wait, that's not quite right, is it? In Greece, the shovels would come soon after the worms, and then the weeping relations, or *arguing* relations, but at least there'd be wine. She tried to summon up some tears for pappous, but all her body gave her was a dull ache somewhere in her abdomen.

She heard footfalls, but didn't open her eyes at first. It was probably Kalliope come to join her, Alexandra thought, as that girl could not bear to leave her American cousin alone for more than thirty minutes. But the voice that called out "Yassass!"—a formal greeting, but in the singsong style of the island's dialect—was a man's. She opened her eyes. He was young, maybe even younger than Alexandra, and excited-looking, all eyes and a mouth full of thick teeth. He wore swim trunks and sandals and was in fairly good shape; he definitely had a physical job down on the pier, or in construction. He introduced himself as Georgios and asked, "*Americanida?*"

That was the limit of Georgios's ability, or at least interest in, communicating verbally. Instead he gestured broadly, wandered over to the large rock jutting out of the sand, squatted and wrapped his arms around it, then with a deep grunt lifted it. He brushed the wayward sand from his chest hair then kneeled next to Alexandra, who smiled and patted her belly. Briefly, she considered saying something in Greek, but decided it was more fun to pretend to know only English. He scrambled to her like a child chasing after an interesting bug.

Georgios was warm, and heavy atop her, and more attentive than Alexandra would have guessed a stranger would be. The pounding, and the sand, kept her from thinking too much about whether this guy had ever had sex with Kalliope, or whether he'd be sniffing around for the rest of her trip. Why not enjoy something, then be gone, the way life itself worked? And with that thought, she came. After, Georgios made a good but too noisy hot-water bottle, so she extricated herself from his limbs, shook him awake and tried to suggest something about the police, which he laughed at, and kissed him good-bye.

It wasn't Kalliope, but Kimon Alexandra encountered on the path leading to pappous's old house. Everyone on the island was a night owl of some sort, as midday was too hot to work and everyone napped through it when they weren't digging up graves. "Cousin," he said plainly. He was smoking a cigarette and didn't offer her one.

"Good evening," Alexandra said in Greek, wondering if it was too formal.

"Popi was worried; she sent me down," he said. "You fall asleep on the beach?"

"No I—"

"Your hair," he said, pointing his chin. "Covered." She ran her fingers through it and sand fell as if blown off a dune. "Yeah," she said.

"Yeah, I saw everything."

Alexandra decided to be Greek about it. "You watched all that, eh? Nothing better to do? You just pull your pants up?"

"Georgios's father…he owns the land," Kimon said.

"Oh? What land?"

"Oh!" Kimon said. "Oh! You don't know village life, American cousin," Kimon said in English. "The cemetery land. He's the one we owe money to."

"Why would he own a cemetery?"

"Pappous was a Nazi-killer, a Red. The church said no. Half the island is Communist and everyone pays taxes to the church and it still says no, so they are all buried in a capitalist cemetery." In English, he added the word "Irony." Then back to Greek: "And this is the man you fuck?"

"*Katse sta avga sou*," Alexandra told him. *Sit on your eggs* was the phrase, *mind your own business* the message.

"We owe him a lot of money, cousin. A lot."

Alexandra shrugged large enough to be seen in the dark. "Not anymore, eh?" She strode past Kimon and headed to the house, her shoulders tight from expectation, but Kimon didn't carry on the argument or chase after her. Kalliope just said "Hi cousin!" as Alexandra walked into the small house; she was hunched over a deck of cards at the kitchen table, playing solitaire. *Everyone here smells*, Alexandra decided sourly, and she took a longer shower than usual, to get the sand and smell of fucking off of her, and to spite her cousins, who had to pay for every drop of water.

The next day was a quiet one, blazing hot. Kimon was grouchy, Kalliope's good cheer rather forced except when she buttonholed Alexandra that afternoon and asked her how Georgios "was", her eyebrows animated and lascivious. They went to the beach to swim and tan, though Kimon stayed perched on a rock, smoking and reading three newspapers, each more full of *malakias* than the last. There was no more talk of pappous, or the flesh sliced from his bones, or money, or sex. Alexandra bought dinner and drinks and drinks and drinks for everyone at a bar with a tiny dance floor that all the islanders referred to as "the discotheque." The cousins had fun, but Alexandra sensed that they were resentfully counting every euro she spent on them. She could drown their contentious conversations in alcohol, but the feelings were like jagged rocks pushing past the surface of the water. *Fuck this place*, Alexandra decided. She meant the entire island.

Outside the bar she bummed a cigarette from a pair of German tourists then turned her back on them and walked off without a word or gesture, even after the catcalls turned to curses. The moon was high and strange, its light setting the pebbles in the unpaved road blazing. The island was small, the village even smaller, and Alexandra was sure she'd find the beach soon enough. Maybe it was just a thing people did—hang out there until an attractive potential sexual partner came walking along. If the shore wasn't crowded with people every night, it was because most everyone was either related or already paired off.

Or both, Alexandra thought for a moment, giving herself a shiver.

And then another shiver, and a quick jerk backward. Before she even knew what she was reacting to, she reacted. "Oh," Alexandra said aloud. The path before her was littered with…not bones. Just stones, slivers of clam shells, and the bleached exposed roots of nearby trees. And a bone after all, a thin rib whiter than a tooth, and fragile-looking. Alexandra gasped. The booze clouding her brain headed right to her knees, and she wobbled. She picked up the rib and stuck it in her fannypack. Probably wasn't even a person's. Certainly wasn't one of pappous's; she had been sitting next to the closed box the entire ride back home.

But who knows how many pappouss are being dug up and brought home these days? she thought. A pick-up truck roared through, and Alexandra had to jump out of the way to keep from being flattened. That sobered her up; it was a long and stupid way home, and what was she going to do at the beach, anyway?

Fucking sleep there.

It wasn't the light of the sun that woke Alexandra, as it was still dark. Nor was it the sound of the sea, which had lulled her to sleep in the first place. She woke to screaming coming from every direction. Just off shore a half dozen boats so filled with people that they were spilling off the sides bobbed low and haphazard in the water. Behind Alexandra came the islanders, some running in pairs with rafts and small rowboats on their shoulders, others barking orders as they pulled first-aid kits, foodstuffs, blankets across the sand toward the shore. There was a well-practiced sense of chaos to it all. She got to her feet and joined the crowd, looking for either of her cousins, or Georgios, while taking an internal inventory. She was still in shorts and tank top, and didn't even have a cough drop in her pocket to offer. No medical skills either, and not strong or fluent enough to seamlessly join one of the response groups. Her phone wasn't even charged, so she couldn't take video or pics for later posting either.

A fishing boat came around the edge of the outcrop of stones in which Alexandra was sleeping and expertly came to a stop near the most distressed of the refugee crafts. Some of the better swimmers cut through the clear water and helped the refugees stay afloat, until they could be loaded onto the fishing boat. The other refugee boats—mostly bright orange rafts, or wooden boats barely buoyant and overcrowded with nervous children in life-vests—headed toward the beach.

Alexandra walked to the water's edge, weaving through bustle and multilingual shouting. A wave lapped against her toes as the first group of refugees were brought onto the shore. One of the women, her hair in knots, salt crusting her features, shouted out a couple of words Alexandra of course didn't recognize. Then she said *le français*, and finally, "English?"

"English! I speak English!" Alexandra said.

"And Greek?" the woman said.

"*Etski-ketsi*." So-so.

It was enough. Who was hurt, who needed medicine, which children had no parents anymore, which few refugees were Christian—and she explained that the Christians had commanded her to identify them to the islanders. Her throat quickly went dry, but the water bottles were for the refugees, so she had to just soldier through. Finally, the fishing boat anchored just off shore, and the islanders formed a chain to shift what few belongings the refugees managed to carry onto the beach, and then helped the refugees to shore. A couple of men came up to Alexandra and began shouting in English, making demands, telling their stories. She took a step back and walked into a pair of hands that quickly grabbed her biceps.

"Yassou!" said Georgios. He was salty and wet, but not drenched. He'd been on the boat. "*Kali koritsi*," he said. *Good girl*. A bit condescending. The men who had been talking to Alexandra reached out and hugged and kissed him, crowding her between their limbs.

"He saved us!" one of them explained as he sidestepped Alexandra's elbow.

"Better captain than you, Sami," said the other. Then their conversation vanished into their own language, except for their non-verbal praise for Georgios—handshakes, tight hand-squeezes, more double-kisses on each cheek, then waving for their women to come join them. Alexandra slid away to see how else she could help.

Kimon was among the crowd of islanders now, holding a small wooden box of oranges. "That's was to be my boat," he said to Alexandra.

"What?"

"Pappous's boat. Georgios's now." A few of the bigger children approached, their hands out. Kimon distributed a couple pieces of the fruit, not making eye contact with the kids, or smiling, or offering extras to take back to their families.

Alexandra glanced over her shoulder at the knot of people surrounding Georgios. Some were crying, one woman was literally on her hands and knees before him, kissing the sand and stroking his ankle, as that was all of him she could reach. "He's a hero, eh?"

Kimon snorted. "I would do the same if I still had the boat."

"How did he end up owning everything? You lose at cards?" Alexandra asked.

"The troika. Pension cuts. Borrowing," Kimon said. He handed out another orange with every word. "At least we still have oranges. Second-most popular present."

"After their lives being saved?"

"After cigarettes," Kimon said. He gave away his last orange, flipped over the box, the drummed his fingers on it. "I'm finished."

"Stay. Your Greek and my English…"

He made a face. "No. These refugees…" He shuddered. Alexandra gasped; she rummaged fruitlessly around her mind for the Greek word for *racist*. She knew Kimon would just pretend not to understand if she denounced him in English.

Kimon saw something in Alexandra's face, and then said something Alexandra didn't understand. He tried again: "Don't get…familiar to these people. They don't stay."

"Where do they go?"

"Nowhere good."

"You're like the sphinx, you know that?" she said.

"Not here," he said, casting his gaze about the busy beach.

Georgios called for Alexandra. "Kimon's cousin! Come help, American!"

"Don't—" Kimon started.

Alexandra gave Kimon the *moutsa*, a wide palm pantomiming shoving a handful of shit into his face. She ran to Georgios, who still had a knot of refugee men around him. One of them spoke English too, and Georgios had an offer to make. Instant money, working in his father's olive grove. No need to go to the camp on the other side of the island, or report to the government at all, not for a couple of weeks anyway, until after the harvest comes in. Georgios's father could pay in euros, pounds sterling, and even American dollars if that's what the men wanted. Most of the men were single, or at least had been separated from their families, so took the offer, and followed Georgois back into the sea and onto the boat. "Come come," he told them, "before the police arrive."

The woman who spoke English ran as best she could up to Alexandra, and stumbled into her arms. "Where are they going?" she demanded.

"With him, to make some money—he has jobs for them, he said."

"Who is he?"

Alexandra realized that despite having fucked him, she really had no idea who Georgios was, or where he lived. "He's rich," she said. "He owns a lot of property around here." The boat roared off in the distance.

"It doesn't matter," the woman said, more to herself than Alexandra. "When will the authorities be here?" With that question came the sound of a siren, and a generalized sense of unease rippling across the crowd. Some of the children started wailing. Alexandra slipped one foot out of her sandal and squeezed the sand of the beach with her toes.

Later, on the roof of pappous's house, where she and Alexandra were smoking the last of a pack of Assos cigarettes, Kalliope announced that she didn't know where Kimon was, and didn't care. She was highly interested in the rib bone that poked out from Alexandra's fannypack when Alexandra reached for her cigarette lighter.

"*Ti einai?*" she asked, grabbing it.

"It's a bone."

"I know *that*," Kalliope said, in English. She peered at it closely. "Where did you find it?"

"On the road…" The island wasn't much for street signs or intersections. "By that curve where you can see the little church on the other side of the harbor. We passed it when we, uh, brought pappous back."

"You collected it," Kalliope said. "You know…"

"The other day…did you count the ribs?"

"This is clean, old," Kalliope said. "No, not clean, it's…" She put the rib up close to her mouth and pantomimed nibbling on it. "But old."

Kimon hadn't done so well with the cleaver, Alexandra guessed. "Should we call someone?"

Kalliope held the bone like a telephone receiver to her ear and mouth. "Hello, police? Anyone missing a rib?"

"Are you drunk?" Alexandra asked.

Kalliope nodded. "Always, cousin." She handed the bone back to Alexandra. "Greece is very old. Many more dead people than living people. Could be from anything. Could be from the Nazis."

"That was seventy years ago!"

"There were many bodies."

"Is that why everyone rushes to help the refugees?" Alexandra asked.

Kalliope shrugged and put her cigarette out on a roof tile. "I don't."

"Kimon does."

"Kimon wants people to think he's doing all right; he spends money he doesn't have."

"Georgois was down there too today. He was recruiting guys to work on the olive harvest," Alexandra said. "I thought that was weird."

"Cousin," Kalliope said. "There's no olive harvest now."

"Well, that's what he said. He took people in his bo—"

"Our pappous's boat," Kalliope interrupted.

"He took them to work on his olive harvest, on pappous's boat," Alexandra finished, huffy now.

Kalliope turned and pointed at a copse of trees two roofs down, on a neighbor's plot. "*Kita*! Olive harvest is in October. It's June."

"Maybe I didn't understand…"

"You didn't understand the word *olive* and you call yourself Greek, cousin?"

"Well, 'harvest'…" Alexandra said in Greek.

"*Therismos*," Kalliope repeated, swinging her hands. "That's not picking harvest, that's cutting the wheat."

"Reaping, yeah. But it means harvest too, right?"

"Yes."

"So it's fine," Alexandra said.

"It's all fine," Kalloipe said. "You leave tonight, no?"

"No, the water-taxi to the other side of the island was commandeered for the refugees for the next two days," Alexandra said. "So, Monday I'll just take the ferry to Piraeus and take the Metro to Athens."

Kalliope didn't respond for a moment. "You could take pappous's boat," she said, finally.

"Trying to get rid of me, cousin?" Alexandra asked, adding a forced giggle as punctuation.

"You can go down there and see if he will; he's a pallikari, and you fucked him, so he will do for you."

"I don't know…"

"Kimon can drive you there."

"It'll be night by the time we get there."

"People fish at night. Pappous fished at night all the time."

"Cousin," Alexandra said, "where's your *philoxenia*, your hospitality?"

Serenity, (1903) by M. K. Čiurlionis

"You know philoxenia—it means friend of the stranger," Kalliope said. "You're family." Alexandra was ready to slap her. "Your phone, is it charged? Don't forget it. Georgios would like to see a smartphone. Show him the game you play on it."

"I don't even know where Kimon *is*!" Alexandra said. "How am I supposed to get to Georgios without a ride?"

Kalliope shrugged. "You walk. It's only three miles."

Alexandra wouldn't beg. She slid off the roof, flicking ash at Kalliope's leg as she descended, then walked inside the small house and collected her things.

"Bye cousin, love you! Say hi to *theos* in America!" Kalliope shouted from the roof at Alexandra's back. Alexandra snorted and flipped her off, American style.

There was no traffic along the single unpaved road, and the moon was as big in the sky as it was the night prior, so the road and nearly everything on it looked white. Alexandra saw bones everywhere, then blinked them out of her mind when she got close to examine a pebble, a bit of wood, or a bleached and empty packet of cigarettes. The *horio* was small—maybe four hundred people, tops, and another twenty to thirty tourists. And thousands of dead, Alexandra was reminded as she approached the cemetery where just two days ago she'd helped exhume her grandfather.

God, there were lots of fucking Commies around here once, she thought, happy to be dismissive and bitter about something other than her cousins. *No wonder it's still such a backwater.* But then, *Is that why their children are so eager to rush out and help the refugees drifting over from North Africa?* slipped in to her mind somehow.

Well, *some* are so eager anyway. Kimon had been petulant, Kalliope absent. Alexandra had done better by the strangers, had shown some real Greek philoxenia. All she wanted to do now is get to the other side of the island and put in some time on the beach. She was ready to forget Georgios and just clamber up one side of the mountain and down the other if she had to.

Then, right by the cemetery gate, she spotted Kimon's pick-up truck, parked in a ditch and behind a shrub. Alexandra approached gingerly; who knew if Kimon was in there crying over pappous, or huffing gasoline, or making out with some secret girlfriend. The car was empty, but now Alexandra was close enough to hear some quiet activity in the cemetery proper.

She froze. Not for one second did she consider the possibility of a ghost. Even if ghosts were real, and they were not, why would Communists leave ghosts behind? *There's a specter haunting Europe...* But she wondered about Georgios, and about the refugees he had hired on the spot, without even a language in common, to...do something.

Anyway, she could find Kimon and make him drive her to their mutual relatives on the other side of the island. She withdrew her phone from her pocket and gave it shake to activate the flashlight, then stepped over the low stone wall into the graveyard.

The sound was digging, and chatter. Not Greek, but a language in which consonants swished about in the mouth like ice slush. And lanterns, on the far end of the graveyard, near the pair of trailers that served as office and equipment shed. Alexandra shut off her light and slid behind one of the larger grave stones. The most reasonable thing to do would be to turn around and go back to the house and beg to be let in, or just sleep on the porch. Second-most reasonable; just wait by Kimon's truck until he showed up, then browbeat him into yelling at Kalliope until she opened the door. In third place, the long walk back to the beach and hanging out there all night, and this time *not* fucking whom ever showed up and flexed for her.

But in a flash, Alexandra realized something about herself—she was not a reasonable person. This was her island as much as it was anyone's, the bones under her feet belonged to some kind of relative, probably. All of them did. It wasn't her fault that she was born in America. Everyone had liked her just fine when she had money to spend or legs to spread, but now she has to deal with this shit? She got up and marched toward the noise, calling out, "All right, what's going on—" Then there was no ground under her and she fell. Something snapped under her. For a moment she was entirely fine, like a rope around her ankle had been untied, but then the pain flooded up her leg.

"Fuck!" The digging stopped, but the talking redoubled. Lanterns bobbled in the night toward her, followed by a voice bellowing in Greek to come back. The first man to come upon her peered down at the shallow grave in which Alexandra had fallen, then turned and rushed away. There was more talking, then some grunting and he appeared again, pulling a wheelbarrow behind him, and with two other men. Alexandra recognized the refugees from the beach.

"Go here," the man with the wheelbarrow said in English, patting the side of it. It was full of something, and had a tarp stretched over the mouth. Alexandra howled as the others lifted her up and tried to place her not too carefully in the wheelbarrow. "Let go!" she shouted as she writhed, her eyes hot from tears. She grabbed at the burlap and snapped it at the face of one of the men.

The wheelbarrow was full of bones. Spines and femurs and pelvises mostly. Four tiny skulls.

Alexandra wrenched herself from the grips the men had on her and fell to the ground. She shouted again and clutched her leg. Confused, the men looked at one another and then backed off, hands up. One of them, Sami, called "Effendi!" and waved for Georgios, who was already rushing up to see what was the matter. Alexandra remembered her phone, and pulled it from her pocket. With a few quick swipes of her thumb, she was recording.

"What's going on here!" she said. "What do you think you're doing?"

Georgios squinted in the glare of the phone's light. "Oh, it's you," he said in Greek. His face was a mask of rage and anxiety, fists huge, chest a bellows. He glared at the men, and their own expressions settled into a simmering malevolence.

"Kimon is here," he said, finally. "Come."

"I can't walk."

Georgios grabbed the wheelbarrow by the handles and dumped the bones into the open grave Alexandra had fallen in, then snatched up the sack and spread it along the bottom of the cart. "Now come," he said. Alexandra shrugged off Georgios's hand and brought herself to standing with the handles of the wheelbarrow. She hopped on her good leg, awkwardly pushing it forward as she used it for balance.

It took a long time for Alexandra to pick her way over the rocky terrain to the trailer. She asked Georgios what he was doing several times, but Georgios just used that word, *therismos*. What was Kimon doing here? Working, Georgios said.

The smell hit Alexandra hard. Then the flies. Kimon stood behind a significant butcher's block, a cleaver in one hand. In front of him, a mass of meat, bones jutting out like winter branches on a fallen tree.

Alexandra reached for her phone again, then stopped. Sami, who had followed her to the shed, yawped, and ran shouting something to the others.

"The refugees won't handle flesh. The Greeks won't dig for their relatives until they have to, not until the very last minute, like we did. This is my job now."

"We're expanding the orchard. We have to plant by autumn to have good growth in the spring," Georgios said.

"Where does it all…go?" Alexandra said.

"Pappous's boat," Kimon said. "From there into the sea."

"My boat," Georgios said.

"At least pappous had you and Kalliope, and the wine, and now he's home. Not all—" he gestured at the mess before him—"mixed up with the others."

"I'm going to tell everyone," Alexandra said.

"Everyone in the village probably already knows," Kimon said. "I told Kalliope yesterday."

Alexandra held up her phone again. "I mean everyone in the world, not everyone on this stupid rock."

"Kimon, control your bitch cousin," Georgios said.

Kimon shrugged. "What will the Internet do, not buy your olives?"

"The police, the detention center officials…they'll want bribes."

Alexandra and Kimon exchanged looks. Kimon put down the cleaver. "I want a bribe too," he said.

"*Gamo to…*" Georgios said. He kicked Alexandra's leg out from under her, then snatched the phone from her hand as she fell and threw it as far as he could. He stepped over her and made a move toward Kimon, towering over him. "The little man thinks he's smart, eh? And I helped you; I let you collect your grandfather first. I'll put you in his grave if you love him so much."

Kimon picked up the cleaver again and looked at it contemplatively. "Go, cousin," he said.

Alexandra scrambled on her hands and knees out the door, watching as Georgios took a spade from its place on the wall and weighed it in his hands. Kimon responded by casually reaching down under the butcher's block and coming up with a still-slick machete in his left hand. Holding both blades, he gestured for Georgios to step forward. Georgios lifted his shovel. Alexandra turned away, hid her gaze behind her hair.

Something like the sound a pig would make if dropped off a roof sent Alexandra scurrying on her belly, her fingers searching for her phone but finding only worms and rock. She nearly crawled into another open grave, but caught herself, and used the stone to get to her feet. Georgios, or much of him, was stumbling after her. Kimon had hacked at him pretty good. He was covered in blood, and clutched the stump of his right hand in the crook of his left arm. But he had Kimon's machete in his left hand now.

"Hey stupid!" Alexandra shouted in Greek. She couldn't recall a more vicious insult. "Let's just call a doctor! You'll go to prison, but you'll be alive! They can sew your hand, maybe!"

"You don't understand. It…" He stopped for a moment. "You know, your pappous wanted us to get married."

"What?"

"It's true," Georgios said. "It's just funny. He talked about you, his smart American granddaughter, to my father, all the time. Kalliope would get mad. We should have gotten married, instead of this."

"Instead of this…Do you want to kill me too?" Alexandra said.

"I want to go back five minutes and give Kimon his bribe. But…" He said a couple of hard-to-translate words. The sort of words mostly men say about how important it is that they be shown respect. The sort of words Alexandra's father used to use to explain why he had to sell the car to pay a gambling debt, why those plane tickets to visit Greece had to be refunded, why if the phone rang he wasn't home. Georgios looked at her, his face twisted in pain, but also with something else—a plaintive demand for understanding, even sympathy. *Please believe this all makes sense*. She knew that face.

"Whatever. You're no pallikari," she said, limping toward him.

"*Koritsi mou*, please," he said. "I'm dying too."

"I'm not."

He lowered his head and rushed her like a bull. He tackled her hard, but yowled. She dug fingers into the stump where his hand had been as she fell back into the grave. There was a rock waiting for the back of her head at the bottom. His breath was near, like it had been the other night. She opened her mouth and started to chew the too-close flesh. There was blood everywhere, hot and salty on the cool earth. Alexandra squirmed down into the soil and then came a roaring sound.

Is this what dying sounds like? she thought. Then came rescue, hands somehow reaching past Georgios and for her, fingers tight around her ankles and wrists, pulling her out of the grave. The smell of salt and a flash of the dark.

But it was backward, she realized. The hands pulled her deeper and deeper into the soil, not out of the grave, but through it. These weren't the hands of the refugee workers, or her cousins come to save her. They were older hands, hard as gnarled twigs, and so many, comrades and cousins passing her along through the sand, past the cages of roots, around shattered boxes and scattered bones.

Up, into the water. The moon a great pearl. Alexandra burst out of a wave—she no longer had lungs to fill. Her name, the x a fuzzed h, the d a lisp the r rolled, and a final pair of hands, pappous's hands, lifting her from the sea onto the deck of his boat. He smiled, even as his face had that now familiar pleading twist. And she understood perfectly. They'd sail around the curve of the island, collect Kimon, who'd be ready in a few minutes, and be on their way.

DEPOSITION OF DARKNESS

Mesándel Virtusio Arguelles
(Translated by Kristine Ong Muslim)

Through the fall, loved ones are cast off.
They dip their feet into the gloom.

Through the next ascent, those desired are pursued.
Anticipating the clarity of their vision.

Looking forward now to the break of dawn.
Even if that meant vanishing again.

Only for a while.
Pure, never-ending

Originally published in Filipino in *Ilahás*, 2004.

THE OTHER TIGER

Helen Marshall

The news creeps through the village.
The last old man has died.
Our village no longer exists.

—From the collected works of Jekaterina Rovenskaya

1.

I was born in the village as the last war began. We were far from the front lines, and, lacking railways or even roads more substantial than footpaths, logging tracks, or frozen rivers, we were hardly touched by it. And yet many of my early memories of the village are inflected by the war, the sense of violence. The possibilities it opened.

The men liked to speak of the war. For the young men it was obvious why. There was little for them to do, though the factories had begun to take on more labourers but those too were far from us and would've required resources or long journeys. The men, though they didn't like to admit it, were scared of leaving home. So some drank. Many fished or hunted: foxes, lynxes, bears, minks, wild boar and grey wolves as well caribou, reindeers and moose. There were also tigers but few hunted them. They were too dangerous and once a hunt was begun it was necessary to finish it: a tiger would remember.

The youngest of the boys, when they were hungry, would pick currants or cranberries from the marshy areas. Ginseng and opium poppies, too, though the growing season was short and they were rare. Some boys would harvest cedar nuts by hand. It was subsidence living. Wages were poor, resources scarce. There was a thriving black market for whatever the President had declared anathema and constant reports of corruption—the tax officials were few and uniformly hated.

In the summer the forests surrounding our village were humid, with a thick bayou languor. There were lush sub-tropical forests that spawned gigantic vegetation: oaks with trunks six feet in diameter, wild kiwis and cherry trees, giant lotus and towering lilacs, fed by typhoons that blustered in for much of the hot months. In the winter the cold was enough to kill. It froze the sap in the smallest of the wind-shorn birch trees, leaving them to hemorrhage or explode like pipe bombs.

Life in the village was hard, our lives trapped within a huddle of huts that had been divided long ago according to their own private geography. I remember as a child being told there were places forbidden to me. I don't know who told me. My mother? I have so few memories of her. She died when I was very young of a disease that could have been treated in a bigger city. But my father had no money for medicine or long travels so he nursed her himself with what he had, which was little enough it turned out. So when she died he buried her in the yard with her sisters, her mother, her grandmother.

Early on I was drawn to those places I was forbidden, the private drinking establishments that admitted men only. The women weren't allowed to enter unless we were called upon for various unfortunate or menial tasks. Then we were barely regarded. We crept in, were told to look at nothing, to touch nothing. The men feared our scent, I think. As we waited outside for permission, our breath would leave smooth swirling contrails. We exuded a presence they feared, an oil on our skin, a sweat, a dank perspiration. We were told we were unnecessary. A village needed a man, we were told, the same way it needed a post office: a man granted a certain kind of authority. A man was necessary for administration purposes.

I married young. I was fourteen, I think, and skinny. I still had scraped knees beneath my thick skirts, and would sometime knock elbows against cupboards, my body was that new to me. But my father couldn't abide me in the house any longer. He'd grown insistent that I should leave but I didn't know why, and the sudden change in his mood scared me. I'd nowhere to go, no proper skills beyond mending shirts, fixing ropes, cleaning guns and cooking. For several years I'd gone to a small girl's school, which was little more than a backroom where gnarled Albina, whose name meant *white*, would help me do sums. Sometimes, if I was very good, she'd read the poetry of the city to me. Most of it was filled with a crazed patriotic zeal, which brought a sheen to her eyes. She was partially blind already so she'd recite the poems by heart. I didn't know they were out of fashion then. She must have heard them during her own youth, which would've been many years ago.

I didn't like all the poems. The war poems, which she loved most, struck me as crude. They intruded into my thoughts like the blast of a horn on a cold, still day. But there were other poems too, ones whose language created a kind of breathlessness around them. When I heard those a space would open inside my mind and I could see clearly, I thought, into the mind of the poet. I would hear his voice speaking directly to me. No women I knew of wrote poetry.

For some time I wanted to become a teacher but there weren't any books in my house. As much as Albina loved me she wouldn't lend me hers. Her little library was precious to her. Without it she would've been like so many of the other old women, who'd tie bright scarves around their head in hopes of appearing young. She told me once she'd had many lovers when she was my age and I believed her. Her features had a regal appearance though they'd softened with time. She'd had two sons. One had died young and the other had left a good while ago. She was proud of him, but apart from her books, Albina was alone.

She did give me one book as a wedding present. It was old and the pages had a soft, velvet-like texture and a smell that was vaguely rank, as if it was fashioned the old way from animal skins. Still I was very thankful for this and I kissed her twice on the cheek. It was a book of love poems. I'd read them to myself in the late afternoons when my husband went to check the traps or do whatever he chose to do in the forest. At first they didn't make sense to me. I'd thought they could help me. When I first met my husband he'd seemed very handsome, very dashing. He had large reddish-brown hands with thick callouses. His beard was large and bushy and there were trails of short black hair in the folds of his neck. His name was Misha which meant *one who is like the Lord*, and also, *little bear cub*. He reminded me of a bear.

My husband liked to speak of the war. He liked to imagine how it was playing out and how he, himself, would be a hero if only the fighting came closer. He imagined himself hunting his prey with a rifle or slipping a noose around the neck of his enemy. He came alive in these moments of imagined gore. You might think otherwise, but he never touched me badly. At heart, I think, he was a gentle man but to him meat was meat and any animal stripped down to its flesh held a strange fascination for him.

He took me away from my father and I loved him for that but my love felt incomplete. I didn't open to his touch as I thought I should. So I read the book hoping it would hold some secret I needed. But the love poems were sad and they didn't help. Once I tried reading him a poem but the words were confusing and he couldn't make heads or tails of them, poor man! But he didn't mind me reading to myself and in fact encouraged me to do so. He believed, I think, I might be a touch mad but this didn't bother him. Many of us were back then.

I don't know how Misha died. This may sound odd to you but it wasn't at the time. Men were always disappearing. Sometimes they'd go into the forest in the winter and they'd lose their way. Drunkenness would make them forgetful. Or they'd stop to take a piss and the cold would creep up on them, thuggishly, and cause them first to sit and then to lie down. It wasn't uncommon for one man to find the body of another in the spring and, thinking he was only asleep, seek to wake him—only to discover his eyes glassy and unblinking, as blue as frozen marbles.

It was late into the winter season and Misha didn't return when I expected. I waited three nights. The fuel began to run low and there was nothing but tins of salted fish he'd traded for. When the last of these was gone I knew he was dead—or as good as.

After that news travelled quickly. I was spotted alone on the streets wearing my red bridal shawl. It was foolish to do that but I'd grown used to only having my husband's company and I'd forgotten how it was to have neighbours watching me. It'd been months since I'd ventured outside. A wiser woman would have kept quiet and left things as they were but I was hungry and it was the warmest thing I owned.

I went to check the traps he'd set. I was lucky. I found a black-and-brown fox but it regarded me with cold and hateful eyes. I'd never eaten fox and wondered if I could do so now. I stared at it as Misha would have, trying to see past the dermis and hair and into its layers of red meat and glutinous fat. I couldn't do. I let the pitiful creature go and it vanished like a scrap of lightning into the forest. I burst into tears at my own stupidity. The creature certainly would've gobbled me up had the situation been reversed!

Raisa found me wandering the trap lines, thank god. She was my husband's mistress. Her name meant *rose* or *carefree* or *beloved*. She was more beautiful than me, two years older, with a full figure and bright red lips I'd always envied. I liked her though we'd never truly spoken and now we stared at each other dumbly, mutely. She fed me dried reindeer and a thick, sweet liquid she carried with her in a little bottle. It made me lightheaded. She took me to the women's quarter where the two of us wept together for a long time over what we'd lost.

You loved three things in life:
pure white snow, the first shoots of spring
pushing through, a fully belly.
How you hated the dark hours of sorrow.

2.

The women's quarter was on the southern edge of the village, close to the river, which flooded frequently in the summer. It had a dark, olid smell to it for this reason and the earth was pitchy. No man would have set his home there.

At first I didn't know what to think. Misha's death felt like a dream. I was haunted by the fact of his absence and the questions it raised for me. Where would I get my food? How would I survive? But mingled with these questions was a less tangible despair. Who was I? It suddenly seemed as if my husband had given me my shape with his presence, his needs. Without them I was a tool that'd been abandoned, a spare hammer, a broken lever.

The women were gentle with me. They poured steaming water into a copper tub and gave me soap to clean myself. One of them toweled my hair while another brushed it and all the while they whispered to me in soft syllables I barely understood. Since I'd been married I hadn't spoken the language of women. It took me time to unmask the words and restore order and sense to them. But among them the curious drone began to resolve itself and at last I calmed.

It was Raisa who uttered the first words to which I could fully respond. She'd been treated the same as I had. Now her skin glowed pinkly and was as smooth as pearl. I could understand why Misha loved her. We touched hands, she and I, and we spoke for a little about him. There were differences already in our memories. He had always been gentle with me, cupping my breasts as if they were small animals that needed to be coaxed. He'd kissed the back of my neck and rubbed his thumb behind my ear. But with her he'd been more boisterous. Almost laughing she showed me a line of bruises he had given her along her thighs. It was strange for me to see those parts of her and to think on what my husband had hidden of himself from me, what he'd shown her. He was a man of two parts, an inside and an outside. The one didn't resemble the other.

I decided to begrudge Raisa nothing. Misha had poured all of that other part of himself into her. It had excited in her some sort of spark of passion and she told me about the marks she had left on him in return. I'd seen these on his skin, of course, the long red gouges. They had been like a foreign alphabet to me. He had told me they were made by tigers.

That first night Raisa and I both slept beneath the same blanket. She curled against me and I could feel the way her body expanded and contracted with her breath. I kept as still as I could so I didn't disturb her. Don't worry, she told me, when she realised what I was doing. I'm used to movement in the night. It doesn't bother me anymore.

In the morning she woke early and she fixed for both of us a breakfast of thick porridge and a single boiled egg which we shared. She asked me if I was still bleeding and I thought about it for some time. Eventually I nodded and she smiled. Afterwards she returned to the men's quarter and I did not see her for many months.

We were your loves.
None other can speak
of your vexed, exalted life.
None other remembers
the strength of your spirit,
the strength of your hand,
the cold wind that blew through you
from which there was no shelter.

3.

In the spring the thaw came quickly and the forest, which had been gripped in a heavy fist of ice, began first to sag and then to spring up with new life. I waited for news but no one discovered Misha's body. I wasn't surprised. There were reports of animals prowling the borders of the village. Men had lost their dogs in the night, had them snatched right off the chain. Eventually I took it upon myself to unravel the wedding shawl he'd bought for me. Some of the other women helped me with this. We took it apart, strand by strand, until the red skeins bloomed. From this I refashioned for myself a hood which was smaller and simpler, as well as a pair of stockings.

As the sun rose stronger and brighter in the sky, I came to my own awakening. I knew I had to make use of myself but I didn't know how to begin. I knew a little of hunting, or rather, of cleaning the spoils of the hunt, and mending traps, making bullets, and twining snares. But the other women told me this was men's work and not fit for me.

Feeling useless and ill at ease, I went to the river to watch the men. Having grown up in my father's home, I felt as if I understood them better. They were busy and raucous, hurling insults and laughs and the occasional blow. They seemed easy with one another and I wished I could feel so easy among them. But my presence changed them. When I came too close a hush would fall. I could observe but nothing more—so that's what I did. I watched them where the river separated us. They glided over the water in birch canoes, hunting for weaker prey than the wolves and lynx of the forest: sluggish, bottom-dwelling sturgeon. One called the great fish to the boat using a torch-lure while the other waited until the beast surfaced and showed her belly. As I watched the forked harpoon landed solidly and whatever it was that lurked

Tiger, (1912) by Franz Marc

beneath them began to thrash about. The boat rocked and the men shouted to one another in loud, excited voices. The man with the harpoon had a good face, a broad forehead and a sizeable nose. The sturgeon began to drag the little craft but he was calm. He waited until she had tired itself out and then dispatched her with a lance and dragged her ashore.

When it was over the man cut off the sturgeon's tail and worked a knife through the meat on both sides. He slit her belly open and rinsed the cavity with clean water. He saw me watching him and he smiled. Once he tried to speak to me but I couldn't understand what he was saying. He didn't give me meat but when he was finished he left the carcass in a tin bucket and encouraged me with gestures to pick through it. I rinsed the bones in the river and gathered them up in my skirt to bring home.

Over the weeks that followed I spent much time by the river, watching the men. The handsome one, I learned, was named Ioann, which meant *God has favoured me*. He asked me for my name and I said he could call me Jekaterina which meant *chaste* but he only grinned like he didn't know what the word meant. This is how we were together, Ioann and me. We spoke but we didn't listen, not really.

When I returned to the women's quarters I often found the others watching me. Instinctively I felt a prickle in the hairs of my neck which told me I'd done something wrong but I didn't know what. Still, together we picked through the bones, taking some for needles and others to fashion into jewelry. What remained was boiled down into glue and made useful. They didn't smile and I could tell they were ill at ease. Still they washed me and combed my hair and they gave me sweet-smelling oils to rub into my chapped skin. I slept alone beneath the blanket and the ground was hard but inside I felt soft and malleable. It was as if I were a flower beginning slowly to unfurl but I didn't know yet of what sort I was or of what use I could be.

One day I stayed late by the river to watch Ioann. He wasn't hunting as he often did but rather he'd taken to mending his nets. His fingers were clumsy so I came to him and I showed him how it was best done. My fingers were littler than his but I'd not worked at this for some time and so they bled easily. I wiped the blood on my stockings so he wouldn't see, or laugh at my weakness. But when he caught me doing this he brought them to his lips and kissed away the redness. He called me his little bird, his sweetness.

He took me back to his home and made me a dinner of pork sausages with chopped onion and stewed beans. While we ate he spoke to me of the war. He told me proudly about his brother who'd enlisted. They'd beaten him every day in training but he'd survived it and now he felt comfortable only among other soldiers. Ioann showed me a letter from his brother and when I couldn't understand them he offered to read them to me:

> *I am here among my people,* said the letter, *and I hope you will join me soon. Brother, it's so much easier this way! My hands can make their own language. They are beautiful. I never knew how beautiful a hand could be but I'm in love with my hands and what they can do.*

That evening I found my book of poems was missing and the women were gathered in a circle around it. At first I was angry but as I looked on I saw the care and reverence with which they touched the pages and mouthed the words to one another. One woman was crying and holding herself away from the others. I went to her and asked her what was wrong. For some time she couldn't answer. After I put my arms around her and rocked her gently she whispered that the book had spoken to her. It told her the story of her childhood which she'd forgotten. It told her of a husband she'd forgotten too, and now she didn't know where he was. It told her of sons that had vanished and of the daughter that had been taken from her and made to go to the city. The woman's name was Kapeka which meant *little stork*.

Together we unstitched the book. Her hands were tiny, her nails bitten down, but we separated the pages and I passed them to the others. One woman brought out the fishbone glue, lacquering slabs of wood, broken furniture and pallets, so the writing would hold fast. A third woman brought out twine so we could hang the pages around our necks like talismans, and when that ran out we undid the threading of my hood.

Be careful, you whispered,
but your hand was empty when we touched.
Now we are half lost in silence
and the dream that was shaped between us.
Night is falling too quickly for pauses.

4.

We learned soon that the war was going badly. In the city there had been a number of terrorist attacks. Bombs had been loaded into schools and public squares, hospitals and there were many deaths. The government blamed the rebels in the east who were hated as much as the tax collectors. But the news came to us slowly and by the time it reached us much of it seemed to have happened long ago.

But then the trucks arrived. They were hulking things, far more advanced than anything we had. The engines purred softly and the cold never bothered them. The soldiers who came wore green uniforms, combat trousers and balaclavas that hid their faces from us. They told us they were going from village to village to seek out recruits. They told us the war had become much worse and men were needed. They asked us repeatedly if we loved the President in odd urban accents and when they spoke his name it sounded strange, like the name of a small bird, not the man whose picture we had seen so many times.

The young men were curious at first and some were excited. I saw Ioann among them but he didn't come to me. Instead he went from soldier to soldier asking them for news of his brother, but none of them had heard of him. The fighting was far away, the commanding officer told him, and if he'd been sent to the front lines he was a hero!

Ioann followed the soldiers into the drinking establishments and late at night we could hear groups of them wandering through the streets, drunk and singing. Raisa was with them too, her lips red and glowing in the night as she joined in the chorus. It was an old folk song, one that Misha used to sing, though his words had been different. The soldiers were singing about the wildness of the steppes and the black birds circling above them, how they longed for home. I struggled to understand the end of it and when I did I couldn't grasp what it meant: my brothers have lain down in the grass, they sang, my brothers have stripped off their clothes, sometimes when I look upon my brother I see the feathers of a white crane straining to take flight.

As the early dawn light began to limn the streets with gold it was clear some of the soldiers were lost. Our village disoriented them. I'd been in the village for many years and so for me it was as easy to navigate as the back of my hand but there were no street signs. They were used to street signs. They were used to maps and they cursed us because we were provincial and didn't have any.

Three brothers came to the women's quarter. They were shouting, they were singing, and one hurled a great heavy bottle against the street. It was strange to watch them carrying on like this. For a while the women wouldn't leave their huts. Come on now, I told them, they're only men and we've all seen men before, haven't we? But the women sheltered in the dark spaces, covering themselves in blankets and whispering to one another. Still their doors were flung open and in came the three men. They didn't know where they were but they looked on us and were amazed by the sight of us. I don't know the last time they had seen real women.

It was terrible at first. Kapeka was crying and the others were all afraid. They couldn't understand what the men were saying to them and the men couldn't understand why the women wouldn't listen. I was the first to go to speak to them because I was still closest to knowing the men's language. I asked them what they were doing here and they told me they were lost. They'd been seeking the river. Their faces had taken on a plaintive, embarrassed look. They seemed so much smaller than they had at first and the youngest said to Kapeka that he was sorry he had smashed the bottle and frightened her.

Why do you want the river? I asked them, curious now. We want to drown ourselves, the oldest told me. They had seen the village and it reminded them of home and now they didn't want to go. They showed me their notebooks and inside they read:

Received censure for sleeping on duty.
Received censure for drunkenness.
Received censure for being the first to stop cheering after an officer's speech.
Received censure for failing to stand up for twenty lashes.
Received censure for writing home too often.
Received censure for the good quality of my penmanship.
Received censure for cursing my homeland and disgracing my family name.

The three were younger than I expected beneath their heavy gear. They were pigeon-chested boys who didn't even have beards. Their Adam's apples were sharp and bulbous, their lips thin, bloodless, their hands large. They had all cut their hair in the style of the President but none of them had the square faces and chiselled jaw they needed to look handsome in it. No, they looked like odd, misshapen fruits, barely covered by fuzz. So we let the soldiers stay with us. The eldest of them was named Ruslan which meant *lion man* and his brothers were Kolya which meant *victorious* and Ermolai which meant *heap of stones*. In the early hours of the morning we sat together and spoke of poetry, what was fashionable in the city. The eldest was a poet himself. He had written many poems about the war but none had been published. We mingled easily and eventually the men calmed and fell asleep.

In the morning there were other soldiers who were out searching for them. They were calling in the streets for men. We told them not to listen and when they began to twitch we gave them new names. We said now you will be called Agafya which means *good-hearted* and Klava which means *feeble* and Nadia which means *full of hope*. Speak only when you must and with these words, we told them, and those were the names they had when the soldiers came. There are only women here, we told the commanding officer. See? And we showed them the names written on their skin. Those others must have thrown themselves into the river, we told them. It's been known to happen.

The light rising behind the hills
and all quiet things coming awake
while the two of us are still abed.
Who could know what sadness lingers
or what joys await
the one who casts aside the covers
and greets the day?

5.

The soldiers left soon after that. I think they wearied of the monotony of village life and there were other places for them to go to. All the young men went with them and many of the old men as well. Ioann was among them. I asked him why he wanted to go when his brother was so unhappy and he looked at me in confusion. He told me he was stronger than his brother was and that he would survive the beatings too. He wasn't afraid of pain and his body would heal. He wanted what his brother had and even though I was beautiful he wasn't in the market for a wife, not while so much of the world lay before him.

On that final hour I saw Raisa with them, blowing circles of smoke from a lit cigarette she had purloined from a soldier. I remembered how it had felt to have her pressed against me, how kind she had been. But when I greeted her it seemed as if her surface was smooth and glittering as ice. Did you know, she asked me, that a tiger's stripes are printed on its flesh? If you strip down a tiger you'll find the same marks tattooed to its naked skin. When I didn't know how to answer this she smiled and shook her head, blowing a ring of smoke that hung in the air like a halo. I'm going with them, she told me.

There were days afterward when I observed from the women's quarter the changing season, the sap beginning to harden once more in the sapwood of the birches and the brief summer bloom of lotuses, which released a thick intoxicating scent. As the weather began to cool I took walks in the forest where I felt comfortable now. No one stopped me, or looked, or stared. The men had vanished and with them gone the old boundaries began to weaken. Soon the forbidden places were just like any other place, neither better nor worse, no more mysterious, no more threatening. No more soldiers came. With the men gone there was nothing left for them here. We might as well have been erased from the maps.

Eventually the other women began to join me. We ventured out into the streets, setting up new homes in the abandoned huts of the men who had left us. Together we would set out in the mornings to gather cedar nuts and set the trap lines. Agafya, Klava and Nadia showed us the best way to do this but soon we were better at it than even they had been. Besides, by that point they were heavy with child and disliked being on their feet for too long.

Those three were much loved among us. We would all gather in the evenings to hear Agafya's poems and to marvel at the newness of their language. Her words were bright and shining and when I heard them I felt a kind of space opening up inside of me. None have written like this before, the eldest said and I put my finger against her lips, saying, of course they have, they have always written like this. Soon after we put aside the talismans we had fashioned and we began to write for ourselves. We wrote on the inside of our skins where no one could see but us. The old words were insufficient for what we were now so we used a new language born neither from war nor love nor loneliness nor loss nor men or women but another thing altogether. From the long silence we shaped our words together, our verses expanding to claim everything around us: the trees, the flowers, the fish, the fields, our own bones and blood.

It was close to autumn when I came upon the bodies of the men in their uniforms, the young boys and the old as well. They had been torn apart by the tigers, by the foxes and lynx and bears and minks and grey wolves, all the wild things that lived in the forest. They had not made it to the front lines. Raisa was not among them though I found signs of her everywhere, her thick sweet scent, the mark of her red lips upon them.

After that there were nights I dreamed the animals had taken on the shapes of men, I dreamed they had found my Misha's body and made a skin of him to wear. I dreamed he might return for me but he never did. There were times as I travelled I spotted a flash of grey or black or—once—bright flame-coloured bands that seemed to glow in the shadows like stoked embers. One day I stumbled upon to the old hut we had shared together so many years ago. It seemed so small and homely without his presence. Nearby I found a yellowed skull with a cracked jaw. It was barely twenty paces from our garden. When I held it in my hands it seemed very large but try as I might I couldn't tell if it had belonged to Misha. I wanted to feel affection for the fineness of its architecture, the narrow channels and familiar contours, but, stripped of its flesh, it could, I suppose, have been any man's.

The news creeps through the village.
The last old man has died.
Soon the snows will come.

UNSTITCHING THE PATRIARCHY:
A REVIEW OF CAMILLA GRUDOVA'S *THE DOLL'S ALPHABET*
Rudrapriya Rathore

Readers looking for likeable characters and neat resolutions should avert their eyes from Camilla Grudova's debut story collection, *The Doll's Alphabet* (Coffee House Press, 2017). Described as "Angela Carter's natural inheritor," Grudova spends thirteen stories carefully constructing a world in which despair, violence, and material ruin govern the lives of individual characters. Here, men bring dwarf corpses home and women stuff them deep into parlour organs. Children invent machines that project hypnotising images onto walls and sit in front of them for years. Costumes, sewing machines, and dolls come alive, grotesquely animated by the fears and obsessions of people surrounding them.

There is very little comfort here. Though no dates or geographic locales are given (the stories take place in "the neighbourhood" or "the factory" or, most often, in homes and apartments in anonymous cities), the atmosphere of a newly industrialized, Dickensian London seems the closest comparison. Part of what appeals about Grudova's aesthetic impulses is her boldness in laying bare the ugliness of this imagined universe. Rations of tinned meat, rat infestations and masses of impoverished citizens abound. It's only appropriate, then, that people do ugly things to each other—in "The Mouse Queen," Peter, a Latin student, leaves his girlfriend when she becomes pregnant with their twins, suspicious that his girlfriend "had betrayed him in a mythological manner." She poses for a photograph after they're born, meaning to send it to him, but finds a wolf's face instead of her own staring back at her from the photo. Later, after purchasing a pink rubber mask of a girl's face from a costume shop, the protagonist finds that her twins have disappeared, and she feels full, "as if [she] had eaten something large."

Many of the stories follow a dream-logic, studded with sinister figures and metaphors of structural social inequalities. Like Kafka's long-suffering "K", Grudova's characters come off as somewhat impersonal, lacking inner traits, as though they could be anyone. And like painter and novelist Leonora Carrington's creepy, surrealist stories, *The Doll's Alphabet* is often edged with a deliberately feminine resistance to patriarchy. Pieces of clothing, for example, carry enormous significance for their ability to transform the wearer. Lingerie, stockings, and new dresses are coveted, since seducing men is necessary for one's social stability. Sewing machines are particularly important: described as giant, black ants, their presence symbolizes all female oppression. When women learn how to "unstitch" themselves in "Unstitching," they leave their false bodies behind to reveal "true, secret selves." But when men try to do the same, they discover that they're made of "only what was taught and known," and end up "wounded and disappointed."

It's clear that Grudova wants to reference an older world while emphasizing her political concerns with the present. Occasionally, her specific approach of ironic allegory takes away from the actual tale by being both on-the-nose and confusing. "All the women looked alike" when unstitched, she writes, compelling the

Cover from
The Doll's Alphabet by Camilla Grudova
(2017) / Coffee House Press

reader to ask: is it patriarchy we're mocking here, or a stagnant white feminism that believes in women's true and yet identical selves?

When she indulges her whimsy, Grudova excels. She turns homes into nightmarish spaces designed for sex and housework, marriage rituals and duties. Pregnancy becomes an archeological horror show: one ultrasound looks like "an ancient, damaged frieze," and its bearer has to find work in a chocolate factory, dreaming of "eating chocolates filled with bird bones, rocks, gold nuggets, Roman coins, teeth." Women live in perpetual fear of being impregnated, and birth control—in an all-too-realistic touch—costs a fortune, both financially and morally. Emmeline, in "The Mermaid," says that "an ear came out of her once, and she put it in a box to keep in case more bits came out and she had to assemble them." It is a mark of Grudova's humour and talent that Emmeline's "labour" is both physical and industrial, that she anticipates having to assemble her child as she would have to do in the kind of factory where innumerable women like her work. At the end of the day, instead of being pure or natural, childbirth is just that—work.

In addition to gender, Grudova is obsessed with materiality. Teacups, clocks, clowns, trains, needles, ships, and doll's houses populate the text, making its imagined space quaint and old fashioned, like an antiques shop. Entire pages are dedicated to listing the precious pos-

Camilla Grudova / courtesy United Agents

sessions of one wealthy industrialist named Baron. (Because he can't stand to lose anything in a shipwreck, he gets each object canned by a factory for an overseas voyage.) People are defined by their ownership of or desperate desire for things, colouring the work with a starkly capitalist brush. Grudova's choices are careful, and the barrage of objects signals who we are as a species, what we care about, and what we leave behind. In fact, the review copy of Grudova's book arrived with a sewing needle and mending kit, as well as a set of buttons. It reminds one that the packaging we place so much faith in is fragile, in constant need of another few stitches, and always in danger of unravelling.

THE EMBOLUS OF CINNABAR

Patricia Cram

It breaks loose from riverbed.
Undulation: white, blistering worm.
Hurl of timeless worm hits a ship,
draws the lives within it to drowning,
but the worm never hears.
Here, in river's water,
Old pagodas wear aeons of mud—
still their sacred tiers bear gifts.
A metallic sound plinks;
an iron kettle tilts from a seventh story.
As the worm passes, roughly flapping,
thick with the slick of passage,
it is suddenly enraged
by the light of the sun pouring
from the kettle into which nuns
had sung it, chanted it so that
one day, this day, the worm
out of time would become
a pendant of light
nailed to pagoda's red lip:
a white cord, billowing

They break loose from scalp.
Her open hands grip
wide braids of black hair falling.
Kneeling at the edge of a plateau,
she leaves what she was
to the god of wind, changing her face
so that it is a moon; shaping her teeth
into stone points; willing the braids
to become dragons in her palms.
She stretches lengthily, and
burial mounds erupt, keloid from bor-
der to border, stiffen with inkstones,
old gold that she will carry.
Into the pitted skin of the dragons,
she presses the red unguent that issues
from between her stretched legs in stringed
masses: fates never lived. The beasts sing and keen,
cycle through euphoria and then misery, spin
many lengths of human life.
When the dragons cease turning, hard-
ening into circles of jade,
she pushes them up her wrists,
sighs, and rises

In the water of their river, the people of a village washed pots large and small. The water seemed hungrier than it had ever been, and it pulled oils from porcelain and stone until its surface foamed. The people scrubbed, sometimes with fingertips, sometimes old rags, taking their time, sharing news with neighbors. Meanwhile, through quiet undulations, the water pushed the foam to shore. What parts were urine, saliva, fish eggs that failed to hatch were all edged to periphery, each lapping feeding the banks this broth of remains.

Cypress trees loomed above, and in their boughs, birds of a dozen varieties let out low songs. What the water discharged now seeped its way through earth and into roots, up veins of xylem, and then was exhaled where the birds now breathed it in. Their songs bowed their vocal cords, escaped horns of beak, and came to vibrating rest in dark fringes of feather. Across time, the people of this land had heard these songs, had put their own words to them until they thought they knew the hearts of birds. Of chosen talon they sang, of course, of stones after impact, of blades at loving rest they sang and they sang.

When the people drank from this river, they found its waters sweet. *It was blood, it was blood, it has always been blood.*

Now hear the crack of lanterns making light. Now feel what has been dropped upon these banks. A swell of red ink rises around a name seal.

Through the forest and mist, the neighbor Lao-Long cried out, "Come quickly!" for there, on the earth, was a fallen man. From his body radiated a strange, faint light; fungal forms already surrounded him, seeming to feed on his body's haze and then glow themselves. As the people approached, their feet crushed a rapidly spreading undergrowth of fungus. The unexpected, ghostly man was unfamiliar, but they were brought to their knees around his aloneness, and their bodies began grieving though their minds did not understand. The song of the many-voiced birds became like dark lengths of silk wrapped around this spiral of mourners, dampening all but this moment. The mushrooms spread, and the people waited, their pots forgotten, sure that something more was to come.

The light of the sun was quickly receding, and the mushrooms were reacting. Filled with the glow of the fallen man, they became the conduits of his decay. His body rippled as the fungi unfurled their mycelium, stretched their roots into his skin. With slipping sounds they drank at his remains—a steady stream siphoned and instantly transformed into growth. The mushrooms, now red, bulged past their usual boundaries and grew steadily more swollen. The corpse-light of the stranger had bloated them past recognition, and they appeared to pulse, perhaps about to burst. As soon as the sun was replaced fully by shadow, in humble silence, the mushrooms ignited—candles of placid, cold flame.

In the sudden brightness and chill, the people hastened to their feet. Freezing air surrounded them, and they rushed to get away, their movements jostling flames and causing the mushrooms to release a drifting red ash. They ran, their feet trampling again, now afraid that this had become no place for them. The man's skin was draped over his bones.

Once freed, the villagers ran to the clearing of the river and picked up the pots they had left behind. But they looked back toward the fallen man and a new grief struck them, released a cord from their centers and seemed to tether them, confused, to this place. They were clutching their pots, unsure whether to leave or stay, staring across flames where the man made a dark center, when a woman floated down to him from the trees. The villagers jumped, took half-steps away but came back exclaiming their surprise. The fabric of the woman's sleeves and dark ropes of hair had streamed behind her as she descended. She was covered in blood, her robe ripped and barely held shut. They could see dark lines of tears on her face, and the people were quickly silenced by fearful reverence.

The woman landed with arms outstretched, stumbling and running the last few steps, paying no mind to the flames or the villagers around her before throwing herself over the fallen man. Her fingers dug at his thinning chest. She pulled and hunched, rising and collapsing, searching him. She whispered, shaking her head, long hair swaying, and it took some time before the people transfixed could hear her. When at last they did, her words struck their centers, at the tragic bells of sentience: despair, powerlessness, the recklessness of fate. "Why didn't I hear you?" she asked, pleading and whispering, voice rising. "I didn't hear you." The people ignored the sound of the river coursing. A few ran toward the woman, but she did not see them, did not accept their hands. With her face in the man's chest, her hands gripping what parts of him they could, the woman's lament became a cutting scream.

Many hundreds of years ago, in the valley between the mountains that formed the goddess's breasts, there was an earthquake. The monastery that was home of stone and gold began its crumbling change back into dust. As soon as the shaking began, the nuns of the monastery stopped whatever they were doing, pivoted wherever they were, and immediately turned toward the temple. Orange robes moved in streams, nuns running toward the meeting place, a room whose edges were painted with dragons, radiating flowers, phoenixes in spirals of cloud. Scrolls of red calligraphy met the prayers of the arriving, echoing them. Wood splintered and murals cracked, things now beginning to plummet to the undulating ground.

Two nuns found each other's eyes and walked steadily toward one another. Simultaneously, they reached out and held both hands together, leaned each forehead against the other's. "I choose this for my end," they said together, and then, euphoric with radiant clarity, let their passion show on their faces for the first time, let their mouths seek and find for the first time. And when the wooden beam cracked above them, it closed its painted eyes and plummeted with a moan, knowing it would end its own life in the broken red of their skulls. The splintering sound was overwhelming. All of the nuns looked toward their sisters, where a cord had become visible between them. The nuns' prayers strained briefly; the women sought to regain control over their own passage, their imminent transition. But an obvious light was pushing at the bodies of the lovers, and when it broke free, it shifted, appearing first as arms, then crowned heads, then countless whipping tails, and then it escaped, surging. One nun jumped to her feet and ran out, quickly returning with an iron kettle. She emptied it as she ran, released the tea she had been pouring just moments ago in ceremony. Arriving at the light that flew from her two sisters, she gripped the kettle's lid and pushed its opening over one powerful ray of light. Now, she changed from prayer to song. The others, understanding the words, knew that their own safe passage must now be second to this sun's. They joined her, by song urging the light into a single stream that poured into the black kettle that would keep it until it was needed again. The women sang until the last one alive used her final gesture to replace the lid.

Outside, water seeped upwards from cracked earth. Something white rippled toward the surface and then disappeared, descending. As if an ocean had been held tenuously at bay by the dirt of millennia, great water broke loose and poured forth, unbridled, rising day after day. It covered low stones, swept over shrubs, mulberry trees and their silkworms, eventually submerging the mountains and all of their flora, their fauna drowned and turned to bone beneath the ebb and flow.

One day, many years later, the earth quaked again, a pale underbelly briefly revealed, and then the water was drawn back into the ground. People returned, erecting their temples, uttering their words. Totems were carved into the bones of water buffalo; divinations were etched into turtles' shells. And then the earth shook again, and there was once more both ruin and renewal. Like this, over and again, earth and water seduced each other until a clear river was made that had, for its bones, sacred architecture, the splintered wood and nails of human worship.

In the time before time, the goddess erupted from the body of her mother, changing her. When the infant passed the threshold of vulva, it had clutched in its hands the viscera of its mother, turning her inside out with the force of its emergence. The mother exploded into darkness, her entrails spraying the universe with the light that became our stars.

The infant floated, suckling at the slick of mother's womb. And mother hung dismembered across eternity, both everywhere and alone.

On the other side of time—not where it is amorphous, but where it is an edge—a family massaged a stillborn boy child. Hands fluttered across his waxen flesh. On a mattress on the floor, his mother teetered in the vertigo between living and dying. Across the muffled, twisting coil of the great in-between, she recognized the spirit of her son, still faintly tethered, and called out. It faced her, overrun with grief, for it knew they could not both live in the same time. In a flash, the mother knew as well, and she stretched every cell toward encircling the spirit. "You go—you be there," she urged it, "You were called here for this." And once her choice was made, the massaging hands pulled back at the sudden and powerful wail that came from the heart of the child. Its father, the god of wind, howled in through the cracks in the walls and wrought a chill across the infant's body. On the stained mattress, the mother's dead eyes wept hot, clear tears every day until finally the others put her on a pyre and freed her to the sky.

When in a vision years later, the boy child, now a man, followed the horizon to a point where lengths of long, black hair hung from the heavens, he found a goddess floating outside of time. She started at his presence, making hair and fabric radiate from her in waves. Blood dried beneath her nails; her face was streaked and her robes stained. A loud pounding began, and the man knew his heartbeat would soon pull him back—he reached out a hand. The goddess took it and was instantly engulfed by a gale. Like this she left the dispersed body of the mother and found herself roaring into the mouth of an earthen cave.

Like this, the wayward rushing, the opening made. It was blood, it was blood, it was blood—and how it came to pour.

They made their home nearby, building a small dwelling at the edge of a human village. Neighbors welcomed the young lovers, gave them chances and work and advice. The goddess learned the way of their words and their walking and their days. Because the man had always straddled two realms, he was able to teach her what he could of this one—cabbage and dumplings, porridge and tea. She made every effort to fit these in her mouth, to fit both these things and human words all day. They walked near the neighbors, discussed clouds and phoenixes as they worked the land. Rice paddies, green vegetables, plump fruits that streamed their juices down her forearms. The man was fast, always eager to learn and work more, for wind moved through him. And she, from the density of a self formed against the formless, was penetrating and keen. He drew her baths daily, helped her wash until the traces of old blood lifted away. And then her own blood came, and then they knew that she could bear children here, and so they did, calling into the void until two voices called back.

As the woman's belly grew, the villagers shared more tales than ever before. She worked to heed their many superstitions, looking only at beautiful things and eating many bowls of noodles to ensure longer lives. But she could feel the two sparks tumbling and increasing within her, and they already knew how to speak within her. The son of wind listened to their dreaming whispers, falling asleep with one arm cradled over her belly night after night.

While earth slept through winter, she fed the sparks from inner light, nurturing and pleasing their different elements, reading the cords they held the longest. She warmed them with soups and contemplated what humans thought of the night sky. When spring came, she sat outside and looked up, singing the songs she had learned from the villagers. Then, on a night of the waxing moon, the twins by long work and great force emerged, pulsing cords gushing from mother, one child as lightning and the other as thunder. At their arrival, the earth beneath their new home rose briefly and then sank again. Layers of clouds were edged above them in light. The twins were alive, ricocheting, streaming through.

One day, the son of wind came home to find the body of the goddess cut open. The children were there on the floor with her, leaning into her, curled and lapping and clenching tiny red fists around her intestines. She moaned and winced and the son of wind cried out, "No, no, no—you don't have to do this." He gently pried open those tiny hands, one finger at a time until the children could be moved safely to a blanket, blood drying on their faces, and their cries of distress ringing at his ears. Over the goddess he knelt, and there he worked to seal her body. "You could have lost yourself here. You cannot do that. You don't have to," he whispered again and again. She was silent, eyes closed, the thumb of one hand weakly rubbing the handle of her blade. After a time, he kissed her face; "I will have to go," he said, "I will take the twins so you can rest, but to heal you, I have to go to the mountain. I will tell Hei-Yu to come." The son of wind wrapped

Daphne, (1921) by Arthur Rackham

his crying children and strapped one to his back and the other to his chest; he grabbed a basket, then a blanket, and went outside to the neighbor to ask her to watch over the wounded goddess.

He walked directly to the foot of the mountain, passed the threshold of the human realm, and entered the place of tall trees. He wound his way through until he reached the staircase of 748 steps, and these he climbed, the twins asleep and his breathing labored by his haste. The trees grew so quickly that he soon felt he was running in place though he was climbing, climbing, breathing in, breathing out, imagining his goddess flayed, guts strewn and dripping, his children fed. When he reached the top of the stairs, he rested his hand upon a deep, black stone as tall as he was and lowered his weeping head.

The next stone was cinnabar, and his heaving outward reached its thick red surface. He put his hands out to the stone, felt its comprehension, its recognition. He stared at the patterns and words that had been pushed into it, or that it had pushed out. Then, with the sudden strike of his elbow, he dislodged a sizeable shard. The son of wind knelt with his children to enter the sacred earth.

Guided he was by the wind that had caressed a thousand healers, his ancestors' knowing, his own, studied hands. Through thick and pounded dirt he dug for roots: ginseng, astragalus, angelica—running from source to source while the twins slept, while he had these moments of silence to be with the ancient instinct to save and heal. In his mind now, the goddess danced as he had seen her before, perhaps long before he himself had been born, and now, in that opal refuge, he saw her with her arms outstretched, her face rapturous, her body moved.

Dirt in his beard, his hair, beneath his nails, up his arms, caked at his knees, in the corners of his eyes. Basket rising with the medicine of the mountain, the trees, the temple gardens, the humble forest floor. A faceted and glowing drop of blood grew heavy at the bottom of a celestial body, and when it had swelled enough, it let itself go, hitting other bodies and gathering matter, gaining in size until it struck the son of wind and his two infant children. With a crack, the lightning child woke and the air around them rippled. When the thunder child woke, the ground buckled. They all three looked upwards, aware that a wide, warm river above them had chosen them as path.

As the deluge threatened to peak, pushing at its confines and bulging over the edge of the sky, the son of wind ran from tree to tree, seeking a hole that could hold him and the twins. By the time he found one, the three were drenched in sky goddess, her cycling, her release. Blood dripped from tree's needles, curtained from branches and clotted where it fell. All creatures faced home and rest, made this a time of dream. To walk a straight line would have been impossible. So the man held his children in his arms, shouldered them into a cave of tree, and there they held their hands out, each gripping a gnarled root. Time rippled and flared as they watched birds spiral down, foxes curl, tall stalks lean and open. Father and children bathed the medicines, imbued the roots with mother healed, channeled the falling sky until, hands full, they fell into sleep.

Sky was dark but still poured blood. From the hole in the tree came warm breaths, synchronized and even. Moisture touched all surfaces, and a light mist of red could be felt in all directions. The silence was profound. But beneath the skin of earth, the worm out of time was drawing near simply because it moved forward. Deliberately, and without motive, it gnawed and swallowed, swallowed and gnawed. All things, at some point in time, would pass through the colorless length of its flickering form. On this night, its jaws met the son of wind and his children. In one powerful movement, the timeless worm broke through earth and knifed straight into the lightning child's body. The infant twitched, dilated as the worm threaded the white mass of its gleaming length through the child's torso. Lunging out of torso and into the son of wind, the worm passed through left shoulder, then out of throat, into and out of the abdomen of the thunder child, weaving between, growing longer and thicker with every hungry thrust, stitching across the three bodies huddled within tree. It seemed to have no end.

In the old stone house that was forever warm, the goddess's eyes flared open. She felt her children's lives flutter in her belly, felt the chambers of her heart heave with adrenaline. Hei-Yu jolted, concerned by the sudden plea in the goddess's eyes. "Call wind," the goddess whispered, "Call wind, call wind," and her eyes rolled back, whites glowing. Hei-Yu leapt to her feet, suddenly aware she was not in the presence of a human being, and ran to the home of the village shamans—women who knew the ways to reach the gods. In the warm house, alone now among humankind, the goddess inhaled and exhaled, by wheezing breath now screaming into the void.

Soon, high above, in whorls of cloud and nitrogen, the god of wind was entered by a bitterness. It gave him the thought of his son, and sharp odors blazed. The god twisted and arced, rushing, loosing the fruit of orchards, splitting banks of mountain snow, finally coming to wrap himself around the tree that held his child. The skin of the worm out of time glared behind the man's eyes, and the god of wind saw that the white worm was sliding through the tunnels of his child's brain. Wind went to his son's nose and blew harder than he ever had before. Something tore. The god saw the worm pitched, from body of son to bed of river, and he felt the worm slip through mud, into the realm of cold, clear water and sinking pagodas. The high peal of infants crying reached his periphery but could not penetrate. As blood poured into its skull, the body before him went gray. The god of wind became a roar, grew to a ripping, and released the dead body of his son, which dropped and hit human-earth with a thud.

The spirits of the four shamans reached the black stone and then the cinnabar stone, their hands sweeping across each as they ran toward the tree their visions had revealed. They surged, shadows like cords braiding and unbraiding, pulsing closed and then open. Tumbling to arrival at the tree, they saw the infant children asleep in a nest of breathing roots, small fists around medicines still clenched, the air around them a slowly circulating warmth left for them by grandfather wind. The shamans thanked wood, then bowed their heads to wind, and pulled the children into the weaving of their tethered spirits. To mother these children would be taken, of matter made, and now by loss to matter they were bound.

TRANSCENDING THE GROTESQUERIE:
THE SURREAL LANDSCAPES OF DAVID WHITLAM

David Whitlam is an artist and illustrator from Manchester. From an early age he showed signs of a vivid imagination, and as a child spent much of his time drawing imaginary landscapes populated by strange creatures. In his teenage years he discovered the Surrealists and became fascinated with their attempts to delve into the unconscious. Although much of his work emerges spontaneously from the imagination, using techniques such as automatic drawing and collage, the subject matter has been shaped by his interests in ancient cultures, mythology and religious symbolism.

It was while studying for a degree in graphic art that Whitlam became transfixed with the Surrealist Movement and the idea of producing artwork from the subconscious. His work is inspired by the technique of automatic drawing, (a concept developed by the Surrealists where the hand moves 'randomly' across the canvas) and generally begins as spontaneous doodles, which are then formed into traditional paintings. Whitlam's work often includes religious and mythological symbols and is often shown in a prosaic setting. He employs a uniquely veristic style, through traditional oil paintings and digital paintings.

Whitlam works off an initial pencil sketch created through 'automatic drawing,' then he spontaneously draws while "largely unconscious in a trance-like state." He is a unique and distinct artist, and we are pleased to showcase some of his work here.

For information on print sales and commission work, please visit www.davidwhitlam.com.

Charming the Empty Vessel

Creature Comforts

Deep Rubbish

Down Devil Bay

Dream Boat

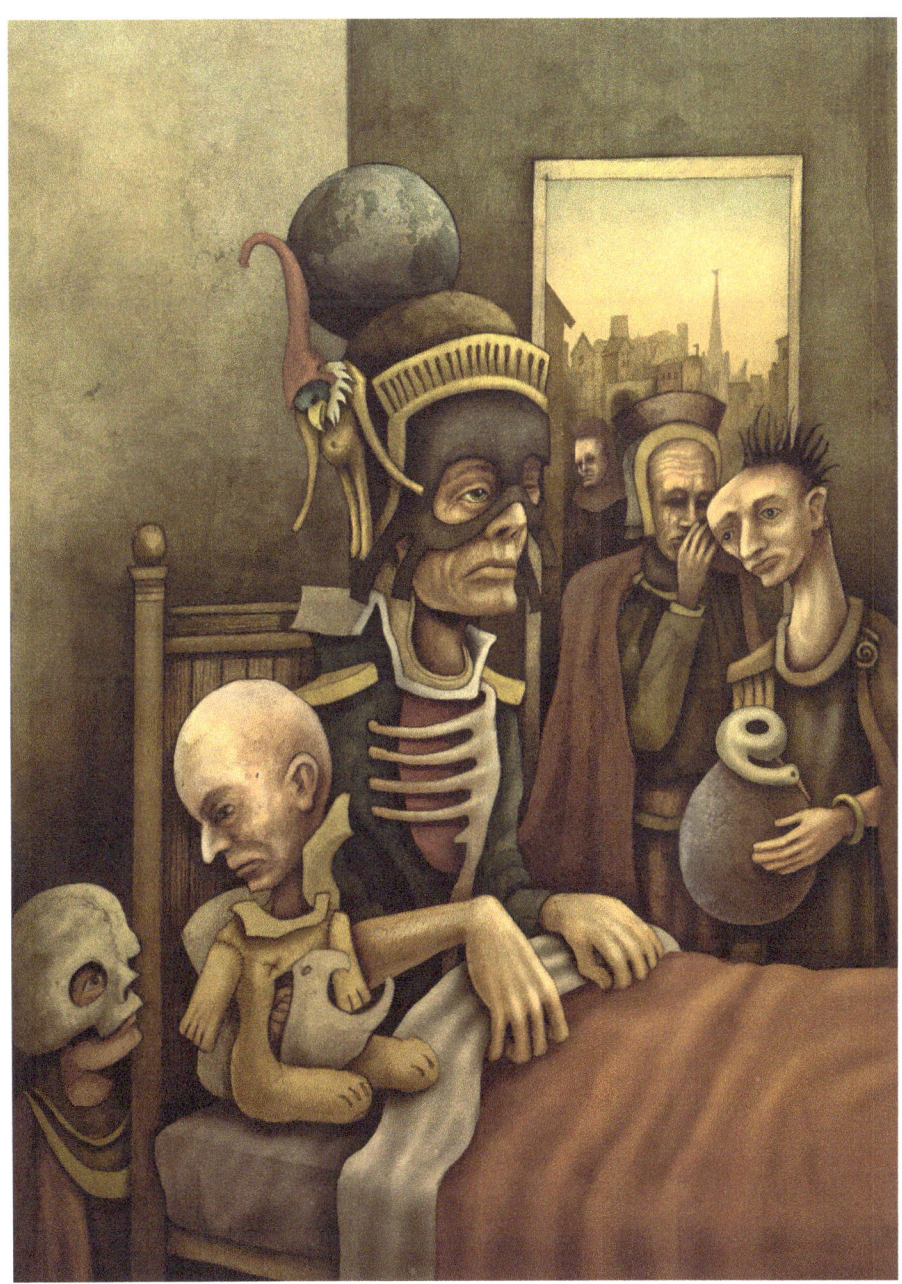

Fading Visionary

Farming Myths

Illuminated Soliloquy

Learn to Swim

Moonlight Sonata

Night Terrors

No Nativity

Psychic Chromatography

TRANSCENDING THE GROTESQUERIE: THE SURREAL LANDSCAPES OF DAVID WHITLAM

Repainting Calvary

Sleep for Breakfast

TRANSCENDING THE GROTESQUERIE: THE SURREAL LANDSCAPES OF DAVID WHITLAM 149

Stilted

The Council of Ten

TRANSCENDING THE GROTESQUERIE: THE SURREAL LANDSCAPES OF DAVID WHITLAM 151

The Happy Event

The Jackdaw Incident

TRANSCENDING THE GROTESQUERIE: THE SURREAL LANDSCAPES OF DAVID WHITLAM

The Persistence of Ego

The Post-Apocalyptic Selfie

The Temptation of St. Anthony

The View From the Pulpit

TRANSCENDING THE GROTESQUERIE: THE SURREAL LANDSCAPES OF DAVID WHITLAM

War and Peas

WAYSTATIONS OF THE HIGH NIGHT

Marcel Brion
(Translated by Edward Gauvin)

This story originally appeared in French in *Les Escales de la Haute Nuit*
published by Éditions Robert Laffont, 1942

The train came to a halt with a limp sound. The rails shivered in the rain, a soft susurration. Then, abruptly, the rain stopped. A green eye winked once, twice, then went out. The brakes strained bitterly. A smell of soot and mud entered the compartment.

I never knew the name of that town. If I decided to stop there, neglecting my intended destination, it may have been to yield to the invitation of the green eye that had opened once more and was now blinking in time like a lighthouse bulb turning with smooth patience in its housing of oil and mercury. There was also something powerfully insidious in the intertwining of the rails that suddenly robbed you of the yen to travel, replacing the desire to arrive somewhere with a temptation to vagrancy amidst the branching of a labyrinth that wrote out, in lazy eights, their predilection for infinity.

A man swinging a lantern at knee height, which made it seem he was striding through puddles of blood, shouted out a few words in a monotone voice and a language I didn't know. He seemed to be inviting all travelers to disembark, but the two men who were sharing my compartment—snoring, crammed into their corners, hunched over their sleep as if to defend it from assault—didn't hear. I had no reason whatsoever to stop in this town; perhaps that was why I opened the door, grabbed my suitcases and went down among the sharp pebbles that gleamed and scraped like chunks of coal.

The train station was fairly far away. I could see it, like a roaring cave, full of light, smoke, and shouts. The crisscrossing rails suggested subtle straying. Red lights raised and lowered their fingers through the fog. A solitary locomotive, launched down its track like a greyhound, brushed breathlessly by. The humbled stars withdrew into the furthest reaches of the sky. A sea monster spat a gush of scalding steam low to the ground. The brass glinted like gold. The black steel melted into shimmers like sealskin.

I walked among these great serene machines at pasture in the night, and heard their peaceful breathing, the breathing of sated beasts. At last, the fanned fingers of the tracks came together, falling by pairs into precise, twinned step. Concrete crushed the pebbles. Smoke fell upon me, shot through with the cries of birds, and a porter seized my suitcases with a series of unintelligible propositions, no doubt the names of hotels.

After the tumult of the station, the vast silence that reigned in the square seemed infinitely restful. Not a single vehicle, not a single passerby troubled this heavy blanket of night. The utter absence of light made the silence even more total, but the sky now rid of its clouds freely paraded its circus of constellations. All the usual stars were there: pets, wild animals, monsters of myth, and the objects the gods had lost one day along a starry route, the lyre a daydreaming poet left at some celestial crossroads, the shield a distracted hero dropped at a bend in the nebular milky way. The sky above had enough lights to make up for the lack of streetlamps.

The square was lined with tall buildings whose windows seemed at first glance exceptionally bright, as if all the stars were reflected in their panes, but upon closer inspection, I noticed that these windows were wide open—gaping, in fact, in the emptiness of the night. What had caught my eye there was no reflection, but the illusory compositions of the constellations themselves in the precise masonry frames. Of these houses, nothing at all remained save their facades, as if some disaster had demolished the entire block of buildings, sparing only their skin, that most fragile and vulnerable layer. Doubtless the ravages of war or an earthquake had caused this horrific disfigurement. And yet the commonplace tragic aspect of ruins was missing from this gathering of solid, solemn buildings; the absence of a body behind the façade in no way made them seem precarious as one might suppose. Nor was it every day wear that had damaged them so, for they seemed new, built with stable, durable materials.

The street I was headed down, following the porter who'd loaded my suitcases onto a small wagon, offered up the same surprising arrangement of façades fronting nothing at all. Whether built from blocks of rusticated or vermiculated stone, brick or cement, marble or half-timbering, the walls never amounted to more than a thin mineral layer this side of the cavernous night. Had some cataclysm befallen this town, I thought, it would have been more fickle. It might have spared half a bedroom or a few steps from a staircase, toppled the columns of that portico, pushed those door jambs apart. But nothing here bore a trace of chance or caprice. Everything had been carefully constructed, meticulously finished. I even noted the fineness of the sculptures that adorned certain houses. The architects and decorators had spent a great deal of effort to raise and embellish these facades flawlessly.

Since I cannot bear being in a basement or a cellar, I could not stay put in the hotel where my porter had escorted me. The graceful, appealing façade sported a sign with a dancing silver unicorn. But descending several floors underground in the elevator, then walking down long hallways with red carpets and blue sconces, to that windowless room, seemingly hewn from rock and filled with the drone of fans, aroused in me so great an anxiety that the thought of spending the night in this luxurious grotto filled me with fear. So I went back up to the surface, returning happily to the vast empty courtyard in front of the entrance to the hotel. The very façades in their blind solemnity seemed reassuring, and the sight of the constellations through the windows could not have been more comforting had the familiar stars given me a friendly wave.

The doorway in the openwork wall invited me to a view of the street; after the blue lights, the buzz and roar of the fans along the hotel's subterranean corridors, there was something restful about its darkness and silence. I was all alone, but the thought of walking the streets by myself at night in a strange town has never frightened me. Quite the opposite, in fact: the intoxicating fortune of all the surprises that offer themselves up to the man who, with neither a companion nor a precise goal in mind, surrenders himself to nocturnal temptations with the relaxed complaisance of someone just about to bed down in the warm sand of his dreams.

Never before had I seen a town like this one. Instead of leading past dark masses of houses, the streets here were dressed in airy lace. Stone lost its substance. Windows opened with an almost delirious joy on the heavens' dark prairies. All around, where we might usually presume the dense uniformity of indoors, with its orderly furniture and the thickness of slumber, was instead vacant space roamed by winds. The fixity of apartments gave way to an ever-changing expanse. Banks, churches, prisons—these offered no more resistance than private homes. The entirety of everyday life was gathered underground. On the surface stood naught but a featherweight fantasy of balconies, terraces, loggias, porticos, pediments, and statues posed like acrobats atop the roofs.

The starlight glided all the way to the ground through enjambed arcades that comprised, almost everywhere, the ground floors of buildings. In the middles of squares were fountains that ran fitfully with the strange sound of a clockwork run down by too much use. During my walk, I saw not a single tree, but I often ran into statues that seemed to be begging or threatening the night.

I no longer remember what part of town I was in when I first glimpsed that little girl. She must have been hiding in the darkness of a doorway, unseen in the shade of a column. For a while she followed me, darting cautiously between pools of shadow, watching my every move, fearful and fascinated. I think that, as the only other living creature out and about that night, she stirred in me a kindred feeling, one almost of gratitude, when she slipped her warm hand into mine.

She was frail and sickly-looking. Locks of hair that trembled in the milky starlight hung to either side of her face, which seemed of another time. Her fragile, misshapen ugliness made her endearing, like a dwarf. She walked with difficulty; every step sent a jolt running from her hip to her shoulder, and at the same time, her lips pressed tightly together in pain. I would no more have dared send her away than I would have a stray dog that had fallen in step behind me. Quite likely she needed protection or simply a human presence, but it was I who felt comforted now, by the twitch of her fingers against my palm.

During our entire walk, she said not a word. Nor did we come across a single living being. The little girl answered none of my questions, not even with so much as a shake of her head that might let me know she'd understood. Words ran off her, indifferent as starlight. In her arms she carried with great maternal caution, a doll wrapped in a scrap of cloth. When I tried, from curiosity or in jest, to peek at the doll's face, she fiercely pulled the cloth over its pale waxen face with its lightly tinted cheeks and eyes, then hugged her toy closer as if she wished to bury it in her chest, in order to shelter it from all defilement. I had given up asking that mute child any questions. We walked in silence, hand in hand. I found her lopsidedness, which became a strenuous limp whenever I unconsciously quickened my step, quite unpleasant, for the jolt from her hip now ran up into my body. I could feel her hand perspiring slightly in my own. Her hair smelled of dust and old age. Sometimes it seemed as if a very elderly dwarf were dragging herself along beside me, but I would not have dared abandon that girl to the tragic severity of the façades.

During my walk, it had surprised me not to come across any of the poor quarters that exist in every town. This one seemed of a solemn and almost sumptuous uniformity. If hovels and slums there were, they were no doubt concealing their wretchedness and poverty below, for none of that showed above ground. The clean, even façades were brusque as masks in the night. And indeed, masks they were, but instead of mouth, nose, and eye-holes cut from cardboard, they offered up the inscrutable emptiness of arcades, steps, windows; while the sky seen through these breaches made their evasive simplicity more mysterious still.

The touch of the child's clammy hand grew so unpleasant at one point that I approached one of the fountains to wash my own in the clear, cool ribbons that ran from the bronze spouts. My fingers met only with a column of smooth, dry glass turning in a dolphin's mouth. There was no water in that fountain, only an illusory spurt of solid crystal, which a mechanism made rotate so that it mimicked the movement of water. What I had taken for the fountain's murmur was but the regular wheezing of the device that brought this bizarre charade to life. I had to lean in very close, almost pressing my ear to the metal basin, to make out the distinctive voice of the flywheels, chains, and counterweights that animated the crystalline cylinders.

All the other fountains were of the same manufacture. Not a single drop of water ran in that town, no grass grew, no tree spread its branches, and if the little girl hadn't been walking beside me, I would've believed that no living creature was to be found that night among its empty streets.

There was a man, however, who just like me was out walking among the houses' empty faces. His voice gave me a start when he called out to me from the depths of a church door where he was crouched. Birds nesting in the nooks of the sculpture fluttered about and cackled with an indignation made languid by sleepiness.

The church looked like a piece of Brussels lace spread out against the velvet night. The filigreed rose windows gave off an impression of extraordinary fragility. The spires rose like fingers of ice, and the tall, narrow windows divided the sky into lancets, trefoils, and flames. The night lent this architecture so unsteady a backdrop that the entire edifice seemed to pitch forward and back, such that sometimes the fantastical tracery of stone and sky seemed about to fall upon me, while at others it seemed to reel backward, snagging the constellations on its carved ridges.

The man emerged from the shadows and walked toward me through the starlight. An expression of spiteful weariness saddened his face.

"Sit down beside me," he said, "and I will tell you the tale of this town."

He spoke with a nonchalance full of trickery and affectation, and with one hand gestured at a hole among the jagged shadow of the pedestals where the statues stood in melancholy soliloquy.

I demurred, claiming I had but a few minutes to make it back to the station.

"The next train isn't until morning," he said peremptorily. "And there'll never be a next train for you, because you won't ever want to leave this town. You'll see. You can't escape its charm. You'll no longer have any desire to go."

His insistence irritated me. I replied, not exactly in a good mood, that this town would never be able to keep me. I was sorry I'd ever come, and would be heading back to the station to catch the first train no matter where it was going. The important thing was to get away from here.

The man snickered. "The same thing happened to me a few years ago. I stopped here by chance, by mistake. A mix-up while changing train. And I never left again. I live with the birds that nest beneath the archways of Gothic doors or in the grooves of baroque volutes. To understand this town, you must wait to see the sunrise, the murderous tenderness with which it brushes each facade. People here haven't the heart to watch. They fear the night as well. They can only stand it when they've got the warmth of the earth all around them. And they never come out until the full radiance of daylight is upon them."

The little girl's hand had become very heavy in my fingers. I felt it insinuating itself like ductile metal into my flesh, with the same weighty authority that was in the man's voice. The night birds twittered, rustling their wings among king's beards and wise men's tiaras. To and fro went the constellations between the towers.

"Come, take a seat right here, next to me," said the man. "It's cool in the dark, and the bird droppings won't stain your clothes. I'll tell you everything I've learned about this town and its people. It's very interesting."

He had taken me by the arm and was trying to drag me toward the steps of the church. The little girl was also dragging me in that direction with an unsuspected strength for her feeble body. As he spoke, the man caressed the fabric covering the doll. The girl showed him none of the anger and repugnance with which she had resisted me when I'd tried to do the same. She gazed at the man, eyes wide with surprise. The tip of her tongue showed between her lips, and I felt her hand trembling in mine. But the man paid her no mind; clearly, he was only interested in the swaddled doll.

The birds, disturbed by our conversation, emerged from the shadows and came to contemplate us, morose and malevolent. The man's fingers stuck to my skin through the fabric of my sleeve like suckers on a tentacle affixed to my flesh and already bending it to their will.

I freed myself with a brusque shake befitting the importunate stranger. When he tried to seize my shoulder, I pushed him back so violently that he tottered. But instead of growing angry at my attitude, he began to laugh, discreetly and intimately, and said once more: "Come."

As I drew closer to that church, I felt such repugnance as only they will understand who have chanced one day to gaze upon a mask the wrong way round. Instead of pressing the cavity to your face, such that your head fits into it, you bring it toward yourself facing outward, as you might a stranger's face, and when your own nose touches its cardboard one, you abruptly discover the twin abysses of the unfilled eyes, the unmoored hollows of the nostrils, a draft through the parted lips. Try it yourself. Gaze upon a mask in this fashion, at least once, instead of looking through it, and you will no doubt experience a sensation like the one that had haunted me since I walked among those façades, and assailed me more violently still when I stopped before that church of lace crochet and night.

Have you ever encountered the autonomy of an empty mask, its uncanny caprices, that play of air and light to which it lends itself, that mystery of a hollow protrusion, an inert shell? Then you know the horror I felt when that man tried to drag me through the mask to the other side.

What lay behind the façade of that church? I had no more wish to find out than I did to hear what he had to say about the fate of that town and the people who lived there. I was seized with horror in the presence of all those façades.

As if he could read my thoughts, the man brought his lips to my ear, and though I drew back sharply, I heard him whisper, "It has another name on maps and atlases, but we who live here call it the City of No Façades."

I studied him, wondering if he took me for a fool, resolved not to question this absurdity. But an old need for logic made me blurt out almost inadvertently, "The City of No Façades? Why, there's nothing else around!"

The man smiled mysteriously. Then, with a very knowing air, he said darkly, "That's exactly right. A city where there's nothing but façades is a City of No Façades."

And he nodded several times, as if quite satisfied with himself, proud of his perspicacity. During this brief exchange, the little girl let out long sighs and clutched her doll even closer to her chest. At the same time, she rubbed her infirm hip against my thigh, which stirred such disgust in me I almost felt nauseous. Brusquely I freed myself of both hands holding mine. The little girl let out a cry, while the man crossed his arms, giving me a sardonic stare. Without so much as a goodbye, I turned my back on my two companions and walked away. But the thought of the façade behind me, pierced by unseeing sockets, aroused such anguish in me that I began to run.

With supple, silent strides the man had caught up to me. I could feel him there beside me, so close he could have touched me with his hand. I could hear his breathing, harsh and irregular.

As for the little girl, I could make out the pained tapping of her heels on the long stone slabs, the lopsided gait of her game leg. Her face as she ran must have been clenched in a tragic rictus. And I would have stopped, out of pity for her, had I not been afraid to see night birds surging from the pages of a stone gospel, the vehement swath of rose windows, the anguished headless martyrs along the balconies and the curt postures of executioners which the empty heavens magnified.

I ran as if my life hung in the balance, less to escape that man and that little girl, who had tangled the threads of their lives with mine, than to flee that town and perhaps to save them, too, from the murderous tenderness of the dawning day. The starlight was fading away even as a greyish glow rose from the ground. Morning was near. The trapdoors to the underground dwellings opened with a thunderclap, and the façades would take on a terrible gravity in the broad light of day. Though night was just beginning to descend from its highest summits, I felt the drear morning chill, its dispiriting insistence on living.

Though almost pressed up against me, the man did not touch me. No doubt he wished to goad me to run even faster, rather than stop. And the little girl, clutching her doll, labored breathlessly behind, in the desperate staccato of her uneven legs.

To lose my pursuers, I threw myself into a structure whose circular façade seemed to offer places to hide. But no sooner had I entered than I saw the trap into which every step I'd taken that night had been conspired to lead me. That structure was a vast circus, not unlike the Colosseum, surrounded by terraces and floors of colonnades. Instead of making good my escape, I had chosen the one place where I would never be able to do so, eternity's serpent folded back on itself, tail tight between its teeth.

The stands were empty, but powerful murmurings rose from the depths. I could hear the cries of gladiators and the roars of beasts, the sharp sound of gates swinging open on hinges. From time to time, a heavy hammering gallop recalled elephants racing through the subterranean vaults. And there were dank nooks slick with water oozing from the porous stone, where intertwining serpents swarmed, an angry hissing from the many heads.

I walked on the sand that nocturnal dew had dampened and fringed with festoons as waves do beaches. I would not have been surprised to spy the elusive constellations of starfish, the milky cowls of jellyfish, the shells of nervous bivalves or unsociable urchins. Sometimes the lions roared like the sea, and had green, frothing waters suddenly surged from the lower arcades, I would not have doubted my eyes.

The tiers of seating sat atop slight columns, such that the enormous amphitheatre gave off a feeling of airy fragility.

There were benches of white marble, smooth and slender as bone, where sculpted monsters exchanged caresses, or tore one another to pieces. In some spots, the sand still bore the impress of great paws, so deeply had their claws wounded the ground, and dew pooled in the hollows. Elsewhere, irregular wheel-tracks attested to sudden chariot turnings, their grand clamor of horseshoes, chains, axles, and whips.

At times the vague uproar from underground would dwindle; then a great and tragic peace fell over the colosseum. At other times, it poured forth in dissonant torrents, smothered under thick carapaces of brick, earth, and rock, like lava seeing an exit, and I thought to hear the rage of wild beasts suddenly hurling themselves against the bars of cages that creaked and rattled.

I remained vulnerable to the mystery of the tumultuous caves and tunnels, but I had outpaced my pursuers. Neither the man nor the little girl had followed me into the colosseum. Freed from their company, I felt a happy relief, but a certain fear as well. I now suspected that once comforted by the sun's stable reign, the citizens of town would flock here, and a flood of wild animals would surge forth from underground, snakes coiled around the elephant's legs, monkeys perched between the ears of giraffes, parrots fastened to antelopes' horns like the plume of a hat. Was I destined to become the sole victim of these bestial games, or would processions of slaves, their round brown heads lined up in stocks, come to join me for the amusement of leopards and the tramplings of hippopotami? Already shapes were emerging from the earth, gauntleted in iron, helmed in leather, with pikes and lassos. Eyes gleamed from behind wire mesh. The smells of oil and wine rose from the cellars. I heard doors rolling loudly aside. All of a sudden, the night was filled with cautious, treacherous cruelty.

The man could have told me what all this was about. The little girl would have left her clammy hand in mine, and I would have found the courage somewhere in myself to protect a child. Perhaps all three of us would have found seats in the narrow stalls to watch the parade of unicorns and gryphons. And then doves would have descended from the skies and, after making several circles in the air, let red roses fall from their beaks into the laps of the prettiest women. But I was alone in this perfect prison, a captive of the arcaded masonry of the night.

Just as I was about to despair of ever escaping the colosseum, waiting for the stampede of sun-bright beasts across sand stripped of its marine maidenhood, a strange apparition approached me in the middle of the arena: a man pushing a cart before him, calling out the same few words over and over in an unintelligible moan. When he drew abreast of me, I recognized the costume of a Scapino: the tight belt pulling in a cotton blouse so as to swell exaggeratedly at the hips and balloon out around the torso. When he saw me, the man stopped moaning, dropped his cart, and began frantically waving his arms, no doubt to tell me that it was time to go. My suitcases were neatly arranged on his small wagon.

Without hesitation, the porter threaded his way among the columns that supported the stands, headed through a large gate, and instantly, the colosseum shut behind him, without a second thought. The train station was so close that some hundred-odd steps took us right up to its bright façade, behind which locomotives were puffing and perspiring.

The porter opened the door to a compartment, carefully placed my bags on a rack, and waved me aboard. No sooner had I taken a seat than the train let out a creak, paused, then started to move. I watched the round, moonlike station lamps fly past, the garish alphabet of signal lights that wrote who knows what message of danger and caution across the skies. There were two other people in the compartment I hadn't noticed earlier. When I turned to look at them at last, I saw the man from town and the little girl sitting next to each other on the banquette across from me. They smiled as if happy to see me again. The man was combing his beard with his hairy hands. The little girl cradled her doll, her scrawny, crippled legs and narrow head rocking to the same rhythm.

I got up to run away, but the train car was an old-fashioned one, without a hallway. Though we were going fast already, I was about to open the door and jump out on the tracks at the risk of my own life when the man said in a gentle voice that for some reason abruptly reassured me: "Sleep. You need some sleep."

"I'm getting off at the next station," I told him.

The man nodded.

"This train won't be stopping before tomorrow night—I mean, tonight," he corrected himself after checking his watch. "A long day's sleep is just what you need. Don't be scared: we won't enter your dreams. We'll be sleeping too."

And with that, the stranger and the little girl moved apart, each curling into their corners and, by all appearances, went to sleep. The man's breathing was slow and regular. The little girl closed her eyes with some effort and began to snore, nostrils tense, lips parted. The fabric covering her doll fell away. I glimpsed a doleful little face with pale eyes and a sullen, sickly mouth, looking back at me with indifference. The light that swung from the ceiling of the compartment went red, then mauve, then blue. Without waking, the little girl instinctively pulled a corner of the rag back over her doll. Beyond the doors, tall trees were falling, one after the other. I, too, toppled into sleep.

When I woke, a night of soot and cotton clung to the windows. Perhaps I'd slept no more than a few minutes. Perhaps a long day had gone by. The events of my dreams piled up like the layers of centuries.

The man, one hand on my knee, was gently shaking my leg.

"The train's about to stop," he said.

And indeed, a few seconds later, it did, as if exhausted from having run all day. The little girl gazed at me with eyes still dazed from sleep. Her skirt, hiked up, showed her pale gray, bony knees.

"Have to get off," the man said. "This is as far as it goes."

I protested, insisting that I was headed to Prague and wasn't about to alight on this deserted moor, but the man simply said in that case, I should've taken another train, and this was the end of the line.

I leaned out the door to see if the other passengers were getting off as well. It seemed to me that aside from the staff, we were alone in the train.

A conductor swinging a reddish lantern came and unlocked our compartment door. A cool, gentle breeze blew in. The man smoothed his sleep-rumpled clothes. The little girl tugged her dress over her bare legs. I stood ready to grab my suitcases, when the man stopped me.

"You won't be needing those. You can get them later."

I shrugged, giving in. My destination no longer interested me. The night had about it some violently evocative force, and this landscape in its very desolation drew me with the same quality of sad, wild nobility, emanating from the dunes barbed with shrubs.

"Look."

A crimson moon was rising. The sand began to glisten. The shrubs lay down their shadows, which spread, stretched, bristling with claws. A smell of marsh and salt lingered in the air. The man breathed deeply of it while the little girl brought one hand to her throat, as if she were choking.

We began walking across the thick sand, which gave way beneath our feet with a crunching sound. Now and then we trod on dry shrubs whose branches shattered, loud as firecrackers. The moon was rising in the sky as if tugged on the end of a string. The little girl had taken my hand once more, as she had in the city of façades, and was limping along beside me, so closely that her bony hip chafed me like a fingernail scratching my leg.

The landscape had the melancholy of unfinished things. It offered up only stunted trees, devoid of living leaves, that flailed about with the envious rage of the infirm. The sand was so soft that I sank up to my knee in places, and insects that dwelled in the underground galleries of dunes pounced upon me fiercely to bite my ankles. The moon yellowed, dwindled, uncertain of its fate.

And on we walked, until at last we reached the shore. Waves made a lapping sound, like kisses. Horned creatures with huge eyes emerged from the sand, gave us a look, then escaped sideways, dragging calcareous housings festooned with baroque ornaments. The man untied a rowboat moored to a large rock, climbed aboard, and took hold of the oars. The little girl got in after him, crouching down in front. I took a seat on the narrow bench in the rear. The oars lifted masses of heavy, sparkling water. The man braced himself and began to row vigorously.

"This is the inner sea," he said after a moment, without my asking a thing.

"Inner to where?"

He shrugged. "I don't know. Inner to ourselves, perhaps."

Then he returned to rowing and said not another word.

Soon enough, we left the shore behind. The dwarf trees grew even smaller, became imperceptible. The dunes flattened. The moon, paling now, seemed lit from within, as if by a bulb. It looked like one of those giant frosted glass lampshades of yesteryear. I recall them from my childhood, and when we would light the lamps at an early hour on winter afternoons, I would say: the moon is rising. And golden dragons would crackle in that globe's icy crystal, but here the moon held only an old blind man tapping his way with his cane past dead shrubs, a lantern in hand and a bundle of sticks over one shoulder, his crippled dog limping along behind.

When we had reached open water, or were so far out that the coast now seemed but a broad charcoal line against a chalk smudge, the little girl rose to her feet and began to unswaddle the doll she held in her arms. The milky body began to gleam in the lacquer of moonlight, but I no longer knew whether it was a doll or a statuette, or a waxen Christ like the ones I'd seen in Austrian convents, that nuns would sometimes borrow to alleviate a painful nostalgia for motherhood.

When the doll had been completely undressed, the little girl delicately rubbed its limbs together, as if massaging them, and then tossed the doll into the water. At first it sank, sending out ripples, and then returned to the surface, as if buoyed by a phosphorescent light rising from the depths of the sea, though perhaps the light emanated from the doll itself. It spun, drifted, surrendering to the whim of the tides, and suddenly, spreading its arms and legs, it started to swim.

This was so sudden that I let out a cry of astonishment. I had leaned over the edge of the rowboat, and was watching that little opalescent shape struggle with a vivacious animal joy. The phosphorescent aura followed it, as if it were caught in a floodlight beam, and the light was so dazzling that I could make out every detail of its body. I could also see schools of fish rising from the depths, drawn by the light, and splashing about her in a great flurry of fins, gills, and tails. So

Cardiff Docks, (1894) by Lionel Walden

vivid was the glow that I discerned the seabed with its parade of sponges, coral spread out like Spanish combs, contemplative crabs and octopi lying in ambush. Everything was bathed in a cascade of green and blue atremble with gold and red shadows from the puppet's every movement.

After watching the tiny swimmer pensively for a spell, the little girl undressed in turn, taking care to fold each item of clothing neatly as she took it off, and setting them all on the bench before her. Her unsightly boniness seemed scrawnier still in the moonlight that highlighted every knob. She disrobed with neither embarrassment nor immodesty. True, the man was rowing with his back to her, but she bared her adolescent nudity before me.

I noted, then, that her paralyzed leg was withered and knotty as a dead branch. The moonlight polished her pallid body, as one might ivory with a velvet cloth to bring out the shine. When she was entirely naked, the little girl climbed toward the prow, wobbling on her uneven legs, and dove into the water.

At first she sank toward the sea floor just as the doll had, disturbing the evenly spread shadows. Then she came straight back up to the surface, and a light accompanied her as well. She swam with a grace I would never have expected from such a misshapen body. The movements of her head, her arms, her legs were of a powerful, assured harmony. Her hair had become a soft blue, and small fish frolicked among its floating strands. Her fingers stirred a foliage of pearls that rose and fell away. I don't know if it was an illusion cast by that miraculous glow, or if some metamorphosis had truly taken place, but in an instant, her unsightly body became one of surprising beauty. All that was knotted loosened, smoothed. Her head swayed gracefully atop supple shoulders. Her long, full thighs moved mischievously. Her breasts brightened like sea flora, her belly lit with fluorescent kelp.

The little girl had caught up with the doll, and the two were now playing. Their naked, shining shapes chased each other about, each trailing a luminous wake shot through with streaks of crimson. Their play was of such extraordinary grace and splendor that I looked on, fascinated, while the man kept rowing. The two swimmers, diving down and returning to the surface, encircled the rowboat in a halo of flame. Undulating, scintillating curves rippled about. The movements of their arms lifted the water and let it fall again like cascades of diamonds. Darker folds of water had the smoky, violet sheen of sea silk. A childlike, joyous, intoxicating lightness emanated from these bodies that seemed of a sudden transparent, incorporeal as jellyfish, whose flesh consists only of light, colors, and water.

They were swimming so fast, the two of them, that the man bent over his heavy oars grew breathless trying to keep up. For a moment he stopped rowing to ask if I, too, didn't want to dive in and join them. I hesitated. It seemed tempting indeed to plunge into the water, those shimmering depths, but I did not know what manner of metamorphosis might await me. I thought of crabs flattened in their blue grottoes, of lurking octopi, sargassum traps.

Was death not a necessary step to attain transfiguration?

When I shouted out "No!" the man nodded with a reproachful air, and I heard him snicker. I almost regretted my decision, but what I saw a moment later taught me that my caution might have been reasonable. I no longer know, now, if I regret not having dived in and frolicked with the swimmers. But countless are the paths that lead us to our fate.

The little girl and the doll had been at play for some time, chasing each other about among the glittering waves that fell in a jeweled rain around their limbs, when I noticed that the girl's movements were slowing, growing clumsier. As if she were starting to tire, or felt a cramp coming on, the child flailed at the water awkwardly, almost convulsively. Gone now were the flowing strokes whose noble, ample harmony I'd admired earlier, given way to a laughable staccato floundering that by turns splashed noisily about or else struggled to maneuver arms and legs grown stiff and heavy as metal. The doll, however, seemed impervious to exhaustion, and its shimmering path retained the same playful, musical grace that had bewitched me. It seemed to fortify itself with the strength the little girl was losing, for now I could see that only with the greatest difficulty was she even keeping her head above water, and that any moment now, weariness would no doubt paralyze her, dragging her down into the depths.

I drew the man's attention to this worrisome weakness, but he wouldn't listen. He just kept on rowing, rhythmically, without seeming to care that, though the doll was still circling our boat as sprightly as a puppy, the little girl had fallen far behind, and was no longer able to catch up. I shouted at him to stop rowing so fast, but he did not lower his speed. The fear of being abandoned must have lent the girl new strength, for in a violent burst of energy she pulled alongside our craft. I noticed, then, how fully her face had taken on an expression of tragic resignation. Her limbs had lost their smooth ivory sheen. A matteness as of marble covered her rounded thighs, a deep groove at the arched small of her back; her hair glistened with blue glints. As her body spent itself in a violent effort, her face with its closed eyes betrayed the profound wisdom of indifference, and the locks of hair pasted to her temples no longer yielded to the water's playful spirit. If I hadn't witnessed her successive metamorphoses, I'd have been hard pressed to recognize the diminutive, limping figure from the City of No Façades in this long, supple, beautiful woman who combined a youthful body with the gravity of an ageless countenance.

Suddenly, she stopped moving her limbs; her legs came together, grew still; her arms fell to her sides and stayed there; her neck stiffened. For a moment she floated, so stiff as to be dead, while the waves passed her from hand to hand. Then she flipped over and dove down headfirst toward the phosphorescent seaweed, which drew her in. Leaning over the water, I watcher that specter of stone sink from sight, her pale feet passing through schools of fretful fish. And then I could no longer see a thing, for the light that surrounded her like a halo had been doused the moment she had dove toward the depths of the sea.

The man had not stopped rowing for even a moment, nor had he said so much as a word. I myself was astonished not to feel more emotion at the disappearance of that splendid creature. I, too, remained unmoved by that tragic accident, as if all this were but a game or a spectacle. Perhaps once she had become so utterly graceful and beautiful, the little girl had ceased to interest me. Perhaps I also believed she would come back up to the surface to play once more with her doll.

At long last, the man let go of the oars, took off his jacket, rolled up his shirt sleeves, and got down flat on his belly, leaning over the front of the boat. With his eyes, he followed the swimming puppet, making quick circles about our unmoving craft, surrounding it in a blue and green circle of liquid fire. He reached out his hands to grab it when it passed within reach, but the clever doll dodged this trap, slipping nimbly away whenever he was about to catch it. This might have gone on for some time, if the man hadn't noticed a net in the back of the boat. He seized it, and while the doll was mocking him, believing itself out of reach, scooped it deftly up, imprisoning it in the netting, then brought it close and grabbed hold of it, though it thrashed about and shrieked like a cat.

At the moment the doll had been torn from the water, the luminous halo around it had vanished. Now it was as if the entire sea had been extinguished, and the moon itself hid behind clouds shaped like hands that expunged the very stars from the sky. In this darkness, the doll's whimpers and piercing cries echoed hideously. But the man had no difficulty quashing the little creature's revolt. He hastily wrapped it up in the clothes the little girl had left on the seat, and then once it was all trussed up, set it down beside him. Smothered moans came from the cloth wound round its head, and the shapeless bundle jerked so furiously it almost tumbled from the boat. But with a few harsh blows, the man brought it to heel, still and silent. Finally, he lit a lantern sad and yellow as the moon and hung it from the prow.

And so we returned to the shore whence we had set sail. The shrubs and dunes greeted us. We leapt ashore. The man moored the rowboat to a rock, carefully knotting the rope to which a tribe of mussels savagely clung. Then we headed for the train.

Before returning to my compartment, which I recognized from the suitcases I'd left there, I passed by a freight car the porters were loading. I made out a long shape wrapped in a soldier's blanket, gray with brown stripes. As they hoisted this bundle aboard, the blanket slipped, revealing a marble shape so beautiful and moving that I drew closer for a better look. I caught but a glimpse, for the chief conductor immediately covered it up, but despite the dim light from the lantern hung outside the door, I saw a worn, weathered statue of the sort that have long sojourned in the ocean depths, where the caress of kelp and the solicitude of sea creatures refine, and strip them of their inert skin. For that statue showed its flayed flesh, eaten away by marine acids, maimed and thus made more human than ones that preserve their crystalline carapace intact.

There was something terrible and heartrending about its nudity. It looked like the little girl, or what the little girl had become in her metamorphoses through life and death. I recognized the locks of hair pasted to her temples, colorless now, pale as marble snow, the deep groove at the arched small of her back, the harmonious swell of her belly, her legs joined in modesty, her arms folded over her torso. Long days underwater had no doubt dulled the blossoms of her breasts and lips, doused the fragile rainbow of the byssus, eroded the nacre of her nails. Light shadows of blue and green lingered in the hollows of the stone, deep in the armpits, imperceptible under the lowered eyelids and between the lips.

But already the coarse blanket hid these troubling wonders once more. The porters rolled the statue into a corner of the empty car with no more care than an empty barrel or a crate of wood shavings. Then they came back out, pulled the door shut, and locked it.

"Come," said the man, tugging my sleeve.

He had the doll tucked firmly under his arm. Not a sound came from the bundle of cloth. Perhaps the doll had suffocated to death, suffocated, or simply resigned itself to its captivity.

He set the bundle down on the seat beside him, right where the little girl had been sitting the night before. I too had taken my former seat. With a gesture of astonishing tenderness, the man peeled back the cloth from the doll's head. Then I saw a small red face, wrinkled and flushed as a newborn's, eyes and mouth pressed shut in a kind of raging fury. The hideous creature was snoring through its nose, grimacing fiercely, caught up in tumultuous dreams, and shivered as much as its close swaddling would allow.

The train cars groaned, bumping and straining, and the train began moving along the dunes. I could no longer see the inner sea, but the smells of salt and silt trailed us for a while. The moon dashed madly after us, across a sky full of obstacles, harassed by clouds that reached out long fingers to seize it. At times, it fell into the clutches of these vaporous hands, but then abruptly broke free, rolling along before the hands caught up, strangled it, set it out on a platter like a severed head.

The man fell asleep. The doll, in turn, stopped groaning and sniffling, and slipped into a thick slumber. I remained awake, alone in the train car, alone in this world beneath the moon's stare, that terrified moon come to beg rescue from the clouds' garrote.

NOX UNA

Marian Womack

1.

You might think that four months is not enough time to exorcise a place, but Arnaud's telegram had not allowed for any hesitation on my part: "Room. Work. Come, Arnaud". Up till that moment all I had done was lick my wounds and think of the city. I can see it even now, as clear as if I were there. The wealthier students heading back from their private dinners with faculty members. They cross the disordered streets, a maze of stone and mud and pigeon droppings. If looked at from above, the avenues and the alleys spread like insect wings around the fortress.

You ask if four months is enough: by then the city, a distant, imagined thing, had wrapped me even tighter in its web. Its mysteries haunted me, even from my self-imposed exile, two countries away. I thought of you often, of Arnaud, of many others at the will of the city's dark embrace. The students with their withered faces, sunken eyes—which we hope is merely a result of their spending long hours inside the rounded library—never arriving to their gilded rooms. And if they make it back it is because they themselves are transformed into unclean spirits, destined to threaten the new crop of ingénues that arrives when the leaves start to fall, with their new rough tweed jackets, those hopeful gazes, unaware that they will soon turn into portions for foxes.

I did exactly what I told you, what you told me: we had been waiting for this to happen. I wasted no time in going to the village post office to send an equally laconic reply: "Train. Friday. Thanks, Jonás." I found somehow the strength to leave the unfurnished flat where I was hiding and head to Killian Engels' antiquarian bookshop in the cobbled square. There I transformed my recent past, heavy books in obscure medieval languages, into the price of a single journey in the express bound for Venice. I would alight in the university town which I loved, which I hated: the stage where all my terrors had recently played out. Even then it all seemed a dream, something that would happen in the distant future. I would leave the next day.

The memories were still pricking me: you, leaving my room after informing me that you never wanted to see me again; Arnaud and his usual satisfied smile; my humiliating expulsion from the fellowship. Now, as then, I was not brave enough to say goodbye, not even to Engels. I disappeared as quietly as I had arrived, and that was it.

A city painted in sepia, with grandiose buildings which somehow managed to exist on a human scale; a damp cloister that was falling to pieces, covered in scuffed shields that resembled boils, marks of a strange skin disease; a beautiful abandoned anatomy theatre, its greatest draw for the tourists; bicycles weaving in and out of the traffic; ash-coloured pigeons. All of this embellished with some old legend about the fortress, and the cursed faculty that had established itself there in the thirteenth century. Monsters that had escaped the plague by unnatural means and diabolical dealings.

Four months is not long enough, you say. In truth, I was not worried about seeing Arnaud, nor was I afraid of those fabled winged creatures that fed on us all. A legend, perhaps, but somehow all those nursery horrors had become true in my case: falsely accused, my carcass had been picked clean by the vultures. And yet, the only one thing that worried me was seeing you again.

"Do you know Professor Scheibert?"

"Justus Friedrich Maximilian Scheibert?" As it happened, a couple of volumes of his work, bound in fine morocco leather, had just monetised themselves into this final train journey.

"You're going to catalogue his personal library."

I had to admit that Arnaud had behaved like a real friend.

The next morning he led me personally to one of the university sites in the town centre, part of a block of nineteenth-century buildings, the heart of the institution. I watched him hobbling off under the dark arcades, his hands in his pockets, looking so like a little boy that I suddenly thought I had no idea how old my friend actually was.

Over the course of our brief walk I had realised something that had hit me right in the heart: the inhospitable city had not changed at all. It was all the same as I had left it: the old dark Renaissance-era buildings, the cars and motorcycles which tormented the cyclists and pedestrians, the permanent labyrinth of arcades, all of them supported on thick Doric columns, covered in rough messages asking for flatmates or offering bicycles (always brand new, in perfect condition). The improvised affectation of these requests, which are unavoidable in cities populated by impoverished students, uglified and saddened the brown and ochre walls, dark with the emissions from cars and motorbikes. And of course, alongside the offers and requests, posters of a different kind: missing students, missing cleaners, missing children and pets.

I crossed the threshold on my own and walked into the long-remembered entrance hall, with its marble walls covered in even more functional notes and timetables, announcements of theatrical productions (which made me think of you, my soul fluttering) and all the signs which diminish the seriousness of these pinkish buildings and shrink them to the needs of the young people who use them. I climbed to the top floor and walked through confused corridors to the back of the building, where the faculty had lodged, just like in English colleges, ever since the fortress had been declared unfit for human habitation. Arnaud had explained everything with his usual efficiency, and soon I was standing in front of the door where his instructions had guided me.

I knocked. No one answered.

I knocked again.

After a while I heard dragging footsteps and a cough, and someone who looked more like a beggar than a world-renowned scholar opened the door, a half-smoked cigarette in the same hand as his coffee cup.

"What do you want?" he grunted. I paused for a second: in spite of my familiarity with this treacherous paradise, this city that I knew all too well to be the very antechamber of hell, I had been naïve enough to think that I might be expected. I panicked: perhaps, all of this could simply be one of Arnaud's jokes.

"My name is Jonás Weber. I'm here to catalogue your books."

"Oh! Good! My books! Those damn things, there's no one who can make head nor tail of them, and if you leave them to their own devices, it's almost as though they breed."

I walked into chaos: ashtrays filled to the brim; half-empty cups of coffee; in the air a sense of urgency that I could not pin down. Strong smells: coffee, tobacco, burnt cooking oil. A little stove on a side table, giving off another smell, both worrying and nauseating. And the books, of course. It was clear that the old man had surrendered himself to the silent onslaught of his library, and its foot-soldiers: papers, piled up without rhyme or reason; dictionaries, heaped so high they almost reached the picture-rails; a huge quantity of newspapers and magazines in various languages.

"Coffee?"

"Thank you."

Scheibert disappeared into the cavernous breakfast room, and I continued my inspection. The arched ceiling cut the straight lines of the corner closest to the windows, which were covered with thick curtains that only allowed one to guess at the rain falling outside. But the noise that carried through them left no room for doubt: the stubborn spring downpour had redoubled its efforts. There were no plaster mouldings or marble statues in the room. Instead the wall was marked by the greyish fingers of a worrying damp patch. Eventually the old man reappeared, and one of the world's most famous linguists, the proud owner of a medal from the King of Spain for his translation of *Don Quixote*, held out a cup that was filled with a dark liquid of unclear taste, which allowed me, briefly and painfully, to remember you, Lucilla, our first meeting: a flurry of confused mugs in the café, me spilling the contents of your tote bag with its unexpected quote (*Le domaine de la liberté commence là où s'arrête le travail déterminé par la nécessité*). The absurd accident worked in my favour, as it allowed your features, perfect as those of a Renaissance miniature, to relax enough to speak to me, the fool who had shed, onto a floor covered in cigarette butts, your very essence—a book with a pencil attached to it by a string, a purse with an embossed picture of Chartres Cathedral, chewing gum and paper handkerchiefs, and a photocopied playscript with annotations on every page.

Expertly, it seems, I put the pain to one side.

I left the professor's lodgings rather late and a little depressed, with my hands covered in dust. An attempt at putting the volumes into some kind of physical order had revealed to me what I had feared from the start: this would not be a job of weeks, but rather months. I felt like Sisyphus: all my work over the course of the day had done nothing to make a dent in the disorder with which I was confronted. Once out in the streets I followed without thinking the winding path that the arcades marked out, and I passed bars and museums and lecture theatres, ending up by the botanic garden. The place had gained such a reputation for being the locus of a number of disappearances that, now dusk was falling, it was firmly locked and bolted shut. Away in the background the unexpected Venetian tower of the university, paid for by those traders who had wanted to soften their bleak reputation, stood tall among the giant trees that surrounded the circular path of yellow dirt.

2.

I woke up in an alleyway. The white light of dawn made everything looked unreal. The cold pavement was wet and unpleasant, and I slowly stood, confused about my surroundings. What was happening? I had obviously slept on the street. A gnashing pain, I put my hand up, and there was blood and sweat on my forehead. Slowly, the pieces came together.

I didn't know how long I had spent laid out flat on the pavement. Images of the previous afternoon filled me with thoughts that were greyer even than the city.

I had not known that you and Arnaud knew one another, unless the meeting I had stumbled upon was somehow connected to me. I had spotted your white tote bag in the window of a coffee shop, and what happened in its faded interior had looked like a theatrical spectacle, a comedy, a dream, more than the impossible reality: you smiling and laughing, and a large bony hand brushing a curl back from your forehead, the same hand that had shook mine, dull and ragged, with nails bitten to the quick, that morning at Scheibert's door.

Everything had started to spin around me, transforming itself into a vortex of dark walls and advertising posters, and the lights of the car against which I pushed myself in a desperate and humiliating attempt to hide down a nearby alleyway. And this was when I saw it: your name, those beloved black letters on a red background, cut out in the shape of a dagger or a sword: "Lucilla Maiorama in *Nox Una*, a new play written and directed by Arnaud Winters". Then the world had turned into a dark and moonless land, like one of those nights on which first-year students like to tell stories whose final moral is always the same: avoid the old fortress at all costs. I must have passed out then and there, and hit my head.

I understood my punishment: to observe this scene, being forever excluded from participating in it, condemned to spend my days engaged in an absurd and impossible bibliographic project which would carry on until the end of time.

After I got up I cleaned the blood as best I could, and I wandered limping through the city, followed by the pigeons. The empty and lonely streets, the pavements as deserted as a theatre after the performance has finished, deeply unnerved me. I only gained some presence of mind when, with worrying calm, everything started to fill with the hubbub of morning. I arrived late at Scheibert's, but the old man did not seem to care: I don't believe that his was a life lived in thrall to the tyranny of the clock, especially since he had started to hand over his duties to the younger and more ambitious members of the faculty of comparative linguistics.

Although I worked hard, caught up in an almost childish urgency, when I left the library that day I despaired at the little I had achieved. Was I dead? Was I in purgatory?

Maybe half the city was already dead, as we had always suspected. Scheibert, engaged in an eternal dialogue with his own shadow, was proof of that. After I left him I went out into a golden May afternoon which spilled its light on the arcades, on the bicycles, and, I supposed, on the botanic garden as well. I recalled our walks along its circular paths. I had escaped early from my punishment among the crepuscular heaps of books, claiming falsely that I had a headache, and the old man had walked me to the door and had said goodbye with an exaggerated politeness that was not usual in him. I could have sworn that he was not in the least fooled by my sudden indisposition.

I took a quick shower and locked myself away in my cubicle. Luckily, Arnaud was not in the apartment. But I soon heard him come in, and, to my surprise, he came right over to my door and started knocking.

"Jonás? Where have you been? You should have called, I was worried."

"I'm sorry to have worried you. I'm fine," I lied, a little stunned by his sudden friendliness.

"You look awful. I'm just going to make some coffee. Come to the kitchen."

Arnaud had, by some uncertain means, turned into the enemy. The play, the connection with you, it was all dubious, otherwise it would have been in the open, I reasoned. But my general apathy prevented me from facing up to the situation, and I would not have been strong enough to stand up to him in an argument anyway. I followed him silently, thinking that we were no more than two strangers united by this city, which breathed and moved only via machinations, murmurs and gossip and revenge.

"You frightened me to death. I thought that the spirits of the fortress had got you," he started, his mouth curved up in a smile. It was typical of Arnaud to make fun of everything, but for some reason his comment unnerved me. "What's it like working with old Schiebert? I thought you'd have fun."

"Yes, it's interesting," I lied again, this time with an ease that surprised me. I watched him

One Summer Evening in Paris, (circa 1880–1890) by Mario de Maria

measuring out the coffee with a carefulness that was almost pedantic. My friend had always been a methodical and meticulous man. The coffee spoons, lined up on the table like two metal stakes, were laden with Russian condensed milk as Arnaud discreetly licked his lips, as though he had just sensed how sweet and sugary they were, before putting them into the liquid with a gesture of satisfaction. This ritual for his coffee must have dated back to his years as an exchange student in Moscow. I imagined him as a callow adolescent, skilled in languages... I put this thought to one side.

The person in front of me must have been born just as he was now, an arrogant incubus cursed with the cold intelligence that kept him separated from the rest of the world. He opened a packet of Turkish pastries and offered me one. Arnaud might have been many things, but he was not miserly. And yet, I could imagine him being so cruel that he had brought me back here in order to stick one final stake into my sad story: my expulsion from this impious paradise; my exile; Lucilla, and now a return in order to—who could tell?—settle various imaginary accounts or else condemn my soul once and for all. I did not know what pleasure he could be getting from this. My friend was a mystery.

Although I sat down at the table, I barely spoke. But Arnaud knew how to fill a conversational void with anecdotes about the classes he was giving, and his never-completed thesis. He didn't mention you, although your presence was the one thing that illuminated the gap between us.

3.

Over the days that followed I buried myself ever more deeply in the cataloguing work. It would be too simple for me to say that I was furious with Arnaud. Millions of ideas, each one more ridiculous than the next, bobbed and clashed in my sick mind. I barely slept, different images competing for control of my agitated imagination: the botanic garden, the Venetian tower, the fortress surrounded by black birds, all too big, all too human. The footsteps of a student on the yellow pavements, wrinkled skin and eyes as large as clock-faces... You, Arnaud, Schiebert.

The old man wouldn't leave me alone. He fluttered around as though he were keeping an eye on me. As always with the inhabitants of this city, his initial friendliness had given way to something more baleful. But for me, as one accustomed to such perfect yet rotten apples, his change of attitude was unsurprising. I spent my days branding the books like cattle, classifying them following a combination of letters and numbers of my own invention, and so the hours went by, in the certainty that the day's work would always come to an end, and time itself would end, and all our lives and all our fears. Nothing else happened in the city except for the disappearance of a young Italian woman on Thursday morning. The news did not affect me as much as it had done in the past. I went to bed that night thinking only of you.

On Friday morning I found an envelope addressed to me, which Arnaud appeared to have slid underneath my door. I opened it, my hands trembling, not at all sure of what to expect—I admit that even then I was hoping for a note begging for forgiveness, offering up some kind of explanation that might be well received in spite of everything. But there was no note in the envelope, rather something else, all the more incredible for its boldness: an invitation to the premiere, that very night, of *Nox Una*. It was a red card, in the shape of a bloody dagger, like the posters I had seen everywhere throughout the ruined city. A monologue, no doubt, as the only name on the posters was yours, Lucilla Maiorama, followed by Arnaud Winters as writer and director. A quotation from Ovid's *Metamorphoses* explained the significance of the title: "A single night", the "nox una" of the title, was a metaphor, a euphemism, for death.

The day passed unbearably slowly. Part of me denied the possibility of hoping for anything, because the most likely outcome was that nothing concrete would take place, nothing connected to me and my circumstances. The most likely scenario was that I would go to the room where the spectacle was being staged and that this, far from being the final act in my personal history, would resolve precisely nothing. Even my outsize egocentrism was not enough to imagine such a sadistic, vandalous act on Arnaud's part. But I had returned; I had this job; there was the play, the invitation… There was a certain sinister pattern to the structure within which I was now letting myself be led.

When I left Schiebert that afternoon I went to an Irish bar and drank three pints, and then, filled with the false strength and enthusiasm of alcohol, I decided to walk to the address that Arnaud had carefully written in pencil on the back of the dagger. Although it was early, I found the building surprisingly empty.

Brandishing my invitation, just in case I came across a drowsy porter, I managed to find the room. It was a large lecture theatre, hidden away in this part of the university; it was unknown to me, belonging, as I supposed it must, to the medical faculty. When I finally reached the Galileo Room I was struck dumb. The door opened onto the anatomy theatre, the tourist attraction that I had never before entered: a result of that sense of security that people have when they are going to live in a place for a long time, and leave without even having been to the local museum.

There was no chance that I had made a mistake: two posters for *Nox Una* were stuck on each of the two heavy wooden doors to the theatre.

The room was dark, and its corners and the last benches on the highest ranks were lost in shadow. The effect was so mournful that I immediately started to feel a little uncomfortable. There was almost no one in the room, but in the centre of the stage you waited, elegantly sitting on a chair. You had your legs crossed, and gave no sign of recognition when I came in. Shaking, I found my place. Arnaud, with his characteristic precision, had assigned a particular seat to each guest. I found the card with my name written on it in one of the last rows. I hadn't been there for longer than five minutes when a flood of people entered and took their seats with eerie speed and precision.

It was only when they were all sitting down in their correct places, just as their portraits might do in the future if ever anyone were to celebrate their passage through the university, that I realized that the entire faculty had come to the production: everyone was there, including my old tutor. I still occasionally thought of his expression of disappointment at my final expulsion. I tried to get up. But the man who was sitting to my right took me by the arm with the surprising strength of an octogenarian, and prevented me from standing.

"Good evening."

Arnaud had entered the round improvised stage to greet us. I was surprised by this old-fashioned gesture, more at home with music halls than proper theatre. I thought briefly of Engels, who retired into the book trade after a career as dramaturge in Munich. A true devotee of Schiller, he would always repeat, when he had drunk too much: *The problem with modern theatre, my dear Jonás, is that nowadays if you go to see a play and don't come out covered in fake blood, or doused in potato salad, then you don't count it as a good night out*. And I immediately knew that I couldn't imagine these old men in the Münchner Kammerspiele, waiting keenly every Saturday night for their ritual bath of potato salad. This, therefore, could not be an experimental, avant-garde production. I had no idea what to expect. And the notion of Arnaud surprising us all was worrying in the extreme.

Were you tied up to the chair? This seemed impossible. Were you there to be devoured by these old crones? My heart started to beat wildly. You weren't moving too much, you weren't speaking. You looked as if you were serenely waiting for something, and looked bored with the whole thing. Was that a smirk in your face?

Even then you knew you would triumph. And triumph you must. I know that now.

But, where did that leave me? *Me, me, me*… Even as if I wanted to see myself as your ally, the cacophony of voices in my head still showed me my true self.

"Tonight we will be witnesses once again to our rebirth," announced Arnaud grandly, turning to look at you in a way that chilled my blood. He then opened a black velvet case and removed what looked like a chisel, or else some other woodworker's tool—his father had been a cabinet maker—and considered it thoughtfully in the light of the candles. A clinking noise to my right made me turn. The old men had started to pass round a decanter of wine and were pouring themselves the liquid, as though this were dessert at a faculty dinner, when the servers have already withdrawn and the time set aside for the most dangerous gossip has begun, those whispers and hints that can make or ruin somebody's career. When it finally reached me, I filled the little glass in front of me with a strange and thick red wine that resembled something else entirely. My stomach twisted unpleasantly.

You considered Arnaud, who was now examining some ancient medical instrument, with an amused expression.

All around me, the remaining invitees started to beat the pulpits with their closed fists, but the noise was not like the dull applause at the end of a distinguished lecture, but more rhythmical, infernally so, a rhythm suitable for the transport of a coffin. Mine, I thought. Yours, I feared.

"There's no room here!" Arnaud announced.

"No room! No room!" the old men in the audience repeated.

No room for what, or whom?

Then I saw it: the ancient eyes, posed over you and resembling those of a wolf, that eternal second before it springs towards its prey.

It was then that you seemed to wake up from your amused slumber.

It was then that you turned to the back doors and opened them, and let in a flock of cavernous looking youngsters.

It was then that you gave orders, imparted instructions, behaved in what looked like a well-rehearsed strategy.

I had been naïve to fear for your safety: it was you who turned the predator, then and there, and the old men who ought to fear for their lives.

The rest passed as if in a dream. I walked on broken glass, the wine decanters smashed on the bloody wooden floor. The old men would not drink anymore, would not behave like the stagnant pack of hounds they had thought themselves to be, their wrinkled faces taken aback by this turn of events. Theirs were the eyes now sinking back into eye sockets, sinking forever. I smelled smoke and saw the anatomy theatre engulfed in an incipient fire. I understood at once: only fire would cleanse the cancerous disease from our city. Over your shoulder Arnaud smiled in my direction, an uncomprehending, terrified smile, his teeth sharp as needles. I had never seen him scared, and gratefully knew that I owed it to you and you only.

And what about me? *Me, me, me!* I had briefly passed out and woke up by my own retching, and by the taste of blood in my mouth. You looked at me and I saw it briefly, there in your eyes. Was it love? I had followed your instructions. I had come back when you told me, your secret message delivered by Arnaud's telegram. Or had I dreamed it all? Perhaps I was deluding myself.

You turned and left me there, in the midst of the destruction. I was part of the town's cancer as well then, although I had thought myself a victim of it.

When I understood, it was too late: there was a locked door between us, between those who would live and those who wouldn't. This was your world now, you had conquered by teeth and claw. This was your world now.

4.

I saw you again, years later. I was engulfed by thick fog, and I thought it was you passing by my side.

"Lucilla!" I shouted. I tried to grab your wrist; but you didn't let me touch you. You looked briefly at me and said… Nothing. Then freed yourself with distressing ease, and back away again into the mist.

THE RAW FOOD MOVEMENT:
COMPARING TRANSFORMATIVE DIETS IN HAN KANG'S *THE VEGETARIAN* (2015) AND JULIA DUCOURNAU'S *RAW* (2016)
V. H. Leslie

"Tell what you eat, and I shall tell you what you are" wrote the eighteenth-century philosopher Jean Anthelme Brillat-Savarin (Ashley, 2004, p.161). It is a truism that resonates on many levels with Han Kang's The Vegetarian and Julia Ducournau's Raw, both of which centre on young female protagonists and the transformative power of food. Han Kang's The Vegetarian, translated from Korean by Deborah Smith, won the 2016 Man Booker International Prize and focuses on a married-women who relinquishes eating meat in favour of a vegan diet, while Raw is an award-winning French-Belgian coming-of-age horror, written and directed by Julia Ducournau about a young vegetarian who starts eating meat. This article seeks to explore moments of consumption and transformation within each of the narratives in relation to feminist theory and to examine how deviant appetites can be seen as a protest against patriarchal structures. Furthermore, despite favouring different diets, both protagonists consume predominantly raw foods. Claude Lévi-Strauss in his seminal essay 'The Culinary Triangle' (1966) put forward the idea that all foodstuffs conform to one of the vertices of his triangle, being either raw, cooked or rotten (Ashley, 2004, p. 30). The process of cooking fulfils a symbolic function, signalling 'the transition from nature to culture' (Ashley, 2004, p.31). In this light, adherence to a raw diet can be seen as a return to a wild, untamed state and as a reaction to civilising practices by which the established systems of control are upheld. Both, The Vegetarian and Raw align femininity with nature and use diet as a way of thinking about female agency.

EATING DIS-ORDERS

The Vegetarian is about a woman trapped in her marriage, whose rejection of meat instigates a series of changes for herself and those around her. The first section of the book is told through the perspective of the protagonist's incredulous husband, Mr Cheong who is first alerted to something being amiss when he finds his wife, Yeong-hye, 'standing, motionless, in front of the fridge' in the middle of the night, on account of a dream (Han Kang, 2015, p.7). Though she returns to bed, she exhibits the first signs of defiance, 'standing there so unnaturally still', as if 'she were some kind of ghost, silently standing its ground' (Han Kang, 2015, p.7). The reason Mr Cheong was attracted to his wife in the first place was due to her passivity, her willingness to perform the domestic duties around the house and to serve and wait on him. Mr Cheong's domestic idyll is subsequently turned upside down along with the contents of the fridge, which he finds strewn across the floor; his wife in the process of disposing of all the meat products:

Around her, the kitchen floor was covered with plastic bags and airtight containers...beef for shubu-shabu, belly pork, two sides of black beef shin, some squid in a vacuum-packed bag, sliced eel that my mother-in-law had sent us from the countryside ages ago, dried croaker tied with yellow string, unopened packs of frozen dumplings and endless bundles of unidentified stuff dragged up from the depths of the fridge...Beef and pork, pieces of chicken, at least 200,000-won worth of saltwater eel' (Han Kang, 2015, pp 9-10).

This isn't the only time Mr Cheong mentions the monetary value of meat, or lists the quantities thrown away, adhering to the idea that the consumption of meat is linked to notions of power and prestige, and by extension, to masculinity, since historically men were the procurers of meat via hunting (Adams, 2000, p.45) Yeong-hye's insistence to rid the house of meat results in her neglecting to iron Mr Cheong's shirt; her meat purge instigating her first rebellion against her domestic role (Han Kang, 2015, p.10). As the novel progresses, Yeong-hye becomes much more assertive on a diet of 'lettuce and soybean paste' and 'plain seaweed soup', refusing to have meat in the house, to wear a bra and to have sex with her husband on account of the 'meat smell' of his body, since he has not adopted a vegan diet like herself (Han Kang, 2015, p. 17).

Despite Mr Cheong's admission that 'going vegetarian was apparently in vogue', Yeong-hye's decision not to eat meat is met with severe opposition, especially from the men in her life (Han Kang, 2015, p.17). Mr Cheong's work colleagues, embarrassed at her inability to coalesce to their dietary standards at a work dinner, muse that, 'meat-eating is a fundamental human instinct, which means vegetarianism goes against human nature' (Han Kang, 2015, p. 23). While Mr Cheong, eager to reassert masculine control and redress the sexual deprivation he has been subjected to, rapes his wife, finding that it produces in him an unexpected appetite he is keen to repeat (Han Kang, 2015, p.31). Similarly, Yeong-hye's father responds with violence, shamed at his daughter's lack of obedience to her husband, by striking her before attempting to force-feed her, evoking in the mind of the reader the force-feeding brutalities that were suffered by the suffragettes in their campaign for women's rights. Significantly, oysters happen to be the viand Yeong-hye's father attempts to feed her, which, with their established feminine allusions, imply that Yeong-hye needs to ingest her gendered role, along with all the cultural obligations and stereotypes that accompany it,

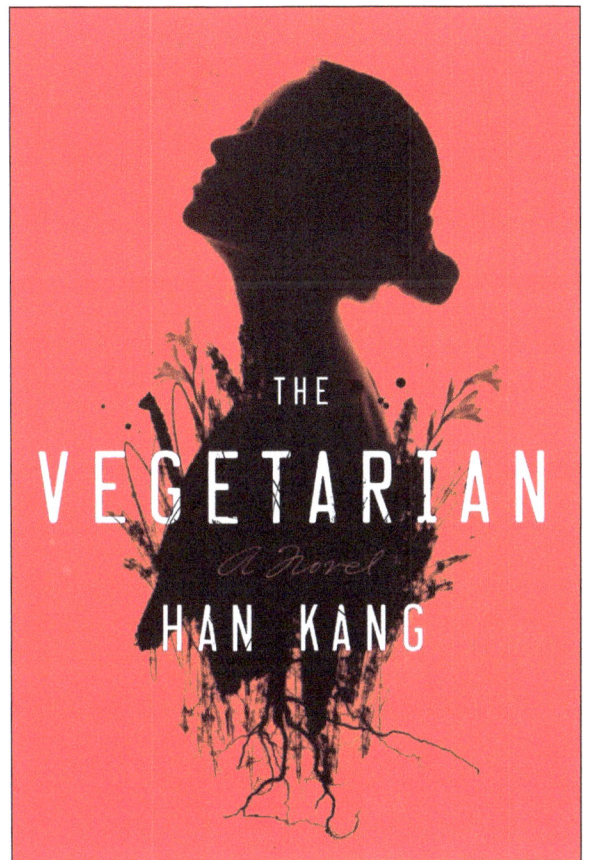

Cover from *Vegetarian* by Han Kang (2016) / Hogarth

especially those that present women as obedient daughters and submissive housewives (Webster, 2006, p. 55).

The force-feeding episode is not the only time Yeong-hye suffers at the hands of her father. Despite refusing to wear a bra, she is visited by recurring nightmares of something stuck in her 'solar plexus', a 'lump' that is the manifestation of her guilt at having been a carnivore:

> Yells and howls, threaded together, layer upon layer, are enmeshed to form that lump. Because of meat. I ate too much meat. The lives of the animals I ate have all lodged there. Blood and flesh, all those butchered bodies are scattered in every nook and cranny, and though the physical remnants were excreted, their lives still stubbornly stick to my insides (Han Kang, 2015, p. 49).

Carol J. Adams' critical theory, *The Sexual Politics of Meat*, explores the correlation between meat-eating and male dominance, and the oppression of women and animals. The language of radical feminist discourse continues this link between animal butchery and female subjugation and sexual violence, 'appropriating the experience of animals to interpret our own violation' (Adams, 2000, p. 57). In this light, Yeong-hye's dreams of animal slaughter can be seen as imaginings of her own suffering, which is supported by the revelation from her sister later in the text, that Yeong-hye took the brunt of her father's anger as a child, 'absorb[ing] all her suffering inside her, deep into the marrow of her bones.' This idea of digesting psychological damage caused by mistreatment and abuse makes her vegetarian stance all the more powerful, a self-determined diet to protest against the abuses of male authority she has endured throughout her life.

But merely changing her eating habits is not sufficient to reverse the damage that has been done. Yeong-hye takes to removing her clothes and sitting outside to 'absorb' the sunlight as a plant would do to induce photosynthesis, a comparison Han Kang makes repeatedly throughout the book. Yeong-hye's mental decline and aberrant behaviour however lead to her admission to Ch'ukseong Psychiatric Hospital, where she spends her time doing handstands, imagining leaves 'growing out of [her] body, roots sprouting out of [her] hands' and flowers blooming from between her legs, before running away into the forest (Kang, 2015, p. 127) Here, the correspondence between women and plants, as espoused by Adams as the opposing binary of men correlating with meat, takes on a more developed, fabulist dimension (Adams, 2000, p. 47). The fact that Han Kang's novel is called 'The Vegetarian' and not 'Yeong-hye', points to the negation of personal identity in favour of the significance of nature. The first lines of the novel also highlight how unremarkable Yeong-hye is until she becomes vegetarian,—though this opinion is told through Mr Cheong's perspective—her diet literally constituting her identity and informing her fantasies of transforming into something more plant-like. To this end, her rejection of meat signals her desire to shrug off her own flesh, the butchered female body and grow into something else.

FRESH MEAT

Julia Ducournau's *Raw* is almost an inversion of *The Vegetarian*, focusing on a young female vegetarian, Justine (Garance Marillier) and the changes that take place when she starts eating meat. The story begins with Justine's arrival at veterinary school and the hazing rituals subjected on new students. Woken in the middle of the night by masked seniors in lab coats, freshers are made to crawl, herd-like, in their nightclothes to a make-shift nightclub. Penned in amidst the blaring music and glaring red lights, and 'shot' with alcohol from water-pistols, animalistic revelry ensues, with Justine increasingly uncomfortable amid the nudity and hedonism. A close-up of a soft toy—a lamb—hangs by the neck from the rafters like a sinister piñata, alluding to the new arrivals as lambs to the slaughter. The next day, the 'rookies' are dowsed in blood for their class photo before being made to eat a raw rabbit kidney as part of their initiation. Justine appeals to her sister Alexia, who also attends the veterinary school, for support. But as with Yeong-hye and the oyster episode, Alexia, now a meat-eater, force-feeds her sister to prevent her from becoming a social outcast.

Justine also undergoes physical changes as the result of eating meat, initially developing a rash, symptomatic of food poisoning, as well as a nascent hunger for flesh. Accommodating this new appetite presents moral difficulties for Justine due to her vegetarian upbringing and her advocacy for animal rights, inducing her initially to steal a burger patty from the canteen before sneaking away from campus to a petrol station with her gay room-mate Adrien. Refusing to let Adrien watch her eat, she devours a shawarma, while Adrien fends off the sexual advances of a drunk trucker; Ducournau drawing attention to the link between meat and sex. Despite confiding in Adrien sufficiently to allow for her new cravings, the extent of her carnivorous appetite is unknown even to him. In an iconic scene, Justine kneels before the fridge eating a raw chicken breast straight from the packet. For the viewer, this is almost as distasteful as later scenes of violence, Stephen Pinker attributing emotions of disgust to the concept of eating raw animal parts as a form of 'intuitive biology', to protect ourselves from harmful microorganisms (Pinker, 1997, p. 383). Interestingly, the fridge functions as a significant symbol in both *The Vegetarian* and *Raw*,—in the latter, preluding another cold receptacle: the morgue—and serving as a liminal space between the world of the living and the world of the dead, where in terms of Lévi-Strauss' Culinary Triangle, the natural shelf-life between the raw and the rotten is extended.

Justine's physical appearance continues to change, this time through Alexia's influence in the form of lending clothes and grooming advice. But a bikini wax accident results in Alexia

Poster for *Raw* (2016) / Focus World

cutting off the tip of her finger and though Alexia's dog gets the blame for eating it and is subsequently put down, since 'once an animal develops a taste for flesh it will bite again', it is actually Justine who is the culprit (Ducournau, 2016). We learn that Alexia shares Justine's cannibalistic instinct but has overcome any feelings of remorse or restraint she may have had in order to accommodate her appetite. Justine however, cannot condone Alexia methods, which include causing car collisions to gorge on the fatalities and the tension grows between the sisters until they are literally taking bites out of one another. This culminates in a very public fight that sees both sisters muzzled like dogs by their classmates. Alexia could be seen as a facet of Justine's mirrored self, a projection of what she could become if she follows in her sister's footsteps. Eating her sister's finger could be seen therefore as consuming part of herself, which she has no aversion to doing, having already ingested her hair and a tooth before biting her wrist as she climaxes during sex with Adrien; his sexual orientation further reinforcing the boundlessness of her appetites. Similarly, Yeong-hye, slices her finger the day before her dream while mincing frozen meat and is left 'strangely pacified' by sucking her finger and tasting her own blood (Kang, 2015, p. 19). For Justine, these moments of self-consumption symbolise her burgeoning autonomy and self-reliance.

Justine's transformation from naïve girl to man-eater, is foreshadowed by another hazing ritual, where she is doused in yellow paint, and coupled with a boy covered in blue paint and instructed to 'make green' (Ducournau, 2016). The painting episode is very similar to a moment in *The Vegetarian*, where Yeong-hye agrees to be the canvas for her artist brother-in-law, who paints the entirety of her naked body with elaborate flowers. Yeong-hye is so enamoured with the transformation that she refuses to wash the paint off, resembling a 'mutant animal that has evolved to be able to photosynthesize' (Kang, 2015, p.91). This blurring of boundaries between human, animal and plant is further emphasised when she has sex with her brother-in-law and he describes a 'green sap, like that which oozes from bruised leaves,' emanating from her vagina, after which, 'the whole of his penis was stained green' (Kang, 2015, p. 96) In both narratives, paint functions as a transitionary layer, concealing the protagonists' exterior at the same time as exposing their true natures. Though the episode in *Raw* has the same green palette and erotic subtext, Justine does not want to make green, but red, and confident in her new skin, she bites off her lover's bottom lip.

As the story progresses, Justine is less able to cover up her sexual desires and her predatory appetite which are presented as one and the same. Drinking to excess and dressing and behaving provocatively, she attempts to bite a neck of a fellow reveller on a night out, only to be swatted away like a mosquito. Ducournau's portrayal of the excesses and anxieties of teenage life are not limited to drink culture. In a moment of dramatic irony, Justine's classmate, hearing her vomiting in the toilets, advises her that using 'two fingers will make it come up faster', assuming her to be a sufferer of bulimia and not a more sinister eating disorder (Ducournau, 2016). Similarly, the presence of social media reinforces the obsession with self-image and lack of privacy, with Justine's drunken antics and the fight with her sister, recorded and shared on her classmates' mobile phones. Ducournau also references the link between video games and violence, depicting Alexia as a keen gamer. When the part-devoured body of Adrien is discovered, Alexia is found nearby, slumped against the fridge, covered in his blood, sated and disorientated with a video game controller in her hand.

Though the female body is important in *Raw*, it is not under attack as it is in *The Vegetarian*. Ducournau's scenes of teenage hedonism present all young people as meat, irrespective of gender. But as the film progresses, it is actually the gay body that is most at risk. Adams identifies 'objectification' as the first stage in a theoretical cycle which links animal butchery to sexual violence, the next stages being 'fragmentation' and 'consumption'. For instance, in reference to women, the metaphorical representation of women 'as pieces of meat', reinforce oppression against them and lead to the continued consumption of these representations, along with the negation of a 'separate identity' (Adams, 2000, p. 58). In *Raw*, the body most objectified is arguably Adrien's, particularly in one scene shot through the diegetic perspective of Justine, who watches him play football shirtless. With ambiguity as to whether it is her sexual or physical hunger that is aroused, the power of her female gaze induces a nose bleed, which could be interpreted as an auto-erotic climax. Adrien is 'consumed' throughout the film, first by other gay men, then by Justine, before being literally eaten by Alexia. But Adrien's isn't the only male body under attack. In the denouement of the film, in a scene that sees Justine back in her family home, sitting across the table from her father, eating a plateful of vegetables she has no appetite for, her father undoes his shirt to reveal his butchered body. We learn that Justine's cannibalism is matrilineal and that her father has acquiesced to his wife's will throughout their marriage. Justine's father preaches the accommodation of appetite, of finding someone who accepts her carnivorous nature and who, like himself, is willing to be meat.

EDIBLE BODIES / EDIBLE HOUSES

To return to Brillat-Severin's aphorism *you are what you eat*, it is clear that the diets of Yeong-hye and Justine are decisive in their various transformations. For Yeong-hye, she replaces the patriarchal diet of flesh she has been fed, with a vegetal one, which ontologically suggests her desire to become something beyond the corporeal. Whereas Justine's appetite for flesh and her self-consumption, speak of her sexual awakening and her developing sense of autonomy. Transformation is a key theme of many of our earliest stories and food often possesses magical powers to instigate change. Film critic Mark Kermode notes the allusion to 'Hansel and Gretel' in *Raw*, referring to Ducournau's film as a 'a gleefully Grimm 21st century fairy tale, subversively told from within the walls of a brutalist gingerbread house' (Kermode, 2017). In folklore and fairy tale, eating in fairy land is taboo, causing the transgressor to become trapped in a netherworld (Guiley, 2009, p. 85). We could interpret Justine's veterinary school as a netherworld of sorts, complete with mortuaries and animal corpses and zombie-like teenagers sustained by a diet of drugs and alcohol. We can also see the fairy tale intertext of 'Hansel and Gretel' in *The Vegetarian*, in which Yeong-hye's initial dream that prompted her rejection of meat, includes a 'red barn-like building' in the 'dark woods' and which, like the gingerbread house, is completely consumable, with 'no end to the meat and no exit' (Kang, 2015, p. 12). *Raw* ends with Justine having escaped her otherworld, though her reluctance to eat her vegetables, means that she is keen to taste the forbidden food again. Whereas, Yeong-hye like the children from the fairy tale, refuses the food of her captors and is able to make her escape back into the forest.

BIBLIOGRAPHY

1. Adams, C. J. (2000) *The Sexual Politics of Meat; A Feminist-Vegetarian Critical Theory*. New York: Continuum
2. Ashley, B. et al (2004) *Food and Cultural Studies*. London: Routledge
3. Ducournau, J. (2016) *Raw*, Focus World, Wild Bunch.
4. Guiley, R. (2009) *The Encyclopaedia of Demons and Demonology*. New York: Facts On File Inc
5. Kang, H. (2015) *The Vegetarian*. Trans. Deborah Smith, London: Portobello Books
6. Kermode, M. (2017) *The Guardian*
7. Pinker, S. (1997) *How the Mind Works*. New York: W. W. Norton & Company
8. Webster, R. (2006) *Magical Symbols of Love and Romance*. Minnesota: Llewellyn Publication

CORUVORN

Reggie Oliver

It is three years ago now since Dennis Marchbanks became a god. Of course he did not know this immediately; the realisation came upon him slowly as such things do and he was decently reluctant to believe it in the beginning. Dennis would have been the first to admit that he is an unlikely god. Do I believe it? Well, that is unimportant; I must simply record what happened, as far as I can.

Dennis and I had been contemporaries at the same Oxford college. We had both read classical "Mods and Greats", and belonged to the same dining clubs and societies. Dennis was highly intelligent, but not very imaginative and, though conventional in most of his attitudes, he liked the company of unconventional and artistic people; hence, I suppose, our friendship.

I graduated from Oxford with a modest second and went into literary journalism while Dennis who had got a first in "Greats" stayed on to take a law degree and studied for the bar. In time he became an eminent Q.C, dealing mainly with commercial cases, hence a rich one. We kept up with each other through college reunions and I would often see him at the first nights of plays when I became a drama critic. We occasionally dined together at Brummell's in St James's of which we were both members. I would not say that our friendship was really close, let alone intense, but it was of long standing and invariably cordial. We were able to share confidences from time to time, partly because our worlds did not impinge on each other's too much. Dennis was unmarried and, though he had met my wife once or twice, he had never visited my home.

One Friday night we happened to meet and have dinner at Brummell's. (My wife, incidentally, was away visiting relatives in Yorkshire for the weekend in case you are wondering if I had callously abandoned her for this still exclusively male preserve.) We ate together at the long table in the Coffee Room. There were several others dining at the table but they were down at the far end, so we could be fairly sure of not being overheard or interrupted. Dennis was not quite his usual genial self and I asked him what was the matter.

He told me that he had just lost a case in the appeal court. He had been representing Centaur, the online retailers, whom their employees on zero hours contracts were suing for better rights and conditions. Centaur and therefore Dennis had lost both in the High Court and on appeal. Representing the workers on both occasions was Dame Maggie Standish Q.C the well-known human rights lawyer and campaigner.

"No, Jack, it's not what you think," said Dennis, taking note of my raised eyebrow. "It was not being bested by a woman or anything like that that irks. As a matter of fact, I think she probably had the better case. Their Lordships certainly thought so. It was the way she treated me. She obviously saw me just as some sort of boss's lackey, a—what is the term they use?—a 'lickspittle'? But, dammit everyone needs legal representation, even criminals, even bosses. It's a human right, after all."

"No doubt Centaur paid you well."

"Well, yes. If you want the best you have to pay for it. But that's not the point. There is such a thing as professional courtesy, professional respect. As far as she was concerned, I was 'less than the dust beneath her chariot wheels.' I think she sees herself as some sort of champion of virtue and anyone who opposes her must therefore be contemptible." There was a pause. "But I am sure she is a genuinely good and highly principled person."

I smiled at his reluctant gesture of magnanimity and he, eventually, smiled back.

"Just unbelievably arrogant," he added in an undertone. We both laughed. Dennis was not without a capacity to see the funny side of himself. We moved on to more benign topics, and though he relaxed a little, I could tell there was still something on his mind.

After dinner Dennis asked me back for a drink at his apartment in Albany, that exclusive and discreet domain of the wealthy and well-connected off Piccadilly. The usual procedure at Brummell's was to have after dinner drinks in the little snug under the stairs at the club, so I sensed that Dennis was anxious to confide in absolute privacy. I just hoped it was not to be any more railing against Dame Maggie Standish Q.C.

We took a cab to The Albany. I would have been glad to walk, but Dennis was never an exerciser and thirty years or so of doing well for himself had expanded his figure considerably. He was, like me, in his mid-fifties. He had a pleasant round face and thinning sandy hair and, if I had been asked about him at the time, I would have said he was the epitome of contented prosperity and success. He was, as he had put it to me once, "not a man of strong urges where human relationships are concerned", so bachelorhood suited him.

We were silent in the cab, and, when we arrived at Albany, barely a word was spoken until we had seated ourselves with a large brandy apiece in armchairs on either side of the fireplace in his drawing room. Coming to Dennis's Albany "set" was like stepping back in time a hundred years or more. The lighting was subdued, the furniture antique but comfortable. Georgian silver gleamed on the sideboard and a faint lustre of gold emanated from the tooled backs of Dennis's antiquarian book collection. An illuminated glass-fronted cabinet glowed with a small but impeccable collection of *famille verte* porcelain. Family portraits hung on the walls, a couple dating back to the 18th century, and one to the 17th. The atmosphere was steeped in wealthy, cultured bachelordom.

"Do you dream a lot, Jack?" asked Dennis when we were settled and had taken our first sip. I was a little taken aback: it was not a familiar conversational gambit of his.

"Yes. No more than most, I suppose."

"I hardly do at all. Or if I do, I remember practically nothing of my dreams when I wake up. At least, I used not to. It all changed a couple of weeks ago. But then, I am not at all sure if it's a dream I am talking about."

He then began to tell me his story. One night he had returned to the Albany rather later than usual having attended one of those legal banquets in Lincoln's Inn. He had given a speech—"rather a good one, though I say so myself"—and was feeling exhausted from his efforts. He could barely remember undressing and getting into bed, but once in bed he fell into a deep state of unconsciousness of this world.

"I found myself in what I can only describe as *another* world. I was walking on a hillside towards evening. The sun was setting and I carried a long staff and wore a blue hooded cloak. The landscape was clothed in peace and the colours were deep umbers and greens and azures, such as you see in a landscape by Claude or Poussin. You may think this all sounds very dreamlike, but it wasn't. It was as vivid as you and I in this room now, if anything more vivid, and, unlike a dream world, it was utterly solid and consistent.

"One thing that appears in retrospect most curious, though not at the time, was that I seemed to see myself standing on that hillside and yet be inside the person on the hill simultaneously. It could be compared to being in a TV studio and being aware of yourself on a TV monitor at the same time, except that I *was* the monitor if you see what I mean. There was no effort involved in this double perception, no sense of a 'divided self': quite the contrary."

The image of himself that he saw was different to the one he presented to me. He saw not a plump, middle aged lawyer but a tall gaunt figure in a long blue cloak with a hood, carrying a staff. He was shod in boots of soft leather and underneath his cloak he wore a closely fitting tunic of dark violet velvet. As he walked, the earth seemed to give way slightly under his feet. "It was like," he said, "walking on water, though naturally that is something I have never actually done, but it's how I imagine walking on water to feel like."

Dennis's descriptions of his experiences were full of these precise and pedantic qualifications. At times it was like listening to Henry James at his most delicate and tentative, so I shall continue in third person précis.

The sun was sinking, salmon pink, below the horizon, as he walked down the hill towards a cottage from whose roof came an aromatic plume of grey blue smoke. The feelings he had were those of immense calm coupled with that of purpose, though to what end? That he could not say, though he tried to at considerable length.

The cottage, perched on the hillside, was surrounded by a small garden fenced and gated. Dennis opened the gate and went up to the door on which he knocked with his staff. He noted that the lintel was only just high enough to let him in without his having to bow his head.

The door was opened by a pleasant looking elderly woman in a brown, homespun dress who welcomed him into a low whitewashed room. Beside an open fire sat an old man, white haired but still hale. When he saw Dennis, he rose, greeted him and told him that he was most welcome under his roof.

Dennis tried to convey to me the extraordinary gratification he felt on being received so courteously. His whole being was suffused with benevolence towards this elderly couple and with this goodwill came a sense of power. The old couple—they were husband and wife—asked him to share their simple meal. Dennis told me that he had rarely tasted anything so austerely delicious. It almost persuaded him to eat less elaborately in future, to order only one plain dish at Brummell's, even to try his hand at cooking for himself occasionally. I took these raptures on the simple life with the scepticism that they perhaps deserved, but he was on fire with enthusiasm when he spoke.

One incident of interest and importance occurred at the end of his stay with these good people. They had finished the meal and the woman of the house was offering to make up a bed for him. Dennis politely refused their kind offer. He told me that he felt not tired in the least. A kind of calm energy was passing through him.

As he was explaining his need to set forth again and his gratitude for their kindness he noticed a small niche in the wall beside the fireplace. It would appear to be some sort of shrine.

In it was a lighted candle and a small figure of a cloaked man bearing a staff, carved in wood. It had been carefully painted in muted bluish colours. The image struck him as vaguely familiar.

"Who is this?" he asked.

"That is our God," said the woman, touching her forehead with her right index finger and bowing to the statuette. "It is Coruvorn, the Wanderer, Lord of the Hills."

At that moment, Dennis told me, he knew that he himself was Coruvorn, and that the image that they were worshipping was an image of himself. "It appeared at the time," he said, "the most natural thing in the world. It was only later and on reflection that the implications seemed rather problematic."

He turned towards the elderly couple, a golden light shone from him and they fell on their knees in adoration.

"This made me feel slightly awkward," Dennis told me, "because, while I seemed perfectly confident that I was—or rather *am*—a god, I was still conscious of being myself, that is Dennis Marchbanks. It's a complicated business. Since then, I have been subject to these visions almost every night. Time is different over there and weeks, months even seem to pass during the time that I am asleep in this world."

I asked him why he was confiding all this in me.

"I couldn't think of anyone else. You are the only person I know who might remotely understand. You are literary, after all: artistic, imaginative. You've even had a novel published."

"I gave you a copy, if you remember."

"Yes, I know. I actually read it. It's really not at all bad, in its way. That's why I thought you might be sympathetic."

"To tell the truth, I don't know what to make of what you've told me."

"That's all right. As long as you don't dismiss it out of hand."

" 'I am a man; I count nothing human alien to me.'"

"Nor nothing divine too, I hope!" He smiled rather complacently at this little joke.

"But isn't there some more 'professional' advice you could seek?"

"Not really. I wanted a lay person. Someone without an ideological axe to grind; someone with no real metaphysical opinions of their own. As you know, I am a Catholic, so this is very disturbing for me. I can't exactly go to confession at the Oratory and tell Father O'Hare that I'm a sort of god. He'd be most offended. We've been friends for ages. I might even be excommunicated."

"Surely an exaggeration."

"Perhaps, but it would be very embarrassing for us both."

"Why not go and see a shrink?"

"Well, you know my views about psychiatrists." I didn't. Dennis had a habit of assuming you knew all about his habits and opinions, most of which, it must be admitted, were extremely predictable. "They'd say it was all due to a mother fixation, or being taken off the breast too early or nonsense like that. It's no such thing. I'm perfectly sane. It's just a—a phenomenon, I suppose. I am an eminent Q.C in this life and a god in another."

I don't think Dennis was a vain man but he was one of those people who, thanks to a trouble-free passage through public school to Oxford and beyond, had a calm and confident sense of his own worth and place in the world. A friend of mine once said of Dennis that he had in life "to take the smooth with the smooth." But everyone has their own particular struggles and difficulties which most of us don't appreciate, being preoccupied with our own. And I suppose you could regard being a god in another life as a peculiar problem: Dennis certainly did.

It was very late, but I asked Dennis to go on with his story.

Dennis, or rather Coruvorn, raised his hand in benediction and then pointed to the figurine in the shrine. It was turned on an instant from wood into gold except for the blue cloak was now of pure lapis lazuli. The ancient couple gazed at their new treasure in delighted astonishment. The next moment Coruvorn was standing on the hillside in the moonlight. The moon was full and low, a pale peach colour. It was beginning to sink below a dun coloured belt of trees before Coruvorn stretched out his hand and raised it a few inches to see it better, then he let it fall into its original position. The earth gave a little shudder, but otherwise there was no disturbance.

Coruvorn took to the air and floated over hills, forests and cities. He visited many homes, answered many prayers, righted many wrongs until he descended once more upon a hillside and stretched himself under a great oak.

"The next moment I was in Albany again in my own bed. My alarm was ringing and I was due for a conference in chambers in an hour. My experience hadn't exhausted me: in fact I felt thoroughly refreshed." He looked at his watch. "Good grief! It's two in the morning! You'd better come back tomorrow and I'll tell you the rest. It's a Saturday. Would you be free for lunch?"

During the course of that weekend Dennis told me much more about his life as a God. Some of it was not that interesting in the way that other people's dreams are always less enthralling than your own. He seemed to spend his time wandering his world dispensing arbitrary and unsystematic benevolence and receiving homage in turn. Not everyone in his world believed in Coruvorn, but he seemed to bear no grudge against the unbelievers. If his acts of random kindness favoured those who acknowledged his existence that was only to be expected. I thought it was genuinely magnanimous of him that he expected no servitude towards him, nor even credence.

I asked him if he regarded himself as omnipotent in his world. Dennis pondered this, genuinely intrigued by my question.

"Well, I suppose in theory, yes," he said. "That business with the moon for example. But I don't exercise it. I want people to be free to worship me or not as the case may be. I must be adored by free spirits or there would be no point in being a god. The same, *mutatis mutandis*, I suppose applies to human relationships."

I agreed that this applied to human relationships as well.

"I see myself, I suppose, as a tutelary deity in the old classical sense. One who stands guard over his people and his planet."

"So you don't command a galaxy, or a universe?"

"Well, I don't think so. I may do, of course, but that understanding has not been vouchsafed me." I found his complacency rather irritating and was beginning to feel that it was my duty to puncture his illusion. Because that was what it was, make no mistake about it. At least, I suppose so. You must judge for yourselves.

I asked him for details of his planet and its people. Did they all speak the same language? Were they all of the same race? In what state of technological and political development did they exist? Were their animals and plants similar to ours? In this way I was hoping to convince him, and myself, that the world over which he presided was simply the product of his rather infertile imagination.

In a way, I was proved right. The world that he described could have been dreamt up by him. Its culture and state of technological development was a mixture of classical and medieval, its language was a version of Latin that Dennis was well equipped to understand. There were cities and city states and kings. There was no established religion, but in small shrines on hillsides or in homes, people paid homage to Coruvorn, the Wanderer, Lord of the Hills. Libations of wine were poured to him and small cakes, not dissimilar to the *madeleines* so beloved of Proust, were placed before his statue in the shrines.

The flora and fauna were similar to those in our world except that in his certain beasts existed which we regard as mythical. There were centaurs, hippogryphs and unicorns. There were also dragons, fire-breathing flying reptiles, but they were no bigger than ostriches and easily tamed.

The world of men and women on his planet was, according to him, peaceable and mercantile. The city states and petty kingdoms rarely had disputes, so there were no wars to speak of. If a crisis threatened between two powers Coruvorn always contrived to have it stopped before it went too far. There was no printing and though there were some books in manuscript, literature was mostly disseminated orally, consisting in long epics or shorter lyrical pieces sung to the accompaniment of an instrument resembling a lyre. The visual arts were on the whole decorative and abstract.

It all sounded very conventional and a little dull, just the sort of world that Dennis's rather staid imagination might have created. When I pointed this out to Dennis, he nodded as if he had considered this already.

"Yes, of course," he said, "I am quite aware that it might well be what you call an illusion, or is *delusion* the word you are looking for? But what exactly do you mean by delusion? If I were to say to you that I was a jar of marmalade, then you could quite easily say I was deluded. I am self-evidently not made of glass and filled with boiled-up Seville oranges; I am not an inanimate object. But when it comes to my experiences as Coruvorn to which I have access mostly at night in some kind of trance-like state, you cannot either prove or disprove their reality. They might appear to *you* to be just a dream, but they are quite unlike any dream I have ever had. They seem to me to be real. Now of course it might be possible that I am suffering from an acute mental illness, but you must admit that I show no signs of it, other perhaps than my so-called 'delusion.' I don't drink to excess; I certainly don't take drugs or imbibe strange herbal concoctions. I am at the top of my profession. You see? You might just as well apply the C. S. Lewis argument to me. You remember.... Jesus claimed to be the son of God. To do so one must either be a lunatic, a knave or the real thing. He was self-evidently not the first two; ergo he must have been the latter."

"There are flaws in that argument. In the first place—"

"But I am not really claiming to be a god; merely that I have experience of godhead."

"A distinction without a difference."

"Possibly. Possibly." He lapsed into deep thought and seemed to be no longer in need of my company, so I left him.

After that he would frequently phone me and tell me of his recent adventures as Coruvorn. I would occasionally take notes and once or twice recorded our conversations, even though what he had to say was not always very interesting. It was the concept that remained intriguing. I confess, I had thoughts of making my friend's strange aberration into a book or a series of articles.

According to Dennis, Coruvorn went about his business in his benign way, pardoning, resolving difficulties, often healing, generally looking after his planet. Dennis would occasion-

Wanderer from the Resplendent City, (1933) by Nicholas Roerich

ally ask my advice about whether he should intervene in some particular issue. I always told him that it was his decision: he was the god, after all and ought to know better. On one occasion he contemplated resurrecting an infant girl from the dead for the sake of her distraught parents. After some discussion, we decided against it, but for what reason I forget. Then something of significance happened.

He rang me at six one morning. My wife to whom I had said nothing about Dennis, other than that he confided in me, expressed understandable irritation and went back to sleep. I went down stairs in a dressing gown and took the call in my study.

"What on earth is all this about? Do you know what time it is?"

"Jack, I'm most terribly sorry about the early hour, but this is important. And time really has no absolute meaning where I have come from. I have just woken up, so to speak, or returned to this world might be a more accurate way of putting it, and I must tell you while it is still fresh in my mind."

Coruvorn had been, as was his wont, wandering the hills towards dusk. The sun was setting in its usual luxuriant way behind a belt of pale violet coloured cloud into the gilded tops of an oak forest. A nightingale was singing in a nearby brake and a faithful rustic was turning his flock homewards towards lower and safer pastures. The god was surveying this gentle crepuscular scene with satisfaction when his eye caught a gleam of bright orange through the oak woods that crowned the hills.

Was it a fire? If it was Coruvorn must hasten to contain it or warn his people in a dream to come and put it out. In an instant he had lifted himself above the trees in the guise of an eagle and was winging his way over the tree tops towards the blaze.

He alighted on the topmost branch of a great elm tree at the edge of a large clearing, roughly oval in shape. Almost in the centre was a great bonfire of felled logs and around it was grouped a large number of men and women standing very still and solemn. In front of the fire at one apex of the oval was a raised wooden platform upon which stood about a dozen women dressed in long white robes. One of the women, older than the rest, appeared to be their leader. She stood in the middle holding a banner which fluttered in the ripples of heat emanating from the fire. On it in silver thread was embroidered the figure of a winged woman holding a sword.

Coruvorn flew down from the branches and assumed the shape of an old man on the edge of the crowd. The white women on the platform began to sing and the congregation was enraptured.

"The words," said Dennis, "as far as I can remember went like this–" And he sang, somewhat tunelessly:

Hail, Thora, our Lady of Wind!
Harbinger of Change, bringer of Purity!
Blow through our hearts, cleanse us with your breath!

"The music sounded to me a little like one of those Soviet anthems that Shostakovich and Prokofiev were forced to produce, but I can't really put my finger on it."

While this chorus was being repeated countless times, according to Dennis, first by the ladies in white then by the congregation, Coruvorn moved among them, picking up their thoughts and murmured conversations. This was a new cult, apparently, that had sprung up and the people were worshipping a deity called Thora, Goddess of Wind.

"Thora, Goddess of Wind?–" I interjected. "Are you sure about this?"

"Yes, of course I'm sure!-" said Dennis irritably. "I was there, wasn't I? So there was another god being worshipped apart from me. It was rather strange that I wasn't aware of it until now, and really I wouldn't have minded... After all, I suppose, two gods are better than one. (Three even better, if you count the Trinity which you shouldn't really.) The trouble was, the chief priestess was requiring exclusive adulation for Thora. Thou shalt have no gods other than Thora, that sort of thing. And I found that her devotees were actually going around and destroying my shrines. Well, naturally this sort of thing has to stop, but I can't use force. Violence is simply not in my nature; besides I felt my powers subtly weakening. I still had plenty of devotees but they began to live in fear of these Thora fanatics who were taking over whole towns and cities, setting up their own political institutions and demanding exclusive allegiance to Thora. Severe penalties were being exacted from those who refused to comply. My faith went underground. I wanted, of course, to get in touch with this Thora but she proves elusive. Sometimes, standing on a hilltop, I felt her pass by in a gust of wind that nearly pushed me off my feet. I tried to stay her and speak to her but she ignored me. She must have known I was there but she would not stop. I am perfectly prepared to come to some sort of amicable arrangement with this goddess, but I am being swept aside. What am I to do?"

Never having faced a remotely comparable situation myself I was unable to help. When I tried to make a joke of it and told him that I was sure "it would all blow over", he slammed down the phone.

I didn't hear from Dennis for almost a fortnight, and I must admit I was rather relieved. I had begun to feel responsible for him. Should I alert some authority—the Bar Council? The Law Society?—that one of their most distinguished QCs was off his head? If Dennis had severed all communication, then it was someone else's problem.

Not wishing to burden her too much I had given my wife Jane a heavily expurgated version of the facts, merely telling her that he was subject to some "strange delusions" and unburdening them on me. Jane suggested I had nothing more to do with him. I sighed as a friend, I obeyed as a husband.

Then he rang again, at three o'clock one morning. Jane advised me to tell him to go to hell. I said I would do my best though I am not a great believer in hell and took the call in the study. Dennis was in a state of high excitement and spoke as if there had been no hiatus at all since our last conversation.

"Jack, I know who she is!"

"Who?"

"Thora, of course."

"Yes. You told me, the Goddess of Wind or something."

"No, no no! Don't be an idiot. I know who she is in *this* world. Just as Coruvorn has an identity here, namely me, so does Thora. You're not going to believe this."

"As you have strained my credulity to breaking point already, I don't think I am going to be that surprised."

"It's Dame Maggie Standish! You know, the Human Rights lawyer."

"Good grief! Really? How can you possibly know?"

"I just do. It would take too long to explain in detail. Suffice it to say that there exist things called astral corridors which link different worlds in space -"

"You mean like... black holes?"

"Yes, something like that. Please don't interrupt. Well once on my planet I managed to catch sight of her goddess form as she streaked across the sky. Incidentally the weather there has taken a marked turn for the worse since her arrival on the scene. Well, at once I set off in pursuit, hoping to have a conversation with her of some sort. She fled from me down an astral corridor but I was close behind. We travelled light years in a few earthly seconds and several times I nearly caught her. The next moment I was standing, still in my divine form as Coruvorn, in a strange bedroom. I was just in time to see the faint silvery form of Thora fly through the open mouth of a sleeping female in the bed. There was enough light for me to see that the female in question was Dame Maggie Standish. The next moment I was in my own bed in Albany."

"I see."

"Well, now I know, I can do something about it."

"What do you propose?"

"Well, I shall just have to confront Dame Maggie with what I know and then we can have a reasonable discussion about it all. One just hopes she will prove to be amenable."

"I'm not sure that's a good idea, Dennis. She could be tricky."

"Oh, I'm aware that this is not going to be easy. Maggie of course is a big cheese in the Labour Party and I, as you know, am a lifelong Conservative." I did not know, as a matter of fact, but I might have guessed. Coming as he did from an old Catholic family, his ancestors had probably been Tories since the days of the Old Pretender. "As you are aware, she almost certainly disapproves of me. You know how priggish and censorious these Socialists can be."

"All political zealots of any persuasion are prigs."

"Exactly. That's the problem. She's a zealot. I'm not and never have been."

"But what if she just says 'you're mad', and tells you to go to hell?"

"I can only hope that she has enough personal integrity not to do so."

"But what if—? What if you are simply mistaken about this whole business?"

"Jack, we have been into this. I know it's hard to believe, but I am not mistaken. I simply am not." The tone of his voice was, I have to admit, level and sane. He told me that he would be encountering her "in the flesh, so to speak" at a Law Society banquet in two days' time, and would "beard her" there. I once again advised caution and rang off. There was nothing more I could do.

My next news of Dennis was through a short piece in the *Daily Telegraph*. Dame Maggie Standish had accused Dennis of sexual harassment and stalking and he was about to appear in court and probably "bound over to keep the peace." He was being investigated and in disgrace. I couldn't imagine what his state of mind was like but I felt guilty about him even though Jane insisted that I had done all I can.

I rang the Albany and was told that Dennis was recuperating at a private sanatorium in Kent called The Cloisters. The man who answered the telephone, an Albany concierge, also told me that I was one of the few people to whom he had been allowed to give this information. The very next day I drove over to The Cloisters.

It was a fine June day. If Dennis needed a refuge from his difficulties, he could have done worse than The Cloisters. Though the building itself, a red brick Edwardian sprawl attached to some monastic ruins—hence the name—was not very impressive, the grounds were extensive and serene. Smooth lawns fringed with deciduous woodland and views of the Kentish Weald beyond might have been vaguely reminiscent of his planet. A nurse showed me to the back lawn where I found him seated on a bench with a plaid rug over his knees contemplating the scenery.

I had expected to find a distraught wreck of a man, for Dennis's reversal of fortune had been dramatic, but it was not like that. Dennis had lost weight dramatically and he had a haggard look, but he was not in any obvious distress. He greeted me with warmth and said he was pleased to see me.

"How are you?" I asked lamely.

"Dying," he said cheerfully. "Inoperable cancer. I've had it for some time apparently, but it's only just been diagnosed. And, no, that does not explain anything at all. The brain has not been infected."

"But you admit that you shouldn't have gone after Dame Maggie in that way?"

"Not at all. I have exposed her for what she is: a ruthless dissembler and a fraud."

"So you accused her to her face of being Thora, Goddess of Wind."

"It was not an accusation, more an assertion."

"Which she vigorously denied, no doubt."

"Not exactly. She told me I was off my head and should see a doctor."

"So why didn't you leave it at that? Why did you persist in harassing and stalking her."

"Because I couldn't stop there. I had obviously rattled her. I was sure I could break down her defences and make her see sense."

"But you didn't. And now you are facing a trial and complete humiliation. I'm sorry; you're ill and I shouldn't be talking to you like this."

"That's quite all right. I know you mean well. As a matter of fact, this case will never go to court. I will either be dead or too sick to plead long before it comes to trial. I am going, as the Bible says, 'to my long home.' I shall be resurrected as Coruvorn, in my own world."

"And what about Dame Maggie?"

"I have exposed her. I have got her on the run. Mind you, I will have to rethink the whole of my religious position. I can't be quite as easy going a god as I used to be."

He seemed positively serene. Our conversation drifted pleasantly into other topics and though he responded amiably and intelligently I could tell that his mind was not fully on them. The things of this world were no longer his concern. I was relieved of guilt.

One morning, barely a week after that conversation a doctor rang me from The Cloisters to tell me that Dennis had died in the night. She said it had been very sudden and unexpected, but it was more of a surprise to her than to me.

As it happened, that evening I was due to attend, in my capacity as literary editor of *The New Observer*, the launch party in the House of Commons for a book by Dame Maggie Standish entitled *Human Rights and Human Wrongs—the Future*. It sounded like one of those books which is destined to be more talked and written about than read; "an important contribution to the debate" no doubt, but probably not a page turner. I had been debating whether to go but Dennis's death decided me.

I had not encountered Dame Maggie in the flesh before, though I had seen her countless times on television. I was impressed. The fluent and passionate address she gave before signing copies of her book was enthusiastically applauded. It was some time before I could get to talk to her, but I managed it eventually.

She was a tall handsome woman and exuded a personality that was certainly forceful but not unattractive. I had been prepared to dislike her, for my friend's sake, but I could not do so. She had a way of fixing her full attention and considerable charm on whomever she was with. It may have been developed for professional purposes but it had a natural origin. I told her that I represented *The New Observer*, a journal for which she expressed courteous enthusiasm. When I casually mentioned my name I saw a slight bewilderment come into her eyes.

"You know Dennis Marchbanks, don't you?"

"How do you know?"

"He mentioned you to me once or twice in his ramblings to me. You're not going to ask me to drop my charges against him, are you?"

"No. There would be no point. He died last night."

"What! Good God! I didn't know that!" It seemed to me a slightly strange reaction.

"Why should you? I only just found out myself."

"Did he...? Was it suicide?"

"Cancer. He'd had it for some time."

"Ah..." She gave a sigh which I thought expressed relief but also a certain irritation. "Well, that's very sad," she added in a flat voice. "If you'll excuse me -" and she left abruptly.

Two days later Dame Maggie was standing outside the Royal Courts of Justice in the Strand talking to a film crew about her latest Human Rights case when a freak accident occurred. A sudden gust of wind blew up and must have dislodged one of the stone finials on the Gothic arches of the façade. It was a heavy piece of masonry and it fell some sixty feet onto Dame Maggie's head, killing her outright.

Dennis Marchbanks's memorial service at the Brompton Oratory under the direction of his confessor Father O'Hare, was a subdued business, but a surprising number of his colleagues were present. His recent aberrations went unmentioned in the eulogy. Death, both his and Dame Maggie's, would appear to have expunged those egregious embarrassments.

After the service, I approached Father O'Hare and asked if I could speak to him about Dennis. He invited me back for a cup of tea in his rooms at the Oratory, and it was to him that I first related all that Dennis had told me. To begin with, Father O'Hare seemed hurt that Dennis had confided in me rather than his true Father Confessor. When I told him that he had been fearful of offending an old friend, Father O'Hare softened a little.

"The poor foolish man!" he said. In the utterance of that phrase I caught for the first time a hint of O'Hare's Irish origins. "Did he think I hadn't heard things like that before? Did he really suppose I was so hidebound and censorious? In my time I've had to cope with much worse delusions from members of my flock . I had terrible trouble once with a young man who thought he was an egg. Well, you can imagine."

As it happens, I could not. "So you think it was just a delusion?"

"Oh, lord, yes! It was all a lot of nonsense." His tone was brisk, dismissive, almost irritable. "Mind you," added Father O'Hare after a long and thoughtful pause, "if one *must* have a god, one could do a lot worse than Dennis Marchbanks."

I was going to conclude there, but only last week I was informed that I had been left a small bequest in the will Dennis had made shortly before his death. I was touched. It consisted of several choice items from his antiquarian book collection, including a complete original set of *The Yellow Book*. There was one other item which was the reason why I had been informed so late, as there had been considerable difficulty in establishing its value for probate purposes. Several experts had been consulted and none could agree as to its date or origin.

Dennis had named it in the will simply as "my gold and lapis lazuli figurine" and there was no mistaking it. It stands about six inches high, the figure of a tall gaunt man in solid gold holding a staff. He has on a cloak of brilliant deep blue, fashioned somehow out of pure lapis lazuli. The experts could agree only on one thing: it is a work of astonishing beauty.

TRANSLATING *THE RITUAL*
J.T. Glover

Do you remember the first betrayal? Maybe it was when you were watching *Salem's Lot* in 1979 and encountered an ersatz Count Orlock instead of Barlow. Or perhaps it came when you saw *World War Z* in 2013 and got a popcorn zombie film instead of a many-voiced narrative of collapse and survival. It could definitely have happened in 1999, when you tried that year's version of *The Haunting* and found yourself numb, wondering where in that farrago of CGI you were supposed to see Shirley Jackson's *The Haunting of Hill House*, against which all other haunted house novels are measured. The taste of these stymied expectations lasts, the bitter tang of something that crackled on the page flickering and dying on screen.

Students of literary translation ponder questions of selectivity, idiom, and words and phrases that are distinct enough to a given language to be dubbed "untranslatable." Translations from page to screen, however, aren't necessarily about fidelity, often jettisoning key elements of stories in order to make more effective films—or at least more marketable ones. Some viewers take changes to source material in stride, but these changes have also irritated countless readers and writers, presumably for as long as prose has been adapted to stage or screen. What's lost or gained in these translations varies by genre, but I've felt it most keenly in the alteration of *frisson*. Sometimes that means Aickmanesque strangeness dissipating into conventional domestic horror, or rubber tentacles substituting for the awe of the eldritch. Other times, though, it can mean new blood for old monsters, a turn on well-known stories that transports them into new territories. And every so often, as with *The Ritual*, things are both gained and lost.

Adam Nevill's *The Ritual* is a striking and strange 2011 horror novel, adapted for the screen by David Bruckner and released in 2018. It traces the misadventures of four middle aged British men on a nostalgic lads' hiking trip through the wilds of northern Sweden. Things go awry, of course, and the first half of the book blends fear of nature and accidents far from civilization with the fear of what may lurk in old places. Readers of James Dickey and Jon Krakauer would find as much to relish in it as readers of Algernon Blackwood or Caitlín R. Kiernan. The second half of the book differs markedly, as the lone survivor, Luke, is captured by a group of Norwegian black metal musicians for sacrifice to an ancient god of the north woods. His ordeal and escape resonate with themes out of both folk horror and survival horror—*Harvest Home* with a side of Annie Wilkes.

Nevill has written about readers' reactions to the book, and many have taken him to task for the book's midstream change of pitch. After the release of the film, he likewise commented that he anticipated another seven years' complaints from viewers of the film. With all sympathy for him in dealing with

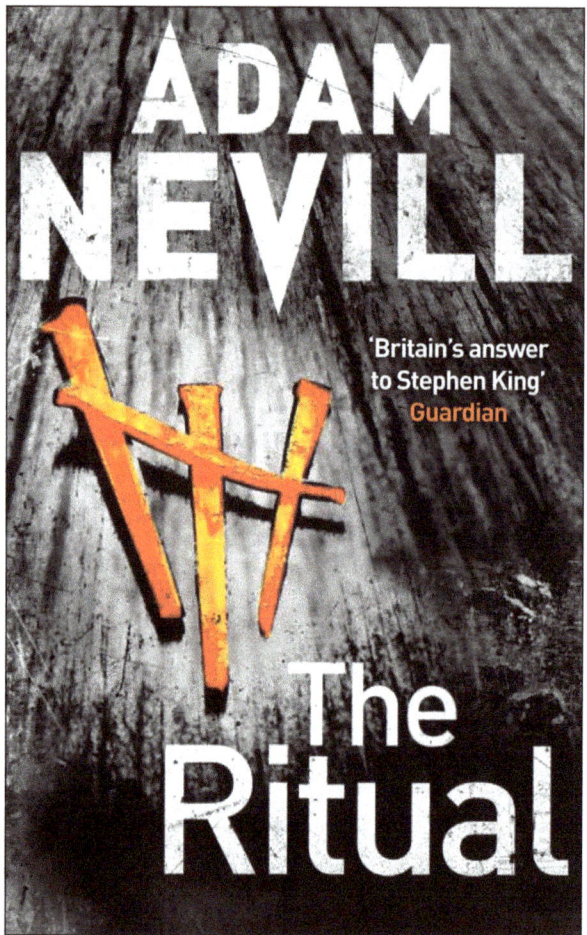

Cover for *The Ritual* (2017) by Adam Nevill / Pan

these complaints, the changes between page and screen are fascinating. The substitution of a village of near-primitive, jötunn-worshipping Scandinavians for a cabin full of black metal musicians shifts the film even further into the world of folk horror, and *The Ritual* can be watched in tandem with films that turn on the survival of old horrors in wild or liminal landscapes, whether *The Wicker Man* or *Pet Sematary*.

By upping this internal genre consistency, however, the film loses the novel's shock. Along with it vanishes the slow build of the novel's first half, with its characters wandering through and getting in lost in a remorseless, ultimately hostile landscape. Many reviewers of the book have commented on the echoes they saw in it of early British weird fiction, and it's an easy leap to make. Algernon Blackwood's love of numinous nature, combined with Arthur Machen's tales of primordial survivals, serve as partial blueprints for the terrors into which Nevill's characters stumble. Nevill's prose echoes this, but a hundred-odd pages of slowly building unease are irreplaceable on screen outside of long-form television or sequential film adaptations. Instead, viewers encounter wide shots to capture the sensation of remoteness: the isolation of a particular mountaintop, a stand of almost disturbingly parallel tree trunks (disrupted by something even stranger), passing in and out of bands of forest where signs of former human presence have been weathered into just another part of the landscape. All are effective, and some provide a certain *frisson*, but nothing on the scale of slow-burn films like *YellowBrickRoad* or *The Blair Witch Project*, where landscapes are given enough time and attention to develop into characters in their own right.

This loss, however, is counterbalanced by the injection of new disturbing elements. While some reviewers have commented on *The Ritual*'s use of imagery and tableaux familiar from films from *Häxan* to *Aliens*, others have also rightly praised its authentically strange creature design. Said by one of the villagers to be a child of Loki, the film's ancient god has strangely placed sets of eyes and limbs, and in a scene near the end, the moment where it rises up and unfolds its full anatomy to demand obeisance from Luke is as authentically weird as anything on screen in recent memory.

Speaking of ultimate forms, some readers of weird fiction have commented on the creature's appearance, and similarities to various semi-divine or chimeric monsters from literature or folklore, most recently the creature at the heart of Laird Barron's "Blackwood's Baby." Whether these similarities are intentional has not been addressed publicly as of this writing by anyone who worked on the film, and surely parallel evolution easily accounts for a giant share of all claims ever made of influence. Large wild animals evoke many feelings in us as we sit in theaters or living rooms, dwelling in experiences and reactions to art that, as Noel Carroll discussed at length in *The Philosophy of Horror*, does not actually threaten our physical safety. The reality of a moose or brown bear twenty feet away from you demands certain precautions and prudence, however, and even the thought of that experience is enough to turn a creative

Scene from *The Ritual* (2017) / Entertainment One

writer's mind toward the dangers of nature. As a matter of reading the beast of *The Ritual*, however, it's useful to think of the Weird as an incorporeal substance, a kind of literary ether flowing from story to story, smuggling itself from one narrative to the next without regard for borders physical or chronological.

The very idea of borders and "the wild" are directly questioned within the film itself. Luke suffers from guilt over the death of one member of the group of friends, Rob, who died in a corner shop in London while Luke hid. That death—new to the movie, and not present in the novel—actually spurred the trip, so that the group could memorialize Rob in a suitable setting. Through Luke's dreams and visions, the contemporary built environment leaks into the wilderness, troubling the idea of primordial *anything*. The landscape of both versions of *The Ritual* is haunted by contemporary human actions, each in different ways. In the novel, the black metal musicians export violent, narcissistic dreams of fame into a zone humans have long identified with envisioning, from Ralph Waldo Emerson to Bruno Latour. The actions of these characters are doubly profane, their adolescent rebellion and grotesquerie performed in a demonstrably sacred world, one where the divine is as tangible as any demon ever combated in the tale of a saint's life.

The film is more meaningfully haunted, however, by specters of humanity. Definitions of weird art (fiction, film, or otherwise) often include a sense of strangeness, something more than mere recombination of tropes, along with the idea that unknown depths underlie the surface of the world, against which humanity is of small, or at least not primary, significance. Early on in the film, the group of friends passes the hulk of an abandoned vehicle, an early signifier of the past presence of humans in the "wilderness" that is redoubled when they stumble across a cabin they at first believe abandoned, but quickly learn is not, and features a fane to the dark god of the woods they will later encounter one by one. The increasing antiquity of these signs of humanity reflect a passage into more primitive time and space, a particular kind of devolutionary narrative that readers and filmgoers have watched for as long as Modernity has had anxieties, whether in *The Heart of Darkness* or *Texas Chainsaw Massacre*.

The shock of irrupting "civilization" is a more consistent theme in movie than book, with Luke's repeated dreams and visions of Rob's death progressively tainting the very place he sought to escape them. This unsettling presence of urban space in the middle of a remote forest isn't new, of course, and one need only think of any number of portal fantasies, featuring misplaced lampposts and other signs of strangeness.

In the cinematic adaptation of *The Ritual*, the urban bleeds more and more heavily into the wild, a rudely metaphysical intrusion that brings with it the intertwining of organic and built environments. In this instance, the Weird is not located in hidden deities or aliens outside of traditional perception, but in the repeated troubling of the idea of "wilderness." To watch this film is to know that humans are part of the world, neither masters of nor apart from it, and that there is no going back to nature for relief from the ills of civilization, because we have always been there, and always take our worlds with us. The would-be innocents who reside in primitive, god-haunted cabins with their ancestors are not safer, happier, or more virtuous than the hikers.

When Luke screams his defiance at the god-thing at film's end, he rejects in one action its tyranny along with his own cowardice that led to his friend's death. Knowing that horror cannot be escaped, and that death can be found everywhere, he finds a new will to live with the help of his encounter with the Weird. In this, the film is akin to recent narratives that have ultimately sympathized with the

Scene from *The Ritual* (2017) / Entertainment One

monstrous or ended in tacit co-existence, from Jennifer Kent's *The Babadook* to Guillermo del Toro's *The Shape of Water*.

Troubled (or at least debated) adaptations have, in my view, greater staying power than straightforward ones. Consider the life of *The Shining*, from Stephen King's bestselling novel to Stanley Kubrick's masterful adaptation to King's legendary frustration with it to Mick Garris' scrupulous television adaptation. The narrative has lived on in various ways, from King's later use of characters from the novel in new works to ongoing study of the adaptations, up to and including *Room 237*, the award-winning documentary about the Kubrick version. For any but novices to horror, it's no longer easy to consume any of these narratives in isolation from the others. At the same time, the number of adaptations, parodies, and riffs is nothing like the proliferation of adaptations of *Dracula*, *Frankenstein*, or similarly iconic works. The number of players in the field of relationships that represent *The Shining* is knowable and manageable in the course of a short or long discussion. There are, when reading or rereading *The Shining*, a limited yet well-imagined set of alternative narratives that must influence that reading.

What will viewers make of *The Ritual* in forty years? It's difficult to say, and dependent on aspects of a media environment that is currently in flux or crisis, depending on who's talking. The swing away from physical media and toward digital—in particular the streaming market and different providers' fluctuating catalogues—means that individual works are not as reliably accessible in the same ways that they tended to be during the decades when videocassettes or discs dominated distribution for home viewing. The constant flood of streaming content threatens to sink individual works' long-term impact. The casual viewer in the current "golden age" of media saturation and high production value television is faced with a selection of good, or at least well made, content so impossibly large that the effort to seek out specific works as entertainment may no longer be as worthwhile as it was in the days of physical media limitations, or as necessary.

Both Adam Nevill's novel and David Bruckner's adaptation of it each deserve attention in their own right, as well as for the ways each informs the other. Now and ever after, of course, some readers will come to Nevill's novel and view it in light of Bruckner's choices. This kind of relationship is both strange and familiar, a sort of backward reading with which we are all familiar, allowing us to see the Livia Llewellyn in Poppy Z. Brite, or the Anne Rice in Bram Stoker. Literary communities tend to ascribe foremost importance to the literary works on which some films are based, but that is, of course, only one of many viewpoints on "source material." Nevill's narrative has within it the potential for various kinds of adaptation. That it found its way into the hands of a cast and crew who created something new of it speaks to the slipperiness of translation, to the truths that may be lies, and to the lies that may be truth.

LA TIERRA BLANCA

Maurizio Cometto
(Translated by Rachel S. Cordasco)

This story originally appeared in Italian in *Heptahedron*
© 2017 Acheron Books

September 19

I wish His Christian Majesty to know that today I have formally taken possession of this land, baptized "Tierra Blanca." I will briefly tell of the vicissitudes that led the crew of the *Rosa del Sol* to land on the shores of what would turn out to be an island.

En route to the New World, we were struck by a storm after just four days of sailing. It was a terrible night. The crew was exhausted, the high and threatening waves didn't let up, the *Rosa del Sol* took on water and rolled dangerously. Suddenly, we were hurled onto a bank of outlying rocks; the hull cracked with the dry sound of death. Some of the crew, desperate, threw themselves into the sea. Others, including myself, remained aboard, and decided to seek a more heroic death. Do not ask me what happened in those moments. It's all a whirling of exhausted bodies, a frustrated shouting of last prayers, followed by the sinking amidst a magnificent maelstrom.

Immediately, we were drowned in the darkness of unconsciousness. His Christian Majesty forgives me if I speak in the name of the whole crew, but later, comparing our testimonies, we realized that it had happened to nearly everyone at the same time.

When we recovered, we found ourselves on an intact *Rosa del Sol*, safe and sound, sailing on a peaceful sea lit by a white light. That light was the Sun, but not the usual Sun. Brighter, yet less blinding, this Sun could be stared at without risk, and would fill one's heart with bliss.

We looked into each other's faces, recognizing one another. There hadn't been any injuries. Our only losses: the cowards who threw themselves into the waves before the supposed sinking. We didn't cry for them: after all, they had chosen it.

We immediately realized that something mysterious had happened to us. That place was not even remotely related to that where the sinking had occurred. The onboard instruments were gone, the starry sky incomparable to any visible from any point on Earth. In addition, the hull of the *Rosa del Sol* looked like new, and this was perhaps the most disturbing thing.

It is said that off the archipelago discovered by Bermudéz, and in the unexplored seas around remote Cathay, mysterious forces have thrown ships into distant worlds, inconceivable by the human mind. What happened to us cannot be like that. Whether it is Divine Will or the Devil's joke, it's not for me to judge; and yet...

The gentle warmth of that white Sun, the mildness of the climate during the day and night, prompted ecstatic abandon; at night an incomparable moon, a generous dispenser of her silvery light, enveloping like a maternal embrace; and besides, there were no storms or dead calms. All of this made us assume a beneficent intervention rather than an evil one.

When we finally landed on "Tierra Blanca" (a trivial appellation, however appropriate), we thought of what the Sacred Scriptures call "Earthly Paradise": the fertile and luxurious vegetation—a tropical kind but everywhere showing an intelligent hand at work; the harmless fauna, consisting mainly of colorful birds and small mammals; the presence of some huts, empty but ready for habitation, curiously equipped with a number of pallets corresponding to the crew, including me. And much more.

As we approached the beach, just disembarked, confused but happy, the foreman approached me and said the following:

"Admiral, I speak for the whole crew, as I always have and always will. It is our general opinion that we have found Earthly Paradise. This sea, this beach, what I'm sure we'll find later... Not to mention this Sun. Well, why don't we stop here, we ask? Why not throw our sorrows behind us, and get drunk on this bliss? Why not spend the few years remaining to us, Admiral, in constant adoration of the beneficial and peaceful Sun?"

I looked around, because the light in his eyes filled me with anxiety. It was an unusual light for the soul of a strong, shrewd, hard-drinking man of the sea. I thought: such a light must have shone in Moses' eyes, in front of the Red Sea that opened at his command. Many of the men were lying on the soft sand and keeping their eyes fixed on the Sun. I didn't respond immediately to the foreman's words. I was confused.

An irresistible force worked in me to dissolve my limbs and abandon myself to the beach to gaze at the Sun, to inhale its light. This force was in agreement with the foreman: it wanted me to stay. On the other hand, the voice of my spirit, which some call clarity, was still strong and alive within me.

I finally managed to answer:

"And our dear ones, who are waiting for us where the stars are in the right places? Are you not thinking about how much they would suffer? And what would they think about our renunciation, our abandonment, our Fall?"

But while I was speaking, I was wondering: would it really be a Fall?

The foreman simply shrugged. He didn't seem distracted or troubled by my doubts. In fact, he then spoke loud enough for everyone to hear:

"Let's go to the island. We have to find the huts. We have to find our beds."

I didn't immediately understand what he was referring to. But later, when we found the huts, the beds, perhaps it was then that I started to surrender. Your Christian Majesty will pardon my

The Sun, (1911) by Edvard Munch

frankness, but it is so: I started to yield, and along with the Fall came an explosion of joy. And I fear, like the others, that I too will soon abandon everything.

A sense of respect almost prevented us from occupying the huts. However, after combing the island, we weren't able to find any other human beings. Then we settled in, finding the huts comfortable.

September 26
The first week of our stay on the island. Your Christian Majesty will forgive the weakness of an Admiral close to retirement, and a crew exhausted from a thousand adventures. As I feared, we have spent the first few days in the most complete idleness, satiating ourselves on the fruits of the land and getting drunk on the light of the Sun. From the latter, I received disturbing signs. It is the source—for me and the others—of sublime bliss, not comparable to any "terrestrial" experience, if I may use the term. My descriptions may seem excessive, but it is exactly what is happening. The foreman and the crew, and myself as well—yes, even me, Carlos Guillermo Rodriguez—spend the days lying on the beach, following the daytime star on his journey across the sky. And such is the joy that infuses us, both individually and collectively, that we even forget to eat. I almost get the impression of a "spiritual hunger," if I may use the adjective, that replaces a "physical hunger."

I spend the nights wondering if this is good or bad. Do not the Sacred Scriptures exhort us to detach ourselves from matter in favor of the spirit? But if it has to do with the spirit, would His Christian Majesty object to the heretic Sun of an alien land?

Meanwhile, the foreman has draped himself in the robes of a prophet. It's as if at the end of so much wandering, we have come to the Promised Land. It's only the crew that shows visible signs of restlessness. Occasionally, he walks around between our bodies lying in the Sun, and pronounces sentences that would be blasphemous to the ear of His Christian Majesty.

I can't refrain from reporting one thing, trusting in His mercy. The foreman, especially in the minutes preceding the dawn and following dusk, falls into a state of joyous exaltation; unlike us, seized by a subtle anxiety. And in that exalted state, he whispers, then declares, then screams, his definitive hypothesis.

According to this hypothesis, the star could be none other than…than…than…

Here, I even lose the courage to pronounce the Sacred Name of the Most High.

But His Christian Majesty will forgive the weakness of an Admiral on the wane, and a foreman made mad by the shipwreck.

September 29
The tenth day of our stay. The star has stopped. His Christian Majesty will forgive the unorthodox syntax of these notes. The star has stopped reclining on the horizon. It hasn't moved from there, and it is watching us. It was the sunset. My companions and I, lying on the sand, waited for it to disappear, as it did every night. With skin burned by the star's rays, which has been passing through our bodies for days—skin burnt but painless, throats dry from lack of water, bodies weakened from lack of food, overloaded minds with no need for sleep—we watched for it to disappear. The foreman waited, standing alone. A wild, unpredictable prophet, his shocked look immersed in the light. He was raising his hands to the sky. He was screaming, realizing it for the first time. "It's the end," he screamed, "the end has come. It is stopping. Our wandering is complete." We waited for it to disappear, but it didn't, to our absolute triumph. And when it was certain, when the hour passed without any change, we stood up. We stood up while the foreman, exhausted, collapsed on the sand. But we ignored him. It's on the horizon and seems like it's calling us. Oh inexpressible joy! We no longer sleep, we no longer eat. Man doesn't need these ballasts. A vicious habit does seem indispensable. And how lightweight we feel as a result! It's as if we have crossed a threshold. There is still one left to cross. There, It. Soon, angels will come to welcome us. The foreman was right, poor foreman. His Christian Majesty will forgive the unorthodox style of these notes.

Rodriguez here. The angels landed on the island. There are three or four per crewmember. Except for the foreman—there were none for him. Because he doesn't need it? Because, unlike the others, he already knows the way? But then why is he left behind, while we rejoice with our angels? I've seen my old man, daddy Rodrigo, in the flesh! And Delfino, and Marcela, the apple of my eye…But the worst was Conte. I had killed him in a duel, during my turbulent youth, over a woman. I have killed many others over the years—in battle, among pirates, in dungeons. But Conte remained in me like a stain, a remorse to which I unwittingly returned in calm moments. Conte landed, held out his hand to me, and said: "I would have done the same to you." Tears came to my eyes. First I embraced him, happy. Then I looked at the Star, genuflected, and exclaimed, "I serve you!"

I felt behind my shoulders, on my back, the silent and perhaps disappointed look of the foreman.

We are boarding now. They are here to guide us toward the Light. The Light, I found, is different for everyone. I am happy to have my Light. It is impossible to describe the color. Perhaps where we come from—where His Majesty still lives—it doesn't even exist. "Your Light is very similar to mine," Marcela confided in me. After all, it's like we're all kids.

Except the foreman. He was a child. Now he has become old.

Majesty, Guillermo here. White light on the horizon. And an increasing sense of peace. Forgive the blasphemy. It's wonderful here. Your kingdoms are nothing compared to this. Is not white the sum of all colors? And then Marcela, and papa Rodrigo. Conte with the wound that smells like chrysanthemums; Delfino playing with the sword, blood draining with none being lost. Without pain. Forgive Christlike words from the spirit. Let's fly in the air. The sea is gone, disappearing beneath us. If I close my eyes I can see my body. It's at the bottom of the ocean, trapped in the rigging. I'm dead. The ship went down, we found peace. Cowards died, but in a different way than us. A blinder way. I will pray for them.

We are all dead, except for the foreman. That's why he hasn't boarded with us. I see the foreman during the shipwreck, thrown from the *Rosa del Sol*. Here he is in the waves, clinging to a tree branch. Exhausted, worn out, but alive, finally picked up by a passing brigantine after the storm.

The foreman, the only survivor of the sinking of the *Rosa del Sol*.

I still see his hand waving from the beach, then his back, then nothing.

Who wanted his ghost, the ghost of the living among the dead, to show us the way?

Yet we need him if we believe.

Before everlasting abandonment. Enclose the card in the bottle, throw the bottle into the sea. Rise, Carlos. Adios.

CONTORTIONIST

Mesándel Virtusio Arguelles
(Translated by Kristine Ong Muslim)

Normally far more malformed than a chimera.
Where does the figure mine its tormented flesh.

The impossible beast of a body twisting
through the pivot joint. Flexed past the limit.

Implicates awe and laced-up grace.
The reward is the dislodged internode.

Slippery is the joint in which the worry of breaking
bone without a cut and without certainty of violating

the law that governs the nature of the creature. Slippery,
yet stuck together. And in his isolation,

one can deduce his sole wanting for an unmarked and
radical construction: one almost lacking a flank, spine.

Originally published in Filipino in *Ilahás*, 2004.

HER BLOOD THE APPLES, HER BONES THE TREES

Georgina Bruce

there in the pines
where no one goes
the ghosts hang sleeping
in the branches and boughs

You will know me by my shade.

The sleepwalking woman stepped from her dream of the apple and the bear and the rose. She stepped into a seam of light that split her head in two, a beaming noise that siren-circled between her ears, a stutter in the speech of the world. A curtain pulled back. Applause, applause. Their faces were smooth, skin like vinyl. Tiny cheers erupting from their stomachs.

She woke in the passenger seat of David's car. They were driving through the desert. Moon flood on the highway, soft music, slow and dreamy. David leant over and patted "her knee. You really are something else, Laura. You know that? You wanna be in one of my movies? It's about a ghost. You can be the ghost.

The ghost-walking woman woke from a dream within a dream within a dream. She walked through many doors, one after another, until she opened the door to the room of her body. It was wearing a red gown, curled on a white bed, face slack and broken. She tried to fall back inside herself, she tried to push back in. But no, no, the body wouldn't yield. Not her body, no, no this body was all dead and wrong. Finger marks on her neck, her face... Her red gown was a dress of blood billowing around her, blossoming from the wound between her thighs, and the beauty—the *beauty* was no longer hers, but had spilled into the waste edges of the dream.

Laura wanted a language for dreaming, one she could speak with her hands. She drove David along a black snake of highway coiling through the woods. She carried a silence as white and coiled as a snake in her heart.

"I mean for dreams," she said. "I mean the only way you would understand."

David sat up straighter. "Laura, please. What are you trying to say?"

She glanced at him. He was frowning at her, chewing on a fingernail.

"Nothing. Just a different kind of story. Just a dream."

"Sounds like a messed-up dream, Laura."

"I guess it was."

Silence fell, and night fell, and the woods pressed in around them. Laura drove on with the radio playing softly, the headlights peeling back the night from the road. Through a winding tunnel of shadow, deep and deeper into the mountains and forest. No buildings, no houses anymore. Only the darkness buzzing with needles and sap. Finally she rounded a bend and glimpsed the hotel, standing alone and awkwardly in the looming shadow of a mountain. The car plunged forward through the narrow winding darkness, along the slip road, steeper and darker, until the darkness gave out and the hotel was there, ramshackle fragments of porches and windows and chimneys and lights. Laura parked the car in the otherwise empty lot. She shut the engine and thought she heard men—their laughter, their voices. But no, nothing out there except a chilly silence. Her mind playing tricks on her.

David slapped his knees and said, "Hey, look at this. Look where we are, Laura! This old place."

That made her smile. "Where else?"

He nodded. "Good to be back. *Watch out for bears!* Remember that, Laura?"

"Sure I remember. I'll always remember that girl."

"Which girl?"

"The *watch out for bears* girl. The one I played."

David smiled, indulging her. "Well, you've lost me there, Laura. I never seem to know what you're talking about these days."

"Oh, don't worry, no, just crazy actress talk. Getting into character."

He laughed, but there was a note of caution there too. "You really are something else, Laura."

She was, she felt it too. She was something else now, something strange, a shape cut out of the night. And as she stepped from the car and breathed in the cold air and the scent of the forest, she felt a physical pull, a tug towards the tangled darkness of the woods. Like before. Like it had always been there, waiting for her to come back.

Movies weren't real, and neither were dreams. But even her memories were strangely vague, floating free of their context, like dresses hanging in the air, waiting to be plucked.

She'd been standing at the window, her reflection doubling her, the lines of her face wavering, the shade of her lipstick darkened by the glass. Her hair messed up, floating round her face. And her hands… a palm pressed against the glass, covering Laura's reflection. She took it away. Breathed a pool of mist onto the glass, and drew a loveheart with her finger. An arrow through it.

"My heart won't stop breaking."

Their reflections overlapped in the glass as Laura approached. Lips crossed and opened. Behind them, in the woods, in the room, shadows moved, branches on the wall, taking shape like the antlers of a great stag. Shapes flickering in the glossy black mirror.

Laura said, "I dreamt I was on stage, somewhere I'd never been before, a grand and enormous theatre. It was a full house, there must have been a thousand, more than a thousand, but all of them were—none of them were real. They were those dolls, you know those Dreemy Peeple, those little plastic girls. And I realised, I saw them all watching me, and I realised, they were waiting. For me. It was the end of the play and I had to say the last line. But I couldn't remember what play it was and I was looking down at my costume, but it was just a red dress and there was nothing on the stage to help me, no one else, no props, nothing at all. And I just couldn't remember—and when I opened my mouth to speak, to try—it filled with ashes and soot and dirt."

"It would have been better if you'd remembered."

"I know."

Laura drew her fingers through the mist on the glass. She was tired, so very tired. It felt like she'd been working on this movie for a long time now. Living in this odd empty hotel that filled from time to time with a scene, with a moment, and then filled back up with silence, with noises from underground, noises from the woods... and why did she feel so drawn to the woods? But she did, she did. And she lay awake, wondering how she should go there, what she would find.

Laura picked through some dusty leaflets at the front desk. Not much going on around here. Not a lot to do. David rang the bell, *ding ding ding!* And a girl came out from the back office. She was young, fifteen or sixteen, maybe. Her hair was long and unbrushed, she was wearing a ratty t-shirt and jeans. Cigarette smoke and peppermint gum. She didn't smile.

"What's that? Can you help me?" David said. "Sure, that would be great. If it's not too much trouble, could you please move me to a different room? I need a room overlooking the parking lot, there are too many trees on the other side."

The girl rolled her eyes. She picked a key from the board behind her and dropped it on the counter. "We cool?"

David turned to Laura, raised his hands in exasperation. "Can you believe this kid? What kind of place is this?"

"Come on," said Laura. "Let's get going. You don't want to lose the light." She smiled at the girl. "He's making a movie about something that happens in the woods."

"Oh yeah, well, watch out for bears," said the girl. She was smiling as she said it, but not in a friendly way.

"Bears? You get a lot of bears around here?"

She rolled her eyes. "I guess. Just don't leave food lying around? I dunno, just don't make them hungry or piss them off. Anything else I can help you with? Okay, have a *great* day." She smiled horribly.

Laura put a hand on David's arm. "Come on," she said.

But the girl had turned her attention to Laura, and the look on her face was different now. "It's not just bears. Things happen in the woods here, you have to be careful. But sometimes you shouldn't be careful. You've never been the Woods Queen, have you, Laura? I hope you can this time."

Laura flinched. Why did she know her name?

"What's that?" David asked.

The girl sighed and turned her attention back to him. "Hey. I watched one of your movies once. It was so fucking boring I swore if I ever met you I'd punch you in the head."

Laura stifled a laugh. "David, come on."

She linked her arm through his and he let himself be led away, out of the hotel, down the steps. As soon as they were outside, he started yelling.

"That jumped-up little..."

"David, she was high as balls. And she's just a kid. Take no notice."

"Call that customer service? What the hell's going on here, Laura? And what did she mean, my movie was terrible? Which movie? She doesn't know what she's talking about."

"David, come on. It doesn't matter. You want me to drive? You can meditate in the car. And let's just go and make this movie, right? Get those ghostseeds fruiting."

"The ghostseeds... Laura, you're crazy, you know that?"

"Loud and clear."

At the bend in the path, Laura turned around to look back at the hotel. The girl was standing at the bottom of the steps. She raised her hand shyly, a tentative wave. Laura waved back.

The mirror was full of shadows. That was all she could see now. Dark and darker, moving like smoke. Lately she'd been forgetting her name. She couldn't remember if she was Laura, or Shelly, or Audrey, or Donna, or Maddy... or was she someone else, was she a person at all, or just a memory, a whisper in another's ear. See how we are indistinct. How we all become nothing. We dissolve into mist, into shadow, we seep into the furniture, we are dust.

How long had she slept in that strange dark pod hanging from a bough. Maybe it was a hundred years. Maybe someone would come after her with a kiss. *A kiss, a curse. Waking is the worst.* She blinked and smiled at her reflection in the window. There she was. *There you are.* Laura, come on. She was always drifting off these days.

The telephone rang and she answered it on the first ring, as though she'd been waiting, but she hadn't, she'd picked it up in surprise, it was right next to her. It was cold against her ear, a cold wind like in a forest clearing, with the trees sighing, creaking, the soft plash of snow falling on snow... and David's voice, counting down four three two one –

He was patting her shoulder. "Laura, honey. You gotta see this."

She opened her eyes, uncurled in the passenger seat. He was driving them through the mountains, the sun sinking, turning the woods to amber and flame.

"The woods are so beautiful," she said.

"They're full of dead girls."

"That's a horrible thing to say."

"Oh no, don't get me wrong. I'm agreeing with you."

"Beautiful dead girls. Exquisite misogyny."

He hadn't taken his eyes off the road, but now he shot her an angry glance. "I wouldn't have expected to hear that word from you, Laura. Of all people. You know who I am, the kind of man I am. You make these movies with me, don't you? If I'm a *misogynist*, what does that make you?"

Laura sighed. "It doesn't matter. You don't know this story."

What did she see in his eyes, in that moment? Only what she'd always seen there but never named. Contempt. Anger. He thought she was crazy. She didn't make sense at all. He said: *you talk a lot, but you're not saying anything.*

She wanted to tell him to stop the car, more than anything she wanted him to stop the car. She wanted to be alone, to run alone through the trees. Lose herself in the woods. The tightening of her core, that pull, that heat. She didn't care what happened to her. She pressed her forehead to the car window, watched the sun burn down the world.

Thinking of the Woods King, thinking of his name—that was all she knew of him, just that, his name and what he was. It was enough for her to bring herself to bed and in the darkness imagine the sweet bite of his kiss... but in the midst of slipping swelling unpetalling—something breathed. She froze. Listened. No, she'd imagined it. Her own breath, caught in unfamiliar quiet. This remote place. Wet fingers, her thoughts running away with her.

It breathed again. A soft snort.

David. His adolescent fantasy. Creeping on a girl. Hiding in the wardrobe. No, he wouldn't. He wouldn't. Watching her through the slatted doors. Sick. Why would she think that?

She flung out her hand, hit the light switch.

Fucking hell, Laura! She was being ridiculous. Nothing there. Just a draft, under the curtain. The scratch of heavy fabric over the floorboards.

Strange how her thoughts had gone straight to David... but he wouldn't. He wouldn't do that. That was a strange and puerile fantasy, something he'd worked through long ago. Not something

HER BLOOD THE APPLES, HER BONES THE TREE / Georgina Bruce

Alone in the Park, (before 1900) by Wladyslaw Wankie

he would actually do. He wouldn't smuggle himself into her room and watch her, like a scene in one of his movies. Close up on her face as she brought herself off. No. The sound of his breath from behind the wardrobe door... he wouldn't do that. How horrible she was, to think that of him.

Nevertheless, she got out of bed and went to the wardrobe. It was empty, only some spare bedding and towels. She went to the window next and pushed aside the curtain. Looked out on the gravel path that led to the front of the hotel. Two figures were walking there. Their shadows fell behind them, long and dark, reaching into the forest all around. The couple walked, but their shadows moved differently. They fell together, wrestled and tore at each other's heads. Laura closed the curtains.

Watch out for bears, the girl had said. She'd known Laura's name. But did she also know that Laura didn't care about the bears. Did she know that Laura still wanted to walk alone in the woods at night? She did, she did. She felt a pull in the core of her body, a physical tug. How strange, how sexual it was, this need and desire. She was afraid of it, afraid of being led away from herself, into the mysteries of the forest. Afraid of her own body. She took two sleeping pills and let them eat her dreams until the morning came.

Fragile white cloud caught among the trees. And the trees crossing spiky fingers against the sky. She was shivering, her bones cold and numb. She was to unfold herself from a shadow hanging like fruit from a tree. She was the first ghost and her revenge was something she carried in her bare hands like a fragile egg. Transparent and teeming with tiny sharp splinters of bone.

David wanted to shoot in the dawn light, to catch the crackle of frost before it softened under the winter sun. The transparency of her dress, her skin translucent, a beam of orange sunlight firing between her legs... that was the beauty, right there. She was barefoot, a ghost. Thin as a ghost. Naked now, always. Because her body didn't matter, after all. They had dragged her into the creek, a gang of them, laughing and roaring. They didn't even stop after she was dead. "The world is a terrible place," David said. "But you see my movies, they are strange but they are also beautiful."

She would unfold from the fruit of the tree, a dark shadow-flower blooming into shade. What would she be, when she crept from her cocoon? A terror, a fierce unloving child. An aching monster. A terrible thing.

David's face next to her face. "Eyes like this. Don't move at all. You're completely dead and no one knows or cares." He moved her arm a little higher, twisted it a little outwards. She was sprawled on the dirt and there was a man on top of her. And there were men all around her. She didn't know any of their names. In the script they were numbers. It could be Rapist 1 or Rapist 21, they all took turns with her. This one rested his weight between her legs for a moment. He was heavy, stacked with muscles.

"Hey," she said.

"You're dead, babe. Be grateful for whatever you get."

They went again. There was blood over his white shirt. The others were cheering him on and then someone said the line.

Oh shit she's dead.

A moment of silence. The guy kept ramming away on top of her. Then laughter. It didn't matter if she was dead or not. It was funnier, now she was dead.

"That's going to get them," David said. "Oh yes it is. That's a real nightmare, right there."

Laura nodded. Okay. She couldn't speak to David at all in that moment. She was disgusted with him, with herself. But it was just a movie, she was being crazy. It was good he was doing this. Drawing attention to this... to... ah she didn't know the right lines anymore. How this was all justified, what to say so that everyone could keep pretending it was okay.

At last she was allowed to get up off the ground. She pushed the men, the actors, away from her. They were laughing, excited. David was watching the footage back, smiling, nodding his head. Someone—a woman—handed Laura a red coat and she wrapped it around herself. They'd been filming for hours. Over and over, playing the scene out from every possible angle. Now someone was touching her hair, dabbing something on her lip. She put her hand up to her face.

"Stop, please."

"You need to take a break, hun?"

No. She needed it all to stop. She looked around her. They were in a part of the woods that led down from the road, where the trees were sparse and a thin trickle of a creek ran through. But beyond that, the woods grew thick and dark and tangled. She wanted to go there, and lose herself inside the forest. But David was calling her again, they were going to go again: he wanted everything to be perfect.

They finished and wandered back to their beers and their fire. They went away, they all left. She took a deep, ragged breath. And felt it breeze through her, cold air whistling through her broken insides. She got to her feet and felt her body fall away from her, like stepping out of a dress. It fell in pieces, slumped face down in the creek. She saw it was a body carved open and emptied. Defiled. Annihilated. Shameful. She felt so ashamed. She'd always been a nothing person, a no one, and now even that was over. It didn't matter now. It had never mattered. Had her body ever been touched with love? No, never. Or with desire? No. Tenderness? Not even a glancing blow. They kissed her with broken glass. Caressed her with knives. That body—worthless. She left it spilling its jewels into the cold creek.

But without her body, she was lost. She didn't know how to move, how to breathe. She was ghost... without form or substance. She felt she could drift, she could disperse. That was the impulse she felt most keenly. But she understood she was tied to her flesh by a gleaming strand of silver that rippled into her empty shape and dragged her to the trees. And the body still cried to her: come back, come back. But no, she couldn't, she never would. And so the silver strand wove the empty space around her, wrapping her into a seed.

She woke in the night, the covers fallen from her. Suddenly, without warning. He was in the room, she was sure. She heard his breathing, the sound of him rubbing himself wetly, quickly, a stifled breath—she reached out and slammed on the light.

Nothing. Silence. The room was empty.

The little light glimmered into the shadows. There really was no one here. But she could smell his cologne, his suede shoes.

She grabbed a shirt and jeans from the floor and went to the window. The full moon washed the woods in an eerie pale light. The trees stood out, glittering and frosted, and from the trees hung clusters of blood-dark seeds, opaque and writhing, each one full to bursting with something moving, pushing against the tough membrane of shadow.

One of the ghostseeds pulsed with light, and split its seam with a jagged scrape. From the tight pod unfurled a long stretch of soft fur and claws and teeth. Velvety silky fur, tumbling to the ground. A creature of some kind... a bear. They were bears! All of them. Bears about to be born from their hanging shells. Little girls with big bear heads and bear jaws and bear bellies and bear paws. They bore themselves out of the seedpods and stretched and limbered and tumbled around the trees.

Laura wanted to get closer, to touch their silky fur and maybe have one curl up in her arms... but they were moving away, into the woods, beyond her sight. She wanted to go into the woods, too. She felt no fear. Not of the bears, not of the stories. She didn't care what happened to her. She just wanted to follow that pull, that call of the darkness.

She would go. Now. No more waiting. She went to her door and pulled it open. Something was moving at the end of the corridor. There was the sound of running, something growling low. A thrumming of blood in her ears. And then she was there, the girl, huge and feral now, taking all the space in the corridor and filling it with her silky fur, her claws, her teeth. There was blood on the white ivory in her mouth. She spat David's watch onto the carpet at Laura's feet. All bloody and covered in chips of bone and scraps of skin.

She ran, her red coat flashing through the woods. Wet leaves and soil under her shoes. *The woods are full of dead girls*. She heard voices calling her back, men trailing her, hunting her. She wouldn't go back. She was pulled onwards, that tugging at her core growing stronger, more insistent. She kept moving, running into the dark dense forest, her heart thundering in her ears and her chest burning and her muscles aching—and she tripped on a tree root and fell, sprawled over leaves and mud.

Her heart thumped in her chest. She felt her pulse in her throat, in her fingers, digging into the dirt. She'd fallen into a natural clearing. She clambered to her feet and raised her head, and he was suddenly there, a shadow in the darkness between two trees. He wasn't what she expected him to be, not really. He was wearing a mask but it was a mask of dreaming. She didn't know him, only from stories. They'd buried the stories so deep, she wouldn't have known him at all if it hadn't been for the apple he held in his hand.

"It's just an apple," he said. "Take it, if you want." His eyes were hidden behind the mask, or she wouldn't have been able to look at him, so fierce, so upright was his bearing. The proud antlers that crested around his head seemed to tangle and weave in and out with tree limbs and branches. As though he wore the whole forest for his crown. The Woods King, his hands full of gifts. "Apples want to be bitten," said he, and held out the fruit. She took it from him, their fingers touching, sliding together and apart. The apple tumbled glossy into her palm. She snapped the skin, bit into the pale heart. Juice flooded her tongue, shone on her mouth. He reached out and slid his thumb over the flesh of her lip, then his own lip, licking off the trembling droplet. An almost kiss. A teasing glance. Nothing more. But it was the same as if he'd pressed his whole mouth against her and tugged at her quivering heart.

This was the forest, too. Not only the bare haunted pines with their ghostfruit hanging like seeds, pulsing with dark blood. But this lush place of deep moss and rough bark, green shadow on green shape, and *him*—he knelt at her parted knees, his hair falling softly over her thighs. And then his mouth was at her ear, and he told her a story. *A girl wandered in this forest*, he whispered. *And do you want to know what happened, when she met the Woods King? We made her Queen*, he said.

His palm pressed upon her. The bone of his thumb slid against her. A long ribbon of flame rose within her, a burning rose unpetaled her from below. The stars were dreaming, silver dreaming scattered in the black silken sky. And they rushed back to her, the stars, the dreams, her blood—and she came, back to her body, crying, weeping for all she had been, all she had lost. Not just her losses, no, but all of them, all—but here was the other side of the story and she was glad and grateful she had made it to the end, to say the last line. She sank into his mouth and he spoke her body back to her with the language of dreaming, until she was under the ground in the rich dark soil, growing roses from her fingers, pushing green shoots up into new life.

ABOUT

Welcome to The Silent Garden.

The Silent Garden is a peer-reviewed journal of esoteric fabulism, edited and curated by the Silent Garden Collective, a professional group of editors, writers, and scholars interested in exploring those liminal borderlands where darkness bends.

The Collective's aim is to provide an annual journal of exceptional writing and art focussed on horror and the numinous, the fabulist, the uncanny, the weird, the gnostic, the avant-garde, the esoteric, and the dark interstices of the known and unknown world.

Each volume of The Silent Garden will feature original, translated, and reprint fiction and non-fiction, including; film and book reviews; essays; opinion and commentary; as well as poetry and art.

All contributions to the journal are peer-reviewed and vetted by the Silent Garden Collective. Contributions are by invitation only. Regrettably, the Collective does not have the time or wherewithal to review open submissions.

The journal is very much a labour-of-love, and its success will depend strictly on sales. The Collective is funding the project out of their own pockets. There was no inclination to crowd-fund the first volume. The Collective believes, (and sincerely hopes) that the volume will be of interest to the many readers of the esoteric.

As the Silent Garden Collective was conceived as an ever-changing and organic group of scholars, editors, writers, etc., further volumes (if sales warrant them) will be curated by a completely different collective.

We do hope you've enjoyed this inaugural volume.

The Silent Garden Collective
July 2018

CONTRIBUTORS

Mesándel Virtusio Arguelles's seventeen books in Filipino include *Pesoa* (Balangay Books, 2014), *Kurap sa Ilalim* (De La Salle University Publishing House, 2016), a volume of selected poems, *Ang Iyong Buhay ay Laging Mabibigo* (Ateneo de Naga University Press, 2016), and a limited-edition release called *Talik* from Balangay Books. A recipient of multiple national awards and fellowships, Arguelles is a two-time Philippine National Book Award finalist. English translations (by Kristine Ong Muslim) of his poems have appeared in *Asymptote*, *Circumference: Poetry in Translation*, *Newfound*, *The Cossack Review*, *Spoon River Poetry Review*, and elsewhere. He is co-editor of the journal *hal.*, works as a book editor, and teaches literature and creative writing at the De La Salle University in Manila.

Essayist, critic, novelist, and historian **Marcel Brion** (1895-1984) wrote nearly a hundred books, ranging from historical biography to examinations of Italian and German art. Later in life, he turned to fiction, distinguishing himself in the domain of the fantastic. A regular contributor to *La Revue des Deux Mondes* and *Les Nouvelles littéraires*, Marcel Brion was for more than two decades also the foreign literature editor for *Le Monde*, where he brought Rainer Maria Rilke, James Joyce, and Dino Buzzati to the public eye. Brion was a member of the Academie Française, a knight of the Légion d'honneur, the Ordre national du Mérite, and the Ordre des Arts et des Lettres.

Georgina Bruce's puzzling fictions are dictated to her by mysterious forces whose cosmic tentacles are entangled in her brains. Her writings have wormed their way into many fine juicy organs of literary and genre houses. In 2017, her short story "White Rabbit" won a British Fantasy Award. A small but viciously devoted internet cult worships her hair as a fiery god. She tweets as @monster_soup. She thanks Paul Jessup for lending her the poem at the start of her story.

Maurizio Cometto was born on September 29th, 1971, in Cuneo, in the Italian region of Piedmont. He's an esteemed Italian author of fantasy and weird tales and novels. His latest publications (all in Italian) are: the novelette *La macchia*, published in February 2016 by Acheron Books; the young adult fantasy novel *Michele e l'aliante scomparso*, published in November 2016 by Delos Books; the short story collection *Heptahedron*, published by Acheron Books. A graduate in mechanical engineering, he lives in Collegno, near Turin.

Rachel Cordasco has a Ph.D in literary studies and currently works as a developmental editor. She's written for World Literature Today, Strange Horizons, Samovar Magazine, and Skiffy and Fanty, and also translates Italian SF. Rachel created and runs the website sfintranslation.com, and can be found on Facebook and Twitter (@Rcordas).

Patricia Cram's work explores the crossroads at which the cultural and political collide with the mythic and magical. She is a writer, designer, event curator, and performance artist. patriciacram.com

Brian Evenson is the author of a dozen books of fiction, most recently the story collection *A Collapse of Horses* (Coffee House Press 2016) and the novella *The Warren* (Tor.com 2016). Other books include *Windeye* and *Immobility*, both of which were finalists for the Shirley Jackson Award, and *Last Days*, which won the ALA-RUSA award for Best Horror Novel of 2009. His novel *The Open Curtain* was a finalist for an Edgar Award and an International Horror Guild Award. He is the recipient of three O. Henry Prizes as well as an NEA fellowship. His work has been translated into French, Italian, Greek, Japanese, Persian, Russian, Spanish, Slovenian, and Turkish. He lives in Los Angeles and teaches in the Critical Studies Program at CalArts.

Edward Gauvin has received prizes, fellowships, and residencies from PEN America, the National Endowment for the Arts, the Fulbright program, Ledig House, the Lannan Foundation, and the French Embassy. His work has won the John Dryden Translation prize and the Science Fiction & Fantasy Translation Award, and been nominated for the French-American Foundation and Oxford Weidenfeld Translation Prizes. Other publications have appeared in *The New York Times*, *Harper's*, *Tin House*, and *Subtropics*. The translator of more than 250 graphic novels, he is a contributing editor for comics at *Words Without Borders*, and has written on the Francophone fantastic at *Weird Fiction Review*.

J. T. Glover has published short fiction in *Best New Horror, Pseudopod, The Children of Old Leech* and *The Lovecraft eZine,* among other venues. His nonfiction has appeared in *Postscripts to Darkness, Thinking Horror, Lightspeed,* and elsewhere. By day he is an academic librarian specializing in the humanities, and he studies literary horror, writers' research practices, and related topics. He lives in central Virginia, and you can find him online at www.jtglover.com.

Angelos Koutsourakis is the author of *Politics as Form in Lars von Trier* (Bloomsbury, 2013, 2016) and the co-editor of *The Cinema of Theo Angelopoulos* (2015). His work has appeared in *Cinema Journal, Film Criticism, SubStance: A Review of Theory and Literary Criticism, Monatshefte für deutschsprachige Literatur und Kultur, New Review of Film and Television Studies, Journal of Contemporary European Studies, Image and Narrative, Studies in European Cinema, Cinema: Journal of Philosophy and the Moving Image,* and many more. His next book is *Rethinking Brechtian Film Theory and Cinema* (2018).

V. H. Leslie's short stories have appeared in a range of publications and reprinted in a number of "Year's Best" anthologies. She is the author of a short story collection, *Skein and Bone* and a novel, *Bodies of Water* and her fiction has accrued a number of awards and nominations. She has been awarded fellowships for her writing at Hawthornden in Scotland and the Saari Institute in Finland and her non-fiction has appeared in *History Today, The Victorianist* and *Gramarye*.

Nick Mamatas is the author of several novels, including *I Am Providence* and the forthcoming *Hexen Sabbath*. His short fiction has appeared in *Best American Mystery Stories, Year's Best Weird Fiction, Weird Tales,* and many other venues. Much of his recent work is collected in *The People's Republic of Everything.* Also an anthologist, Nick's most recent projects include the hybrid fantasy/crime Locus Award nominee *Hanzai Japan* (co-edited with Masumi Washington), and the hybrid flash/fiction cocktail recipe book *Mixed Up* (co-edited with Molly Tanzer).

Helen Marshall is a Senior Lecturer of Creative Writing and Publishing at Anglia Ruskin University in Cambridge, England. Her first collection of fiction *Hair Side, Flesh Side* won the Sydney J Bounds Award in 2013, and *Gifts for the One Who Comes After*, her second collection, won the World Fantasy Award and the Shirley Jackson Award in 2015. She recently edited *The Year's Best Weird Fiction* and her debut novel *The Migration* will be published by Random House Canada in 2019.

Daniel Mills is the author of the novels *Moriah* (2017) and *Revenants* (2011) and of the short fiction collection *The Lord Came at Twilight* (2014). He lives in Vermont.

Kristine Ong Muslim is the author of nine books, including the short story collections *Age of Blight* (Unnamed Press, 2016), *Butterfly Dream* (Snuggly Books, 2016), and *The Drone Outside* (Eibonvale Press, 2017), as well as the poetry collections *Lifeboat* (University of Santo Tomas Publishing House, 2015), *Meditations of a Beast* (Cornerstone Press, 2016), and *Black Arcadia* (University of the Philippines Press, 2017). She is poetry editor of *LONTAR: The Journal of Southeast Asian Speculative Fiction* and co-editor with Nalo Hopkinson of the British Fantasy Award-winning anthology *People of Colo(u)r Destroy Science Fiction*. Her stories have appeared in *The Cincinnati Review*, *Tin House*, *Weird Fiction Review*, and *World Literature Today*. She grew up and continues to live in a rural town in southern Philippines.

Reggie Oliver, according to Ramsey Campbell, "...quite possibly our finest modern writer of spectral tales," is an actor, director, playwright and award winning author of fiction. Published work includes six plays, three novels, seven volumes of short stories, including *Mrs Midnight* (2012 winner of *Children of the Night Award* for best work of supernatural fiction), and, the biography of Stella Gibbons, *Out of the Woodshed* (Bloomsbury 1998). His stories have appeared in over sixty anthologies. Recent work includes *The Boke of the Divill*, a novel (Dark Regions 2017) *Holidays from Hell* – a collection of stories from Tartarus & *The Hauntings at Tankerton Park and How They Got Rid of Them* – a children's book with over 80 illustrations by the author (Zagava Press). Forthcoming: *Madder Mysteries and More* - a new collection from Tartarus.

Rudrapriya Rathore's writing has appeared in *Joyland*, *Hazlitt*, *This Magazine*, the *Literary Review of Canada*, *Quill & Quire*, and *The Walrus*, among others. She lives in Toronto.

D.P. Watt lives between Scotland and England in an otherworldly, misty borderland. His collection of short stories *An Emporium of Automata* was reprinted by Eibonvale Press in early 2013 and his second collection, *The Phantasmagorical Imperative and Other Fabrications*, was published in 2014 with Egaeus Press and is now available in a paperback edition. His third collection *Almost Insentient, Almost Divine* was published in 2016 by Undertow Publications and was nominated for a Shirley Jackson Award. You can find him at The Interlude House: www.theinterludehouse.co.uk

Ron Weighell has published four short story collections: *The White Road, The Irregular Casebook of Sherlock Holmes, Tarshishim* and *Summonings*; three novellas for Sarob Press, *The Chapel of Infernal Devotion, The Letter Killeth* and *The Asmodeus Fellowship*. A new revised edition of *The White Road* has also been published by Sarob Press. Short stories have appeared in anthologies for Michael O'Mara, Ash Tree Press, Aegeus Press, Ex Occidente, Tartarus Press, Sutton Hoo/Alpenhouse Apparitions, Zagava, Hieroglyphic Press, and 'Year's Best' anthologies edited by Karl Edward Wagner and Stephen Jones.

David Whitlam is an artist and illustrator from Manchester. From an early age he showed signs of a vivid imagination, and as a child spent much of his time drawing imaginary landscapes populated by strange creatures. In his teenage years he discovered the Surrealists and became fascinated with their attempts to delve into the unconscious. Although much of his work emerges spontaneously from the imagination, using techniques such as automatic drawing and collage, it's subject matter has been shaped by his interests in ancient cultures, mythology and religious symbolism.

Marian Womack is a bilingual writer of speculative fiction. She is graduate of the San Diego Clarion Writer's Workshop and of the Cambridge University Creative Writing MSt. Her fiction has appeared in *Weird Fiction Review, The Year's Best Weird Fiction vol. III, Ecopunk! Speculative tales of radical futures, LossLit* or *Apex Magazine*. She has contributed non-fiction to *The Times Literary Supplement*, the *Science-Fiction and Fantasy Network*, and has written for video games. Her collection of short fiction about ghosts, giant insects, and disappearing nature, *Lost Objects*, was published by Luna Press this year. Marian was born in Andalusia and lives in Cambridge, where she works as an academic librarian. She is a co-founder of Ediciones Nevsky/Nevsky Books, a publishing project based in Madrid and East Anglia, which mostly publishes speculative fiction in Spanish and English translation. She tweets as @beekeepermadrid and her website is marianwomack.com

Nothing is Everything
Simon Strantzas

$17.99 US

Short Stories

ISBN 978-1988964034

8.5 × 5.5 Inch

274 PP

Trade Paperback

Available October 16, 2018
Through Ingram

"Simon Strantzas captures the creepiness of small town Ontario; there is something of Seth, of Alice Munro in his work, wonderfully tangled with the likes of Aickman and Jackson. Uncanny as a ventriloquist's doll, but with a real, beating heart."

— Camilla Grudova,
author of *The Doll's Alphabet*

www.ingramcontent.com/pod-product-compliance
Lightning Source LLC
Chambersburg PA
CBHW061405160426
42812CB00089B/2592